D0472825

DESOLATION JONES
MADE IN ENGLAND

Warren Ellis: Writer

J.H. Williams III: Artist

Jose Villarrubia: Colors

Todd Klein: Letters

DESOLATION JONES created by Ellis & Williams
Original series covers by J.H. Williams III
Collected Edition design by Ed Roeder

Jim Lee, Editorial Director
John Nee, VP-Business Development
Scott Dunbier, Executive Editor
Kristy Quinn, Assistant Editor
Ed Roeder, Art Director
Paul Levitz, President & Publisher
Georg Brewer, VP-Design & DC Direct Creative
Richard Bruning, Senior VP-Creative Director
Patrick Caldon, Executive VP-Finance & Operations
Chris Caramalis, VP-Finance
John Cunningham, VP-Marketing
Terri Cunningham, VP-Managing Editor
Stephanie Fierman, Senior VP-Sales & Marketing
Alison Gill, VP-Manufacturing
Hank Kanalz, VP-General Manager, WildStorm
Lillian Laserson, Senior VP & General Counsel
Paula Lowitt, Senior VP-Business & Legal Affairs
David McKillips, VP-Advertising & Custom Publishing
Gregory Noveck, Senior VP-Creative Affairs
Cheryl Rubin, Senior VP-Brand Management
Jeff Trojan, VP-Business Development, DC Direct
Bob Wayne, VP-Sales

ISBN: 1-4012-1150-X   ISBN-13: 978-1-4012-1150-9

DESOLATION JONES: MADE IN ENGLAND, published by WildStorm Productions. 888 Prospect St. #240, La Jolla, CA 92037. Compilation copyright © 2006
Warren Ellis and J.H. Williams III. All Rights Reserved. Desolation Jones, all characters, the distinctive likenesses thereof and all related elements are
trademarks of Warren Ellis and J.H. Williams III. WildStorm and logo are trademarks of DC Comics.

Originally published in single magazine form as DESOLATION JONES #1-6 copyright © 2005, 2006 Warren Ellis and J.H. Williams III. All Rights Reserved.
The stories, characters, and incidents mentioned in this magazine are entirely fictional. Printed on recyclable paper. WildStorm does not read or accept
unsolicited submissions of ideas, stories or artwork. Printed in Canada.

DC Comics, a Warner Bros. Entertainment Company.

I dedicate this book to the memory of

Leticia Blake
1973 - 2005

"For years the children and old people will talk about the lady up the street
who spent her fortune on this big crazy house, and then one day she just
disappeared...and the only thing missing was the telescope."

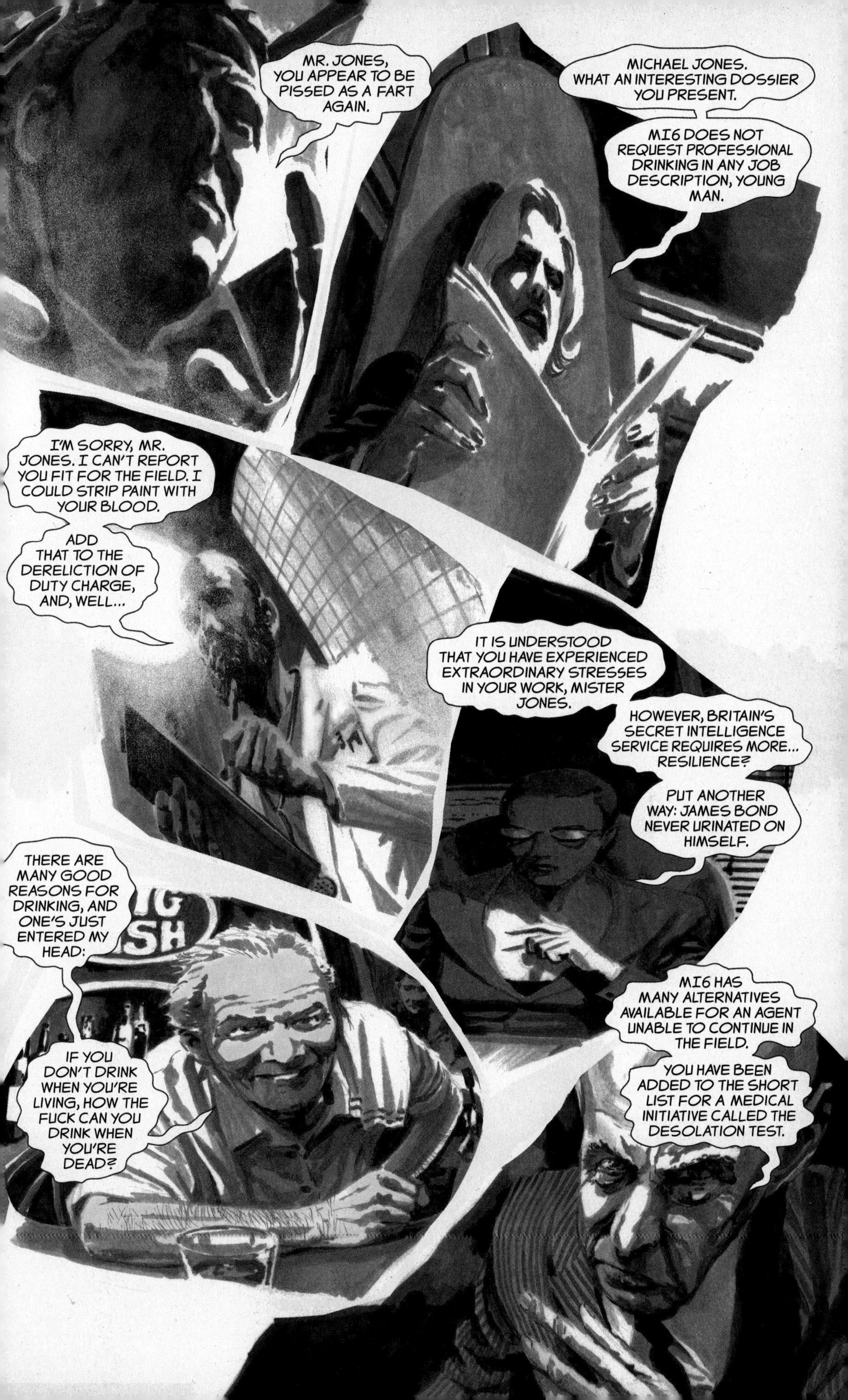
MR. JONES, YOU APPEAR TO BE PISSED AS A FART AGAIN.
MICHAEL JONES. WHAT AN INTERESTING DOSSIER YOU PRESENT.
MI6 DOES NOT REQUEST PROFESSIONAL DRINKING IN ANY JOB DESCRIPTION, YOUNG MAN.
I'M SORRY, MR. JONES. I CAN'T REPORT YOU FIT FOR THE FIELD. I COULD STRIP PAINT WITH YOUR BLOOD.
ADD THAT TO THE DERELICTION OF DUTY CHARGE, AND, WELL...
IT IS UNDERSTOOD THAT YOU HAVE EXPERIENCED EXTRAORDINARY STRESSES IN YOUR WORK, MISTER JONES.
HOWEVER, BRITAIN'S SECRET INTELLIGENCE SERVICE REQUIRES MORE... RESILIENCE?
PUT ANOTHER WAY: JAMES BOND NEVER URINATED ON HIMSELF.
THERE ARE MANY GOOD REASONS FOR DRINKING, AND ONE'S JUST ENTERED MY HEAD:
IF YOU DON'T DRINK WHEN YOU'RE LIVING, HOW THE FUCK CAN YOU DRINK WHEN YOU'RE DEAD?
MI6 HAS MANY ALTERNATIVES AVAILABLE FOR AN AGENT UNABLE TO CONTINUE IN THE FIELD.
YOU HAVE BEEN ADDED TO THE SHORT LIST FOR A MEDICAL INITIATIVE CALLED THE DESOLATION TEST.

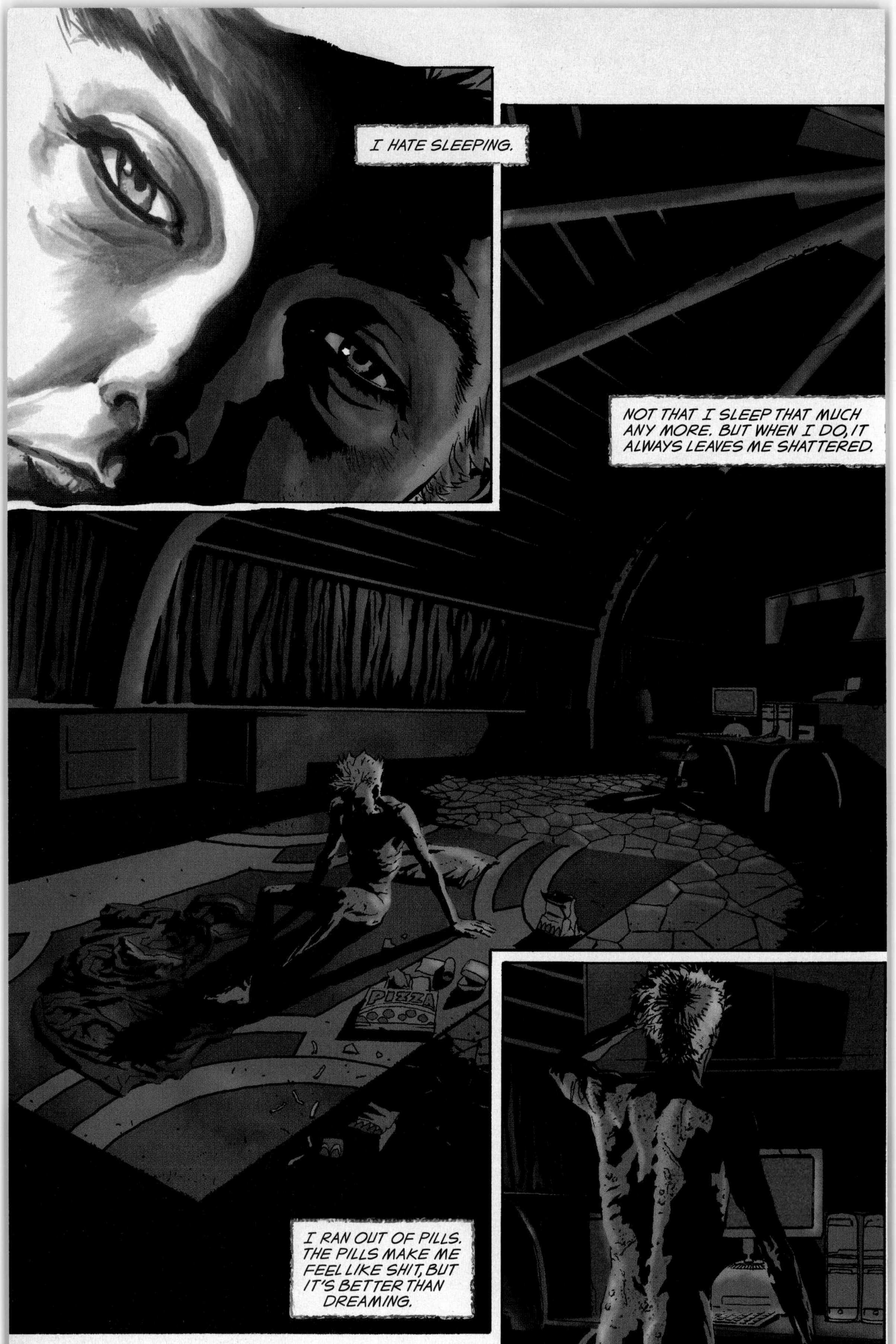
I HATE SLEEPING.
NOT THAT I SLEEP THAT MUCH ANY MORE. BUT WHEN I DO, IT ALWAYS LEAVES ME SHATTERED.
PIZZA
I RAN OUT OF PILLS. THE PILLS MAKE ME FEEL LIKE SHIT, BUT IT'S BETTER THAN DREAMING.

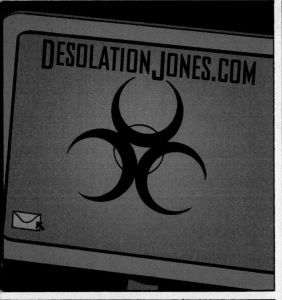

DESOLATIONJONES.COM

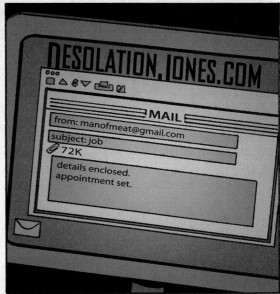

DESOLATIONJONES.COM

MAIL

from: manofmeat@gmail.com
subject: job
72K

details enclosed.
appointment set.

CALLING ROBINA...

BLOODY HELL, JERONIMUS...

ROBINA? JONES.

GODDAMMIT, JONES, DO YOU KNOW WHAT TIME IT IS?

UM... NO.

YOU USELESS LIMEY BASTARD. IT'S TEN AFTER EIGHT, GOD-DAMMIT.

MORNING OR EVENING?

MORNING! I'VE BEEN IN BED FOUR GODDAMN HOURS!

SHIT. SORRY. LISTEN, I NEED A RIDE OUT TO THE HILLS. JERONIMUS HAS HANDED A JOB OFF TO ME.

I NEED TO BE THERE FOR NINE-THIRTY. HELP ME OUT? YOU KNOW I CAN'T FIND MY WAY AROUND THIS BLOODY PLACE...

ALL RIGHT, ALL RIGHT. TWENTY MINUTES.

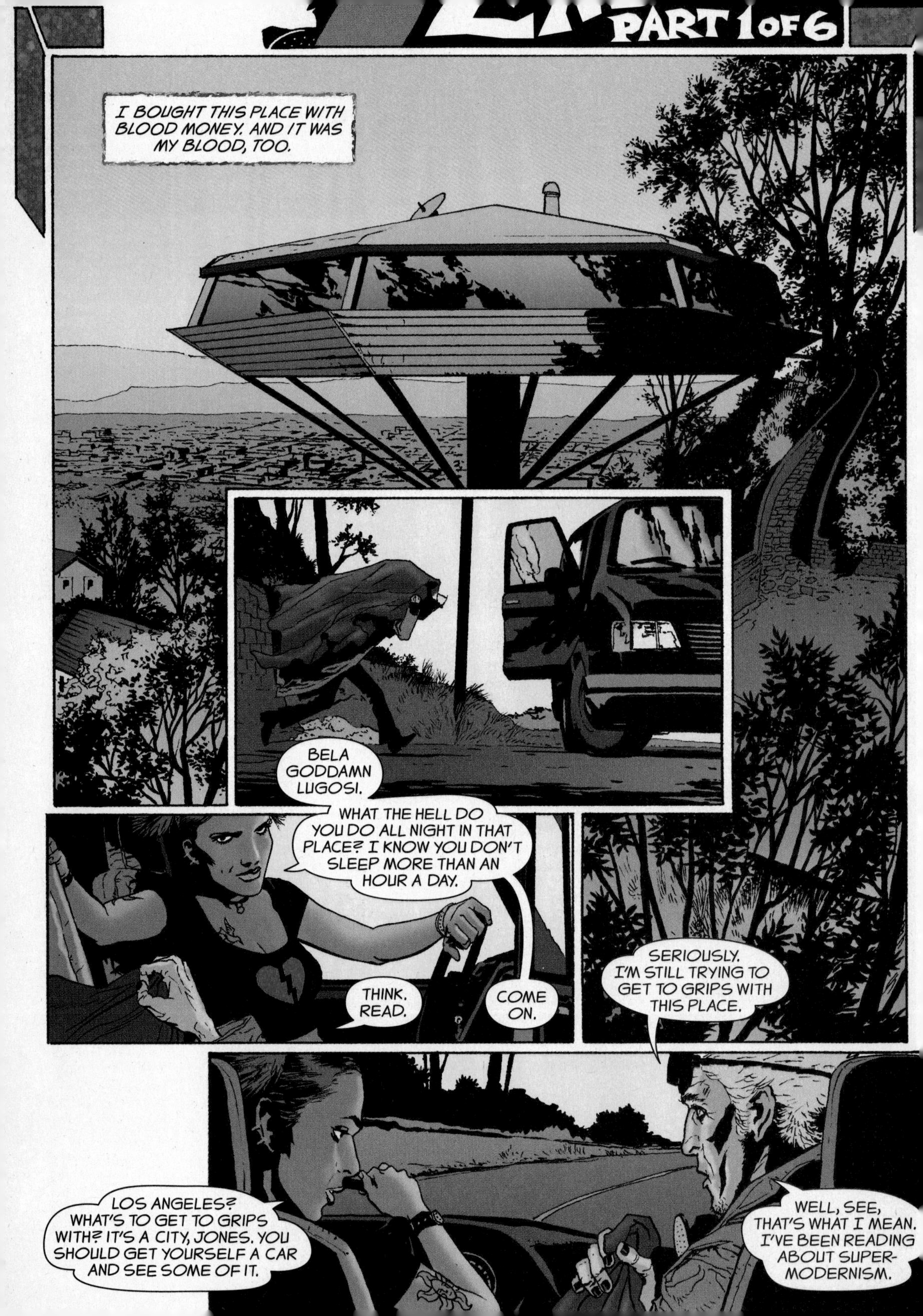

PART 1 OF 6
I BOUGHT THIS PLACE WITH BLOOD MONEY. AND IT WAS MY BLOOD, TOO.
BELA GODDAMN LUGOSI.
WHAT THE HELL DO YOU DO ALL NIGHT IN THAT PLACE? I KNOW YOU DON'T SLEEP MORE THAN AN HOUR A DAY.
THINK. READ.
COME ON.
SERIOUSLY. I'M STILL TRYING TO GET TO GRIPS WITH THIS PLACE.
LOS ANGELES? WHAT'S TO GET TO GRIPS WITH? IT'S A CITY, JONES. YOU SHOULD GET YOURSELF A CAR AND SEE SOME OF IT.
WELL, SEE, THAT'S WHAT I MEAN. I'VE BEEN READING ABOUT SUPER-MODERNISM.

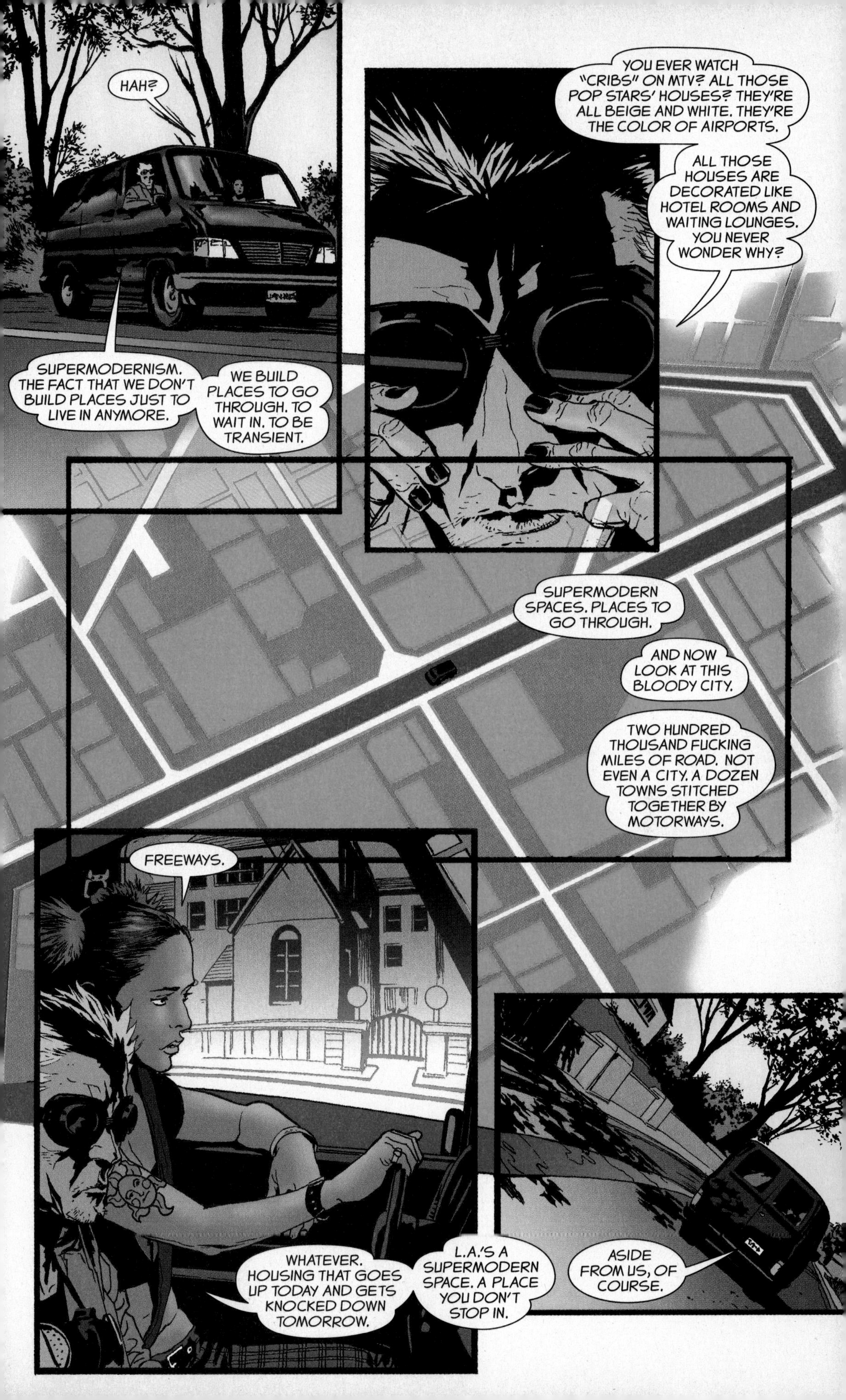
HAH?
YOU EVER WATCH "CRIBS" ON MTV? ALL THOSE POP STARS' HOUSES? THEY'RE ALL BEIGE AND WHITE. THEY'RE THE COLOR OF AIRPORTS.
ALL THOSE HOUSES ARE DECORATED LIKE HOTEL ROOMS AND WAITING LOUNGES. YOU NEVER WONDER WHY?
SUPERMODERNISM. THE FACT THAT WE DON'T BUILD PLACES JUST TO LIVE IN ANYMORE.
WE BUILD PLACES TO GO THROUGH. TO WAIT IN. TO BE TRANSIENT.
SUPERMODERN SPACES. PLACES TO GO THROUGH.
AND NOW LOOK AT THIS BLOODY CITY.
TWO HUNDRED THOUSAND FUCKING MILES OF ROAD. NOT EVEN A CITY. A DOZEN TOWNS STITCHED TOGETHER BY MOTORWAYS.
FREEWAYS.
WHATEVER. HOUSING THAT GOES UP TODAY AND GETS KNOCKED DOWN TOMORROW.
L.A.'S A SUPERMODERN SPACE. A PLACE YOU DON'T STOP IN.
ASIDE FROM US, OF COURSE.

MY NAME'S JONES. I HAVE AN APPOINTMENT TO SEE THE COLONEL.

INDEED, SIR. I AM GRAHAM, THE COLONEL'S MAN.

CAN I TAKE YOUR, AH, BLANKET?

YEAH. I'M NOT GOOD WITH DIRECT SUNLIGHT.

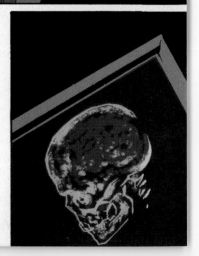

ONE WONDERS WHY YOU WOULD LIVE IN LOS ANGELES, MR. JONES.

LIMITED OPTIONS. YOU'RE ENGLISH?

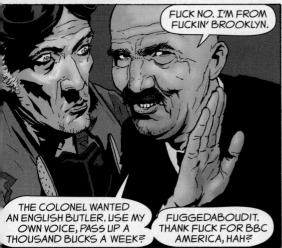

FUCK NO. I'M FROM FUCKIN' BROOKLYN.

THE COLONEL WANTED AN ENGLISH BUTLER. USE MY OWN VOICE, PASS UP A THOUSAND BUCKS A WEEK?

FUGGEDABOUDIT. THANK FUCK FOR BBC AMERICA, HAH?

THE COLONEL WILL RECEIVE YOU IN HIS STUDY, SIR.

I WILL HOLD YOUR BLANKET UNTIL YOU RETURN.

DON'T WASH IT. I'VE ONLY JUST GOT IT THE WAY I LIKE IT.

COLONEL NIGH?

I'M JONES. JERONIMUS CORNELISZOON REFERRED YOU TO ME.

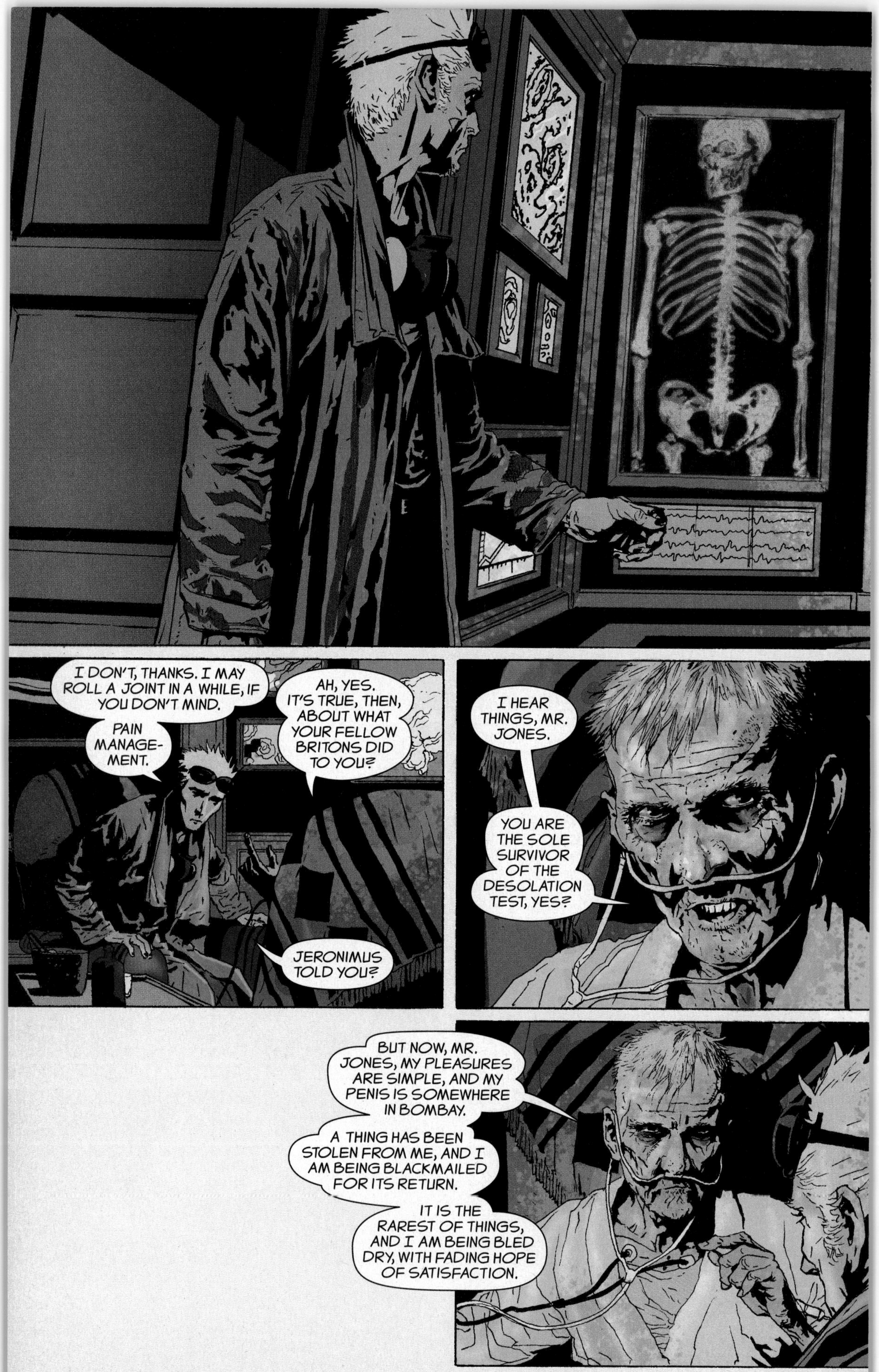
I DON'T, THANKS. I MAY ROLL A JOINT IN A WHILE, IF YOU DON'T MIND.
PAIN MANAGE-MENT.
AH, YES. IT'S TRUE, THEN, ABOUT WHAT YOUR FELLOW BRITONS DID TO YOU?
JERONIMUS TOLD YOU?
I HEAR THINGS, MR. JONES.
YOU ARE THE SOLE SURVIVOR OF THE DESOLATION TEST, YES?
BUT NOW, MR. JONES, MY PLEASURES ARE SIMPLE, AND MY PENIS IS SOMEWHERE IN BOMBAY.
A THING HAS BEEN STOLEN FROM ME, AND I AM BEING BLACKMAILED FOR ITS RETURN.
IT IS THE RAREST OF THINGS, AND I AM BEING BLED DRY, WITH FADING HOPE OF SATISFACTION.

MR. JONES, YES. EXCELLENT.

PLEASE HELP YOURSELF TO A DRINK.

I'D JOIN YOU, BUT ALCOHOL MAKES MY LIVER CONVULSE LIKE A SPIDER WITH A PIN IN IT.

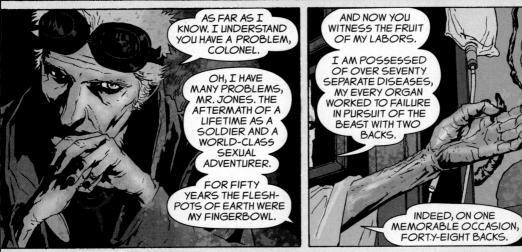

AS FAR AS I KNOW. I UNDERSTAND YOU HAVE A PROBLEM, COLONEL.

OH, I HAVE MANY PROBLEMS, MR. JONES. THE AFTERMATH OF A LIFETIME AS A SOLDIER AND A WORLD-CLASS SEXUAL ADVENTURER.

FOR FIFTY YEARS THE FLESH-POTS OF EARTH WERE MY FINGERBOWL.

AND NOW YOU WITNESS THE FRUIT OF MY LABORS.

I AM POSSESSED OF OVER SEVENTY SEPARATE DISEASES, MY EVERY ORGAN WORKED TO FAILURE IN PURSUIT OF THE BEAST WITH TWO BACKS.

INDEED, ON ONE MEMORABLE OCCASION, FORTY-EIGHT BACKS.

IN 1944, ADOLF HITLER--

OH, COME ON...

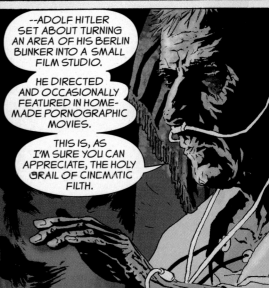

--ADOLF HITLER SET ABOUT TURNING AN AREA OF HIS BERLIN BUNKER INTO A SMALL FILM STUDIO.

HE DIRECTED AND OCCASIONALLY FEATURED IN HOME-MADE PORNOGRAPHIC MOVIES.

THIS IS, AS I'M SURE YOU CAN APPRECIATE, THE HOLY GRAIL OF CINEMATIC FILTH.

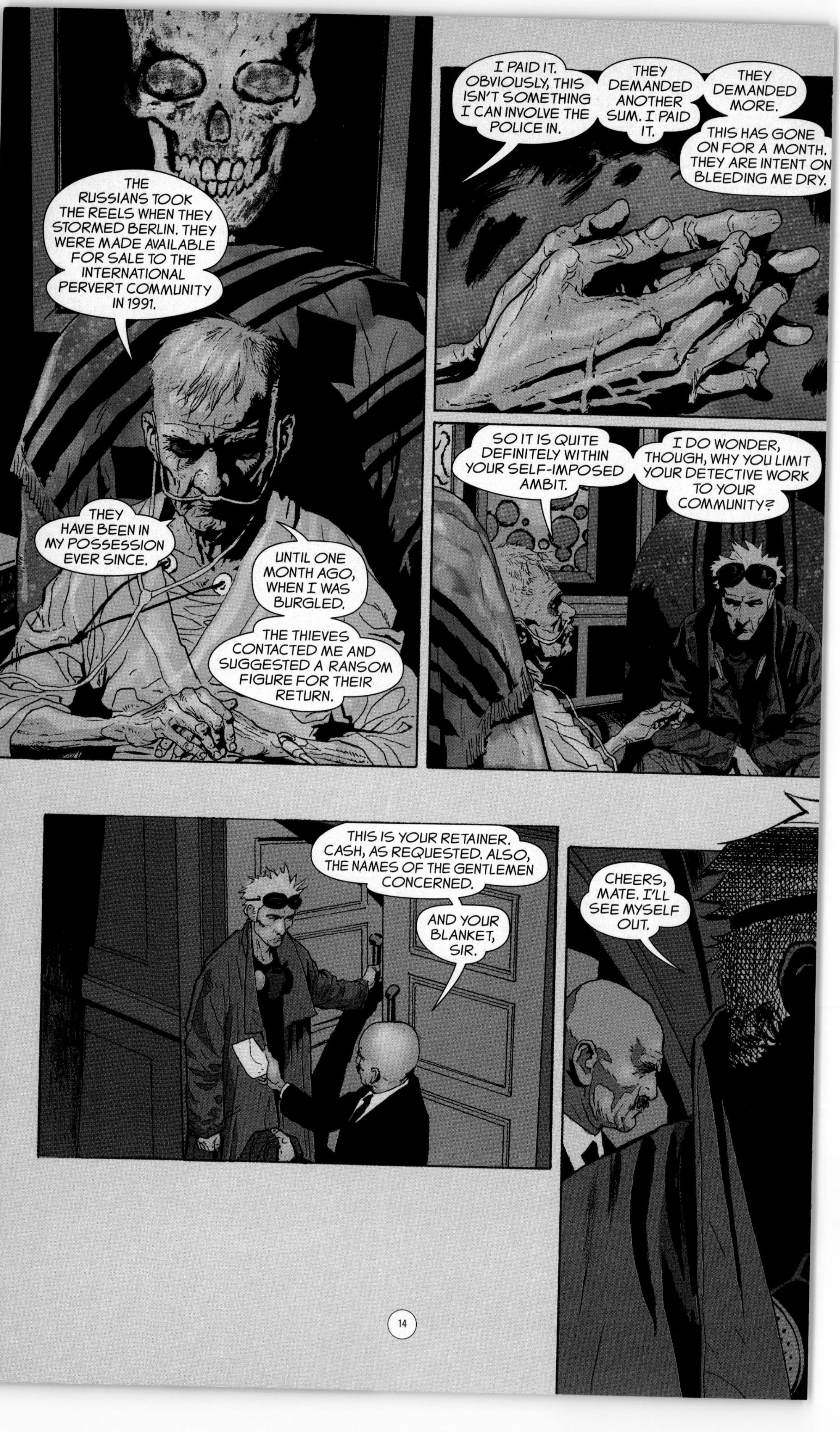
THE RUSSIANS TOOK THE REELS WHEN THEY STORMED BERLIN. THEY WERE MADE AVAILABLE FOR SALE TO THE INTERNATIONAL PERVERT COMMUNITY IN 1991.
THEY HAVE BEEN IN MY POSSESSION EVER SINCE.
UNTIL ONE MONTH AGO, WHEN I WAS BURGLED.
THE THIEVES CONTACTED ME AND SUGGESTED A RANSOM FIGURE FOR THEIR RETURN.
I PAID IT. OBVIOUSLY, THIS ISN'T SOMETHING I CAN INVOLVE THE POLICE IN.
THEY DEMANDED ANOTHER SUM. I PAID IT.
THEY DEMANDED MORE.
THIS HAS GONE ON FOR A MONTH. THEY ARE INTENT ON BLEEDING ME DRY.
SO IT IS QUITE DEFINITELY WITHIN YOUR SELF-IMPOSED AMBIT.
I DO WONDER, THOUGH, WHY YOU LIMIT YOUR DETECTIVE WORK TO YOUR COMMUNITY?
THIS IS YOUR RETAINER. CASH, AS REQUESTED. ALSO, THE NAMES OF THE GENTLEMEN CONCERNED.
AND YOUR BLANKET, SIR.
CHEERS, MATE. I'LL SEE MYSELF OUT.

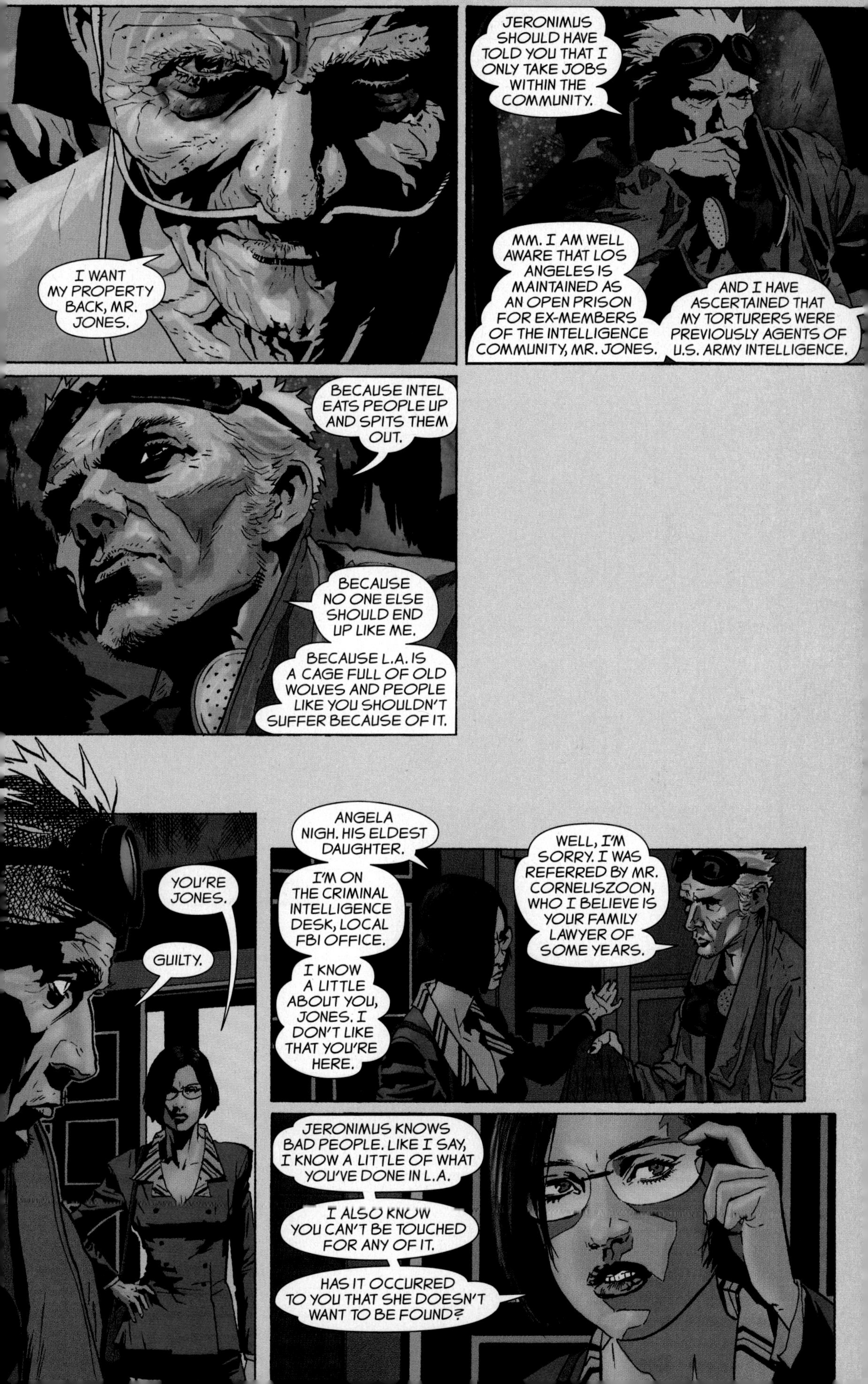
I WANT MY PROPERTY BACK, MR. JONES.
JERONIMUS SHOULD HAVE TOLD YOU THAT I ONLY TAKE JOBS WITHIN THE COMMUNITY.
MM. I AM WELL AWARE THAT LOS ANGELES IS MAINTAINED AS AN OPEN PRISON FOR EX-MEMBERS OF THE INTELLIGENCE COMMUNITY, MR. JONES.
AND I HAVE ASCERTAINED THAT MY TORTURERS WERE PREVIOUSLY AGENTS OF U.S. ARMY INTELLIGENCE.
BECAUSE INTEL EATS PEOPLE UP AND SPITS THEM OUT.
BECAUSE NO ONE ELSE SHOULD END UP LIKE ME.
BECAUSE L.A. IS A CAGE FULL OF OLD WOLVES AND PEOPLE LIKE YOU SHOULDN'T SUFFER BECAUSE OF IT.
YOU'RE JONES.
GUILTY.
ANGELA NIGH. HIS ELDEST DAUGHTER.
I'M ON THE CRIMINAL INTELLIGENCE DESK, LOCAL FBI OFFICE.
I KNOW A LITTLE ABOUT YOU, JONES. I DON'T LIKE THAT YOU'RE HERE.
WELL, I'M SORRY. I WAS REFERRED BY MR. CORNELISZOON, WHO I BELIEVE IS YOUR FAMILY LAWYER OF SOME YEARS.
JERONIMUS KNOWS BAD PEOPLE. LIKE I SAY, I KNOW A LITTLE OF WHAT YOU'VE DONE IN L.A.
I ALSO KNOW YOU CAN'T BE TOUCHED FOR ANY OF IT.
HAS IT OCCURRED TO YOU THAT SHE DOESN'T WANT TO BE FOUND?

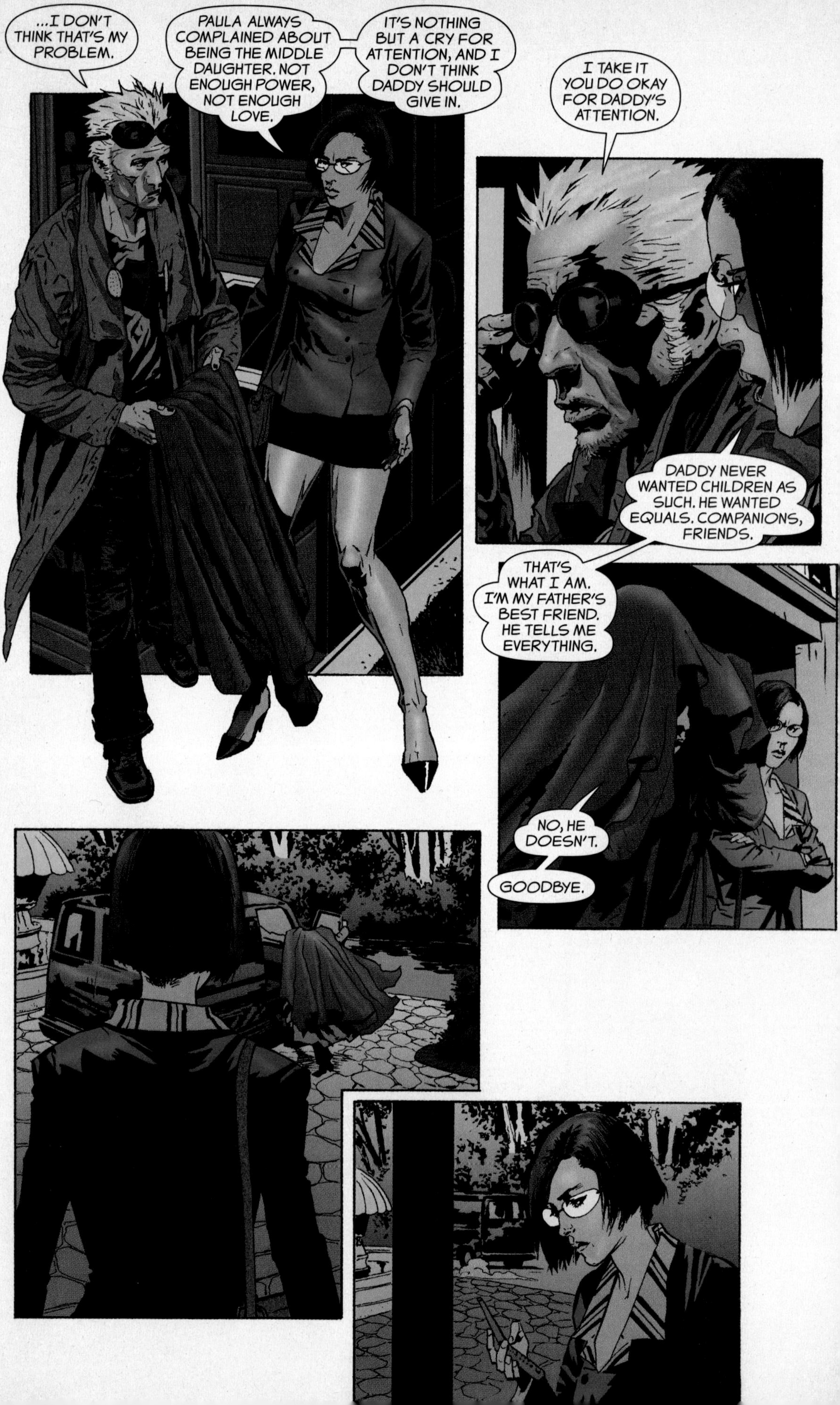
...I DON'T THINK THAT'S MY PROBLEM.
PAULA ALWAYS COMPLAINED ABOUT BEING THE MIDDLE DAUGHTER. NOT ENOUGH POWER, NOT ENOUGH LOVE.
IT'S NOTHING BUT A CRY FOR ATTENTION, AND I DON'T THINK DADDY SHOULD GIVE IN.
I TAKE IT YOU DO OKAY FOR DADDY'S ATTENTION.
DADDY NEVER WANTED CHILDREN AS SUCH. HE WANTED EQUALS. COMPANIONS, FRIENDS.
THAT'S WHAT I AM. I'M MY FATHER'S BEST FRIEND. HE TELLS ME EVERYTHING.
NO, HE DOESN'T.
GOODBYE.

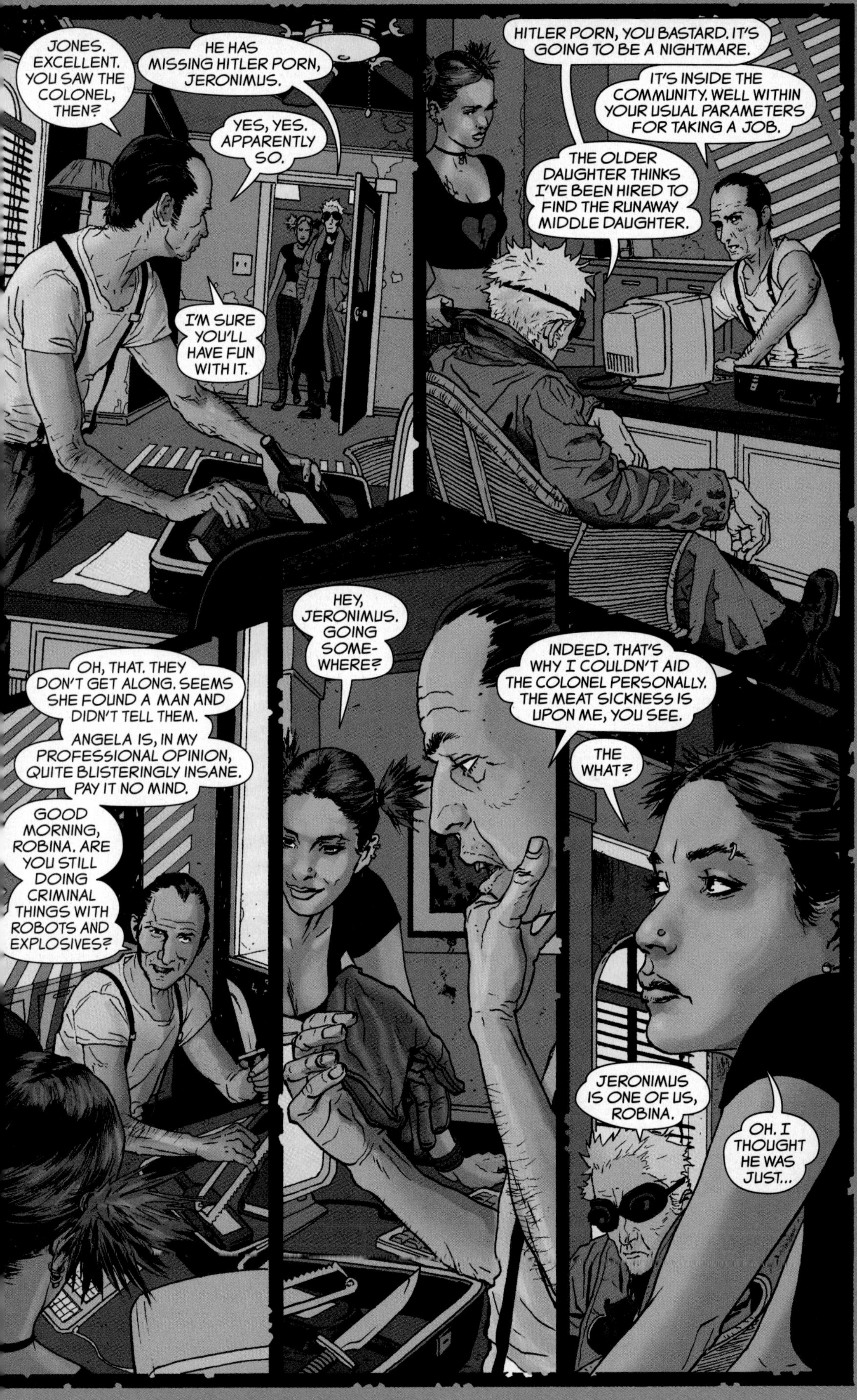
JONES. EXCELLENT. YOU SAW THE COLONEL, THEN?
HE HAS MISSING HITLER PORN, JERONIMUS.
YES, YES. APPARENTLY SO.
I'M SURE YOU'LL HAVE FUN WITH IT.
HITLER PORN, YOU BASTARD. IT'S GOING TO BE A NIGHTMARE.
IT'S INSIDE THE COMMUNITY. WELL WITHIN YOUR USUAL PARAMETERS FOR TAKING A JOB.
THE OLDER DAUGHTER THINKS I'VE BEEN HIRED TO FIND THE RUNAWAY MIDDLE DAUGHTER.
OH, THAT. THEY DON'T GET ALONG. SEEMS SHE FOUND A MAN AND DIDN'T TELL THEM.
ANGELA IS, IN MY PROFESSIONAL OPINION, QUITE BLISTERINGLY INSANE. PAY IT NO MIND.
GOOD MORNING, ROBINA. ARE YOU STILL DOING CRIMINAL THINGS WITH ROBOTS AND EXPLOSIVES?
HEY, JERONIMUS. GOING SOME-WHERE?
INDEED. THAT'S WHY I COULDN'T AID THE COLONEL PERSONALLY. THE MEAT SICKNESS IS UPON ME, YOU SEE.
THE WHAT?
JERONIMUS IS ONE OF US, ROBINA.
OH. I THOUGHT HE WAS JUST...

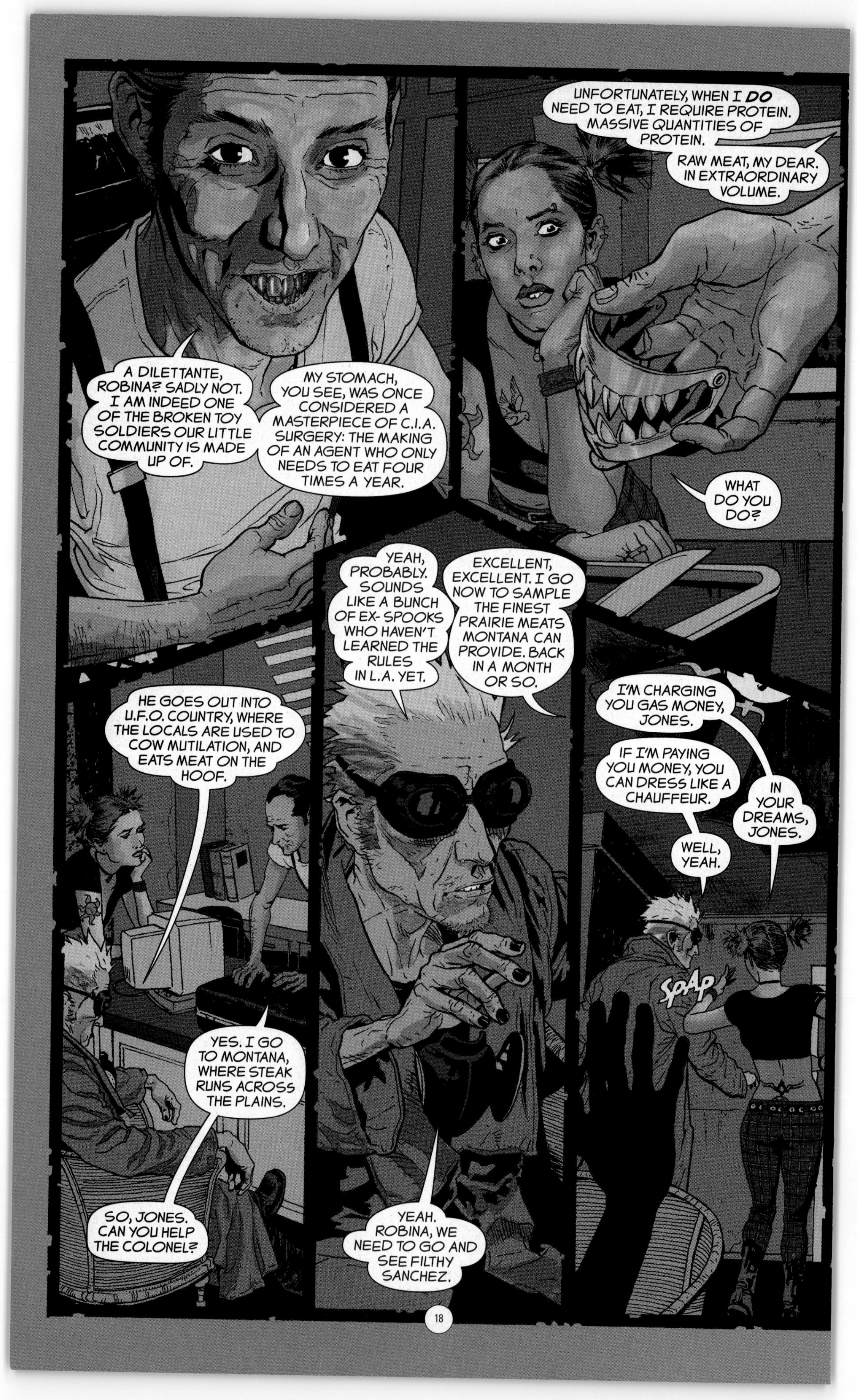
A DILETTANTE, ROBINA? SADLY NOT. I AM INDEED ONE OF THE BROKEN TOY SOLDIERS OUR LITTLE COMMUNITY IS MADE UP OF.
MY STOMACH, YOU SEE, WAS ONCE CONSIDERED A MASTERPIECE OF C.I.A. SURGERY: THE MAKING OF AN AGENT WHO ONLY NEEDS TO EAT FOUR TIMES A YEAR.
UNFORTUNATELY, WHEN I DO NEED TO EAT, I REQUIRE PROTEIN. MASSIVE QUANTITIES OF PROTEIN.
RAW MEAT, MY DEAR. IN EXTRAORDINARY VOLUME.
WHAT DO YOU DO?
HE GOES OUT INTO U.F.O. COUNTRY, WHERE THE LOCALS ARE USED TO COW MUTILATION, AND EATS MEAT ON THE HOOF.
YES. I GO TO MONTANA, WHERE STEAK RUNS ACROSS THE PLAINS.
SO, JONES. CAN YOU HELP THE COLONEL?
YEAH, PROBABLY. SOUNDS LIKE A BUNCH OF EX-SPOOKS WHO HAVEN'T LEARNED THE RULES IN L.A. YET.
EXCELLENT, EXCELLENT. I GO NOW TO SAMPLE THE FINEST PRAIRIE MEATS MONTANA CAN PROVIDE. BACK IN A MONTH OR SO.
YEAH. ROBINA, WE NEED TO GO AND SEE FILTHY SANCHEZ.
I'M CHARGING YOU GAS MONEY, JONES.
IF I'M PAYING YOU MONEY, YOU CAN DRESS LIKE A CHAUFFEUR.
IN YOUR DREAMS, JONES.
WELL, YEAH.
SPAP

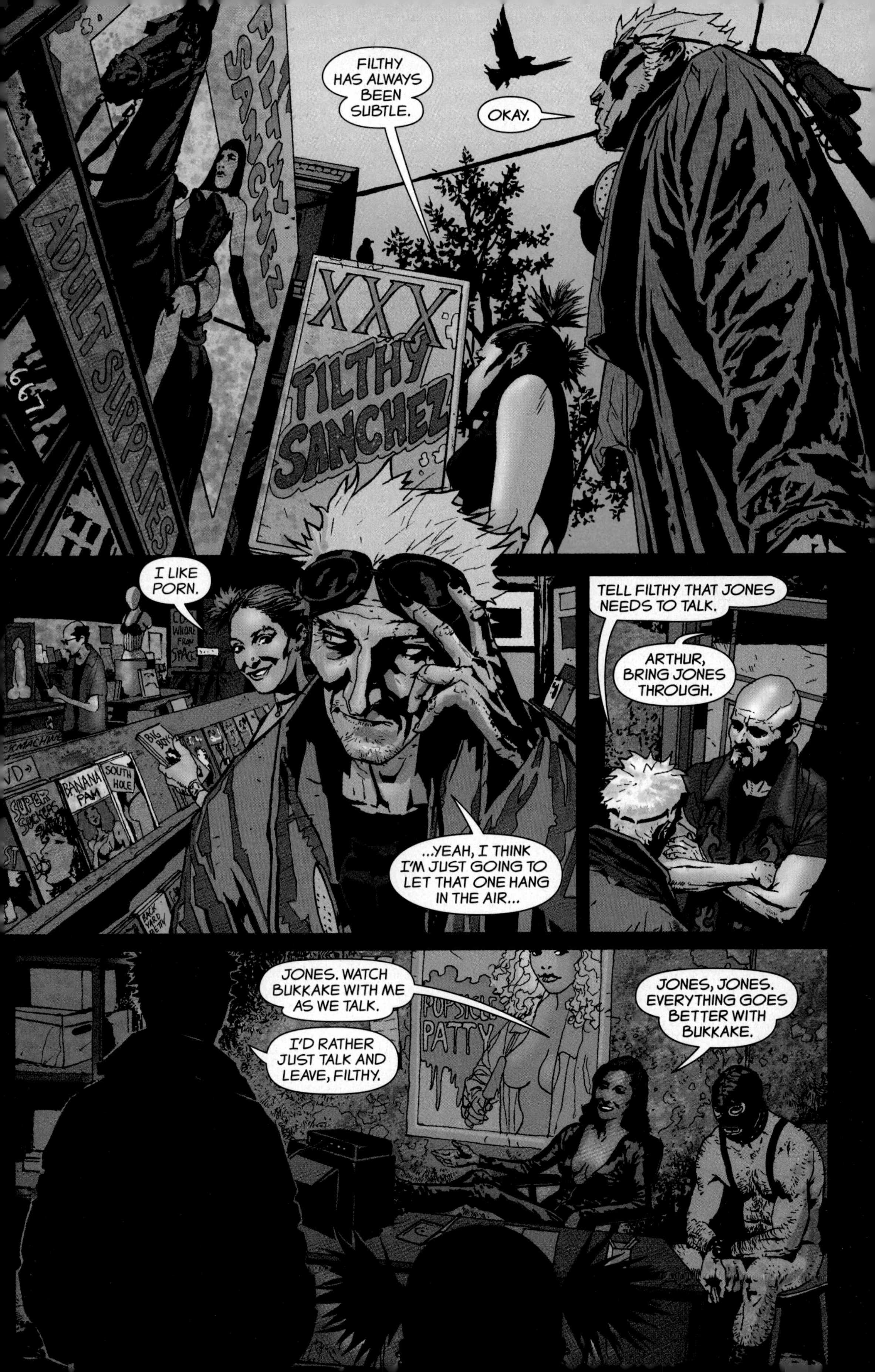
FILTHY HAS ALWAYS BEEN SUBTLE.
OKAY.
ADULT SUPPLIES
XXX
FILTHY SANCHEZ
I LIKE PORN.
BIG BOYS
BANANA PAM
SOUTH HOLE
...YEAH, I THINK I'M JUST GOING TO LET THAT ONE HANG IN THE AIR...
TELL FILTHY THAT JONES NEEDS TO TALK.
ARTHUR, BRING JONES THROUGH.
JONES. WATCH BUKKAKE WITH ME AS WE TALK.
I'D RATHER JUST TALK AND LEAVE, FILTHY.
POPSICLE PATTY
JONES, JONES. EVERYTHING GOES BETTER WITH BUKKAKE.

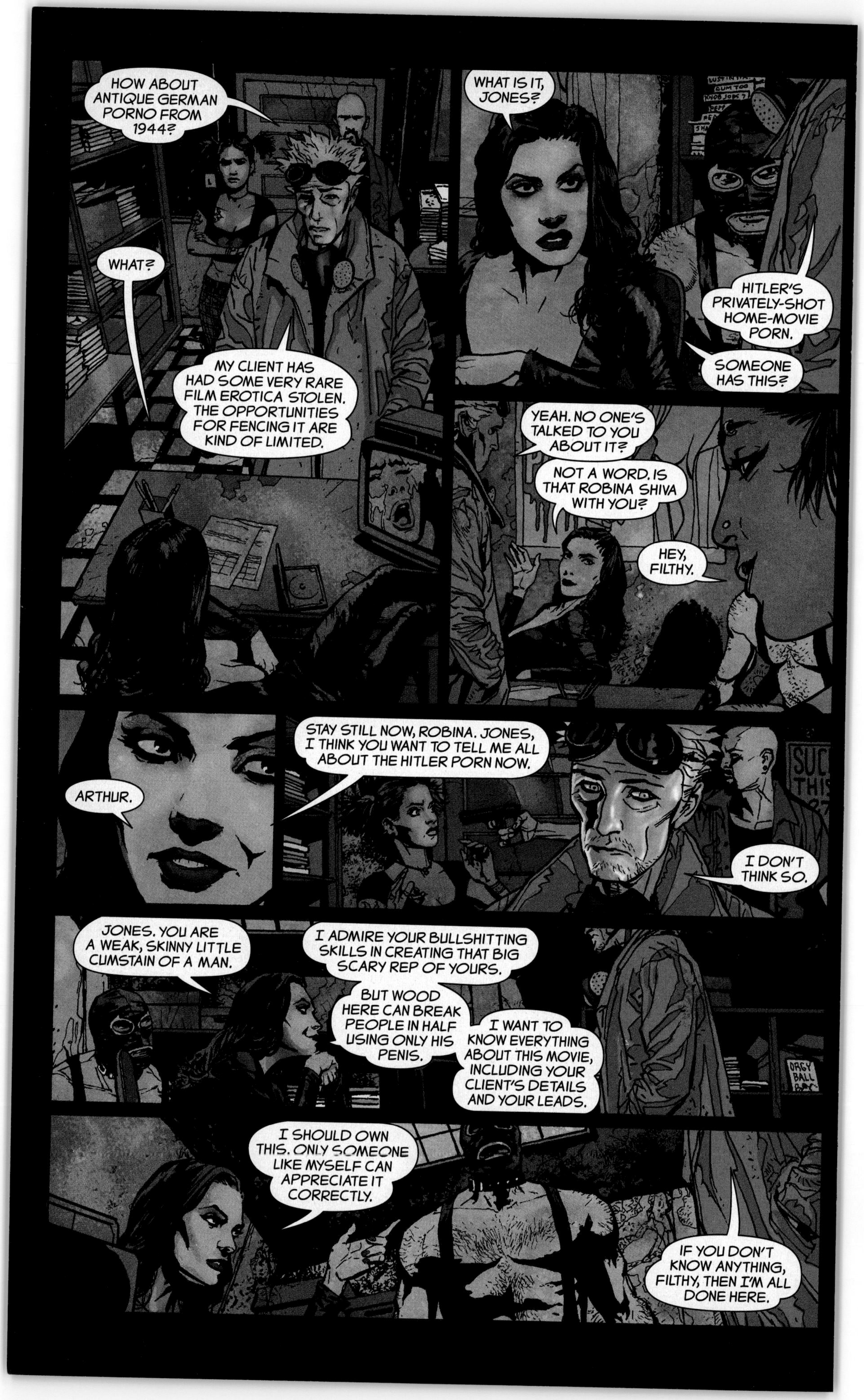
HOW ABOUT ANTIQUE GERMAN PORNO FROM 1944?
WHAT?
MY CLIENT HAS HAD SOME VERY RARE FILM EROTICA STOLEN. THE OPPORTUNITIES FOR FENCING IT ARE KIND OF LIMITED.
WHAT IS IT, JONES?
HITLER'S PRIVATELY-SHOT HOME-MOVIE PORN.
SOMEONE HAS THIS?
YEAH. NO ONE'S TALKED TO YOU ABOUT IT?
NOT A WORD. IS THAT ROBINA SHIVA WITH YOU?
HEY, FILTHY.
ARTHUR.
STAY STILL NOW, ROBINA. JONES, I THINK YOU WANT TO TELL ME ALL ABOUT THE HITLER PORN NOW.
I DON'T THINK SO.
JONES. YOU ARE A WEAK, SKINNY LITTLE CUMSTAIN OF A MAN.
I ADMIRE YOUR BULLSHITTING SKILLS IN CREATING THAT BIG SCARY REP OF YOURS.
BUT WOOD HERE CAN BREAK PEOPLE IN HALF USING ONLY HIS PENIS.
I WANT TO KNOW EVERYTHING ABOUT THIS MOVIE, INCLUDING YOUR CLIENT'S DETAILS AND YOUR LEADS.
I SHOULD OWN THIS. ONLY SOMEONE LIKE MYSELF CAN APPRECIATE IT CORRECTLY.
IF YOU DON'T KNOW ANYTHING, FILTHY, THEN I'M ALL DONE HERE.

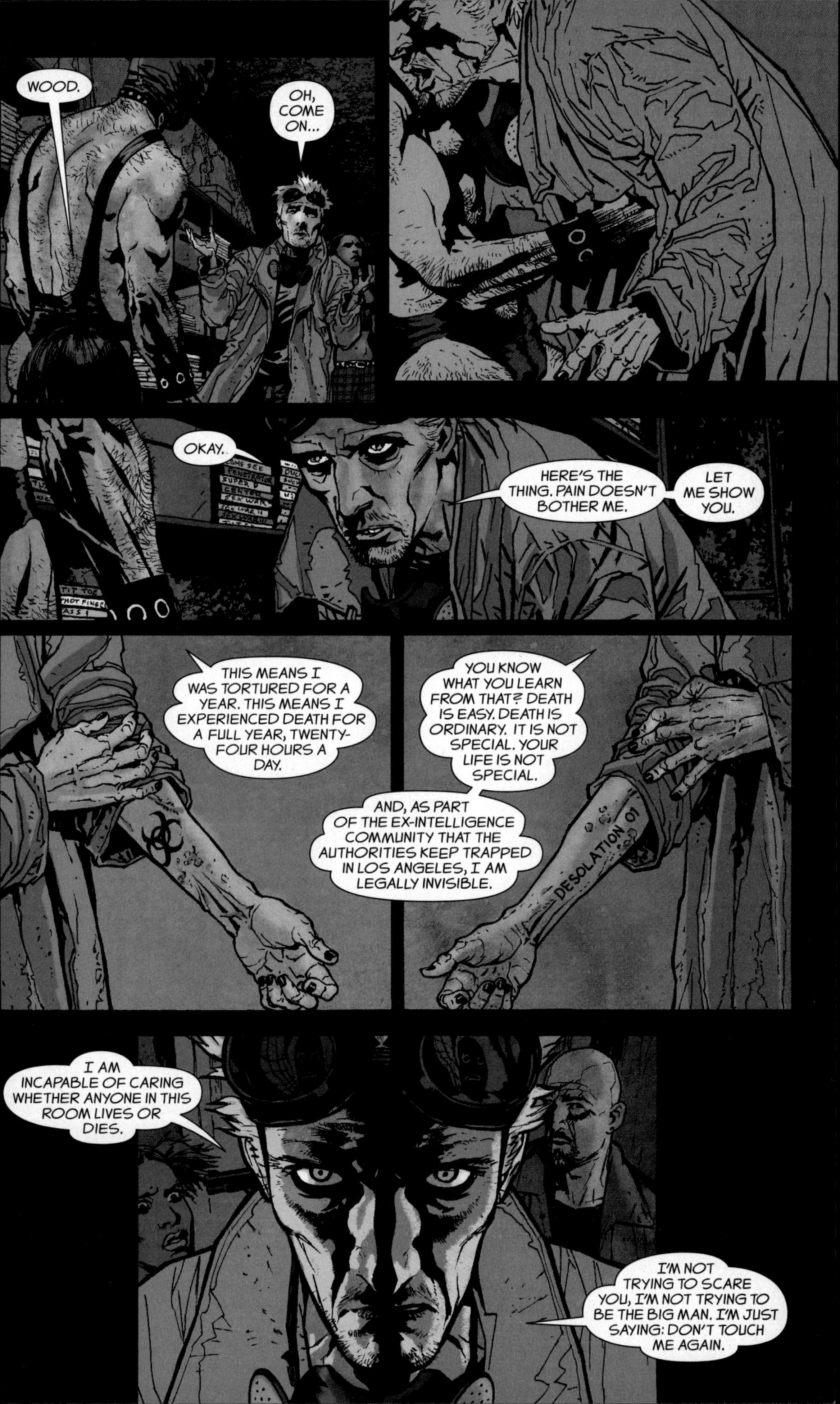

WOOD.
OH, COME ON...
OKAY.
HERE'S THE THING. PAIN DOESN'T BOTHER ME.
LET ME SHOW YOU.
THIS MEANS I WAS TORTURED FOR A YEAR. THIS MEANS I EXPERIENCED DEATH FOR A FULL YEAR, TWENTY-FOUR HOURS A DAY.
YOU KNOW WHAT YOU LEARN FROM THAT? DEATH IS EASY. DEATH IS ORDINARY. IT IS NOT SPECIAL. YOUR LIFE IS NOT SPECIAL.
AND, AS PART OF THE EX-INTELLIGENCE COMMUNITY THAT THE AUTHORITIES KEEP TRAPPED IN LOS ANGELES, I AM LEGALLY INVISIBLE.
DESOLATION 01
I AM INCAPABLE OF CARING WHETHER ANYONE IN THIS ROOM LIVES OR DIES.
I'M NOT TRYING TO SCARE YOU, I'M NOT TRYING TO BE THE BIG MAN. I'M JUST SAYING: DON'T TOUCH ME AGAIN.

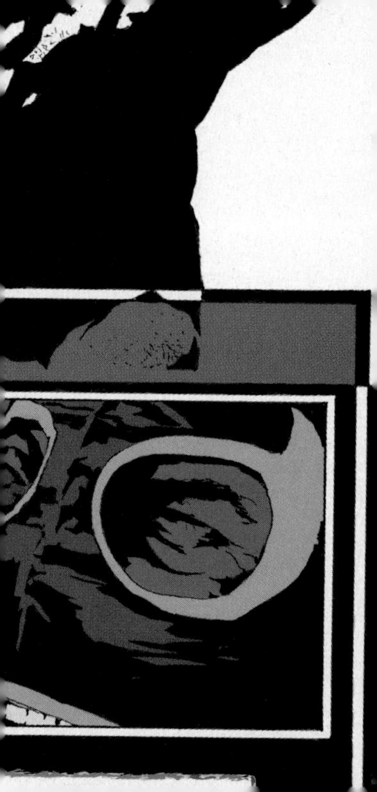

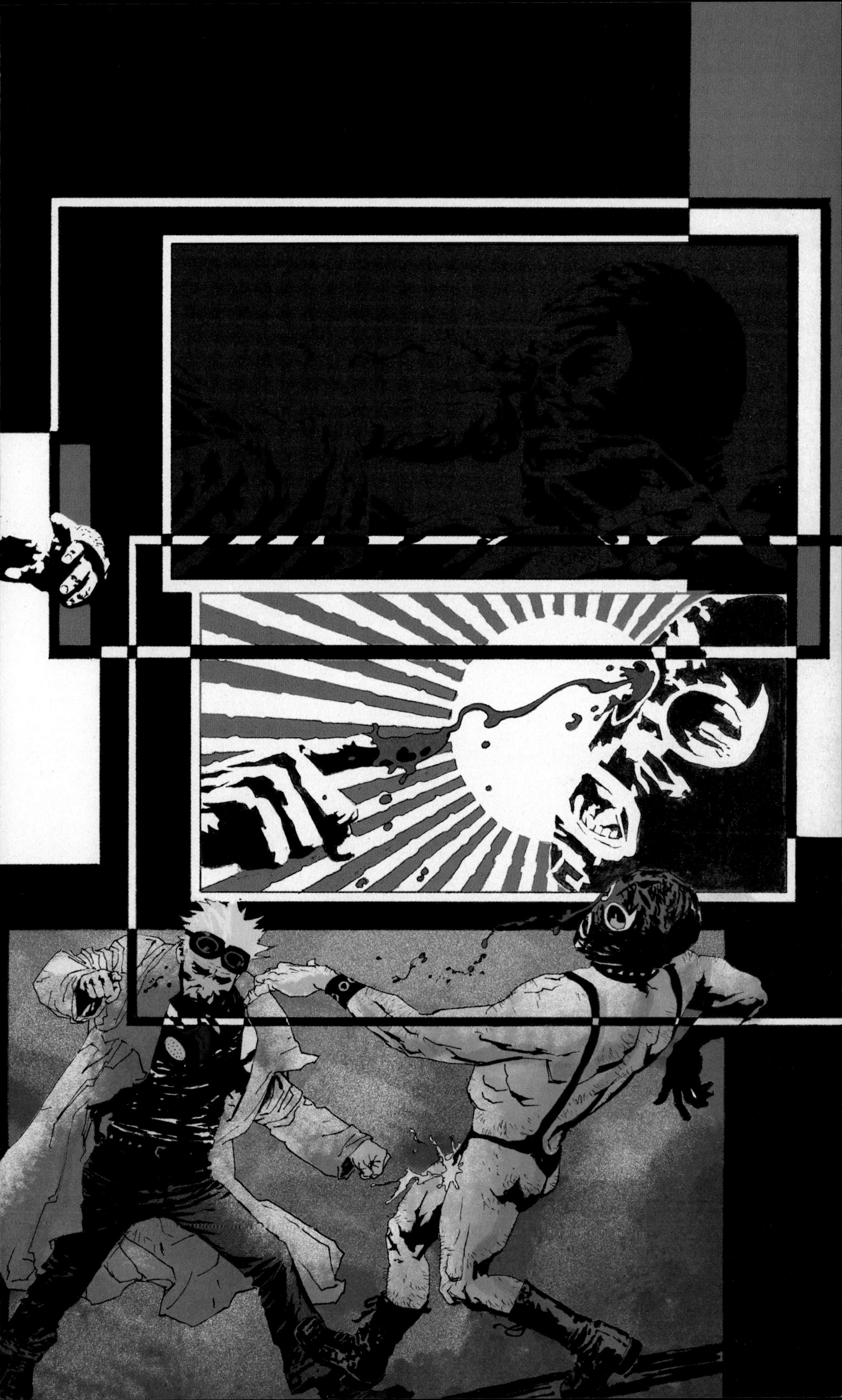

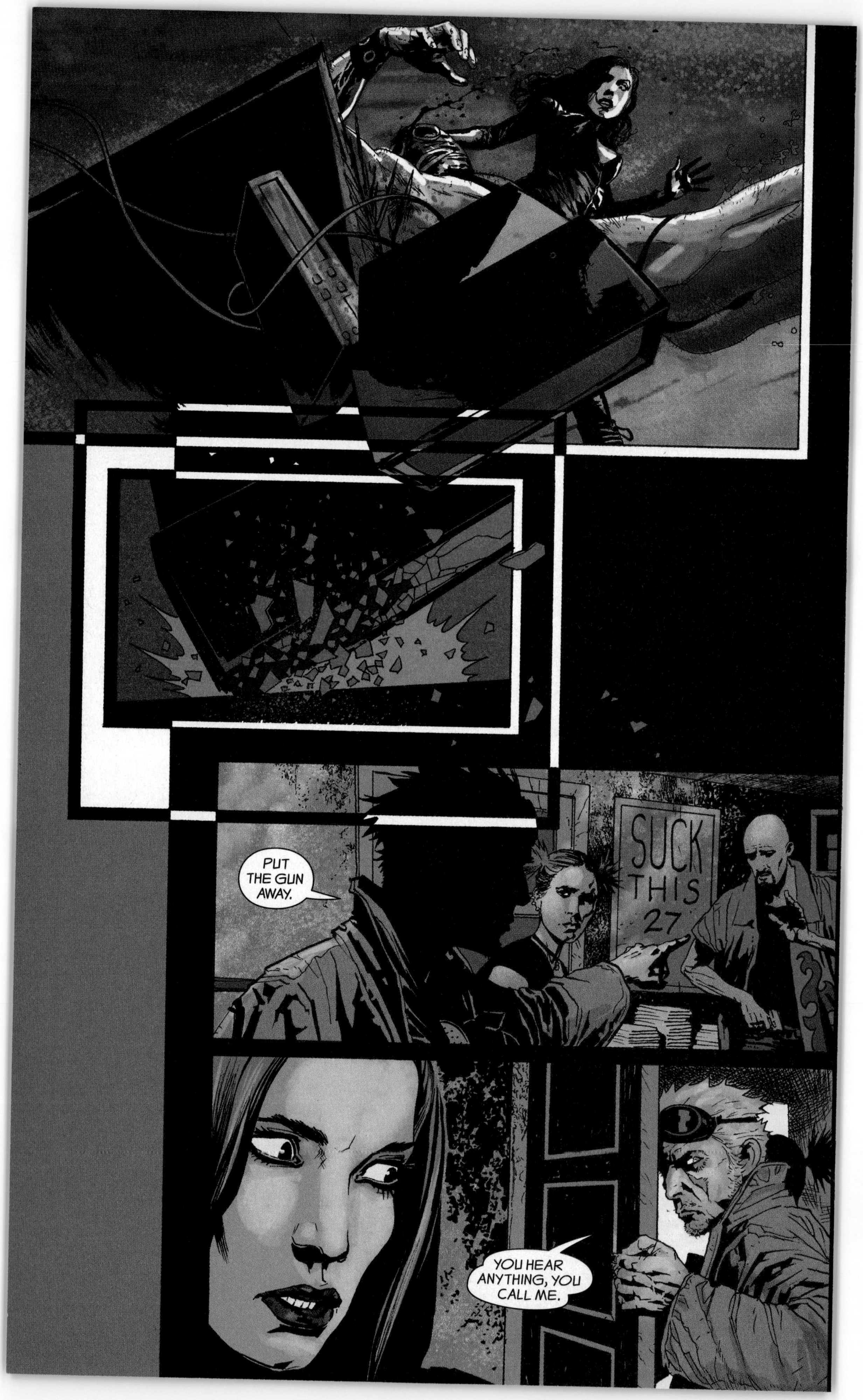

SUCK THIS 27
PUT THE GUN AWAY.
YOU HEAR ANYTHING, YOU CALL ME.

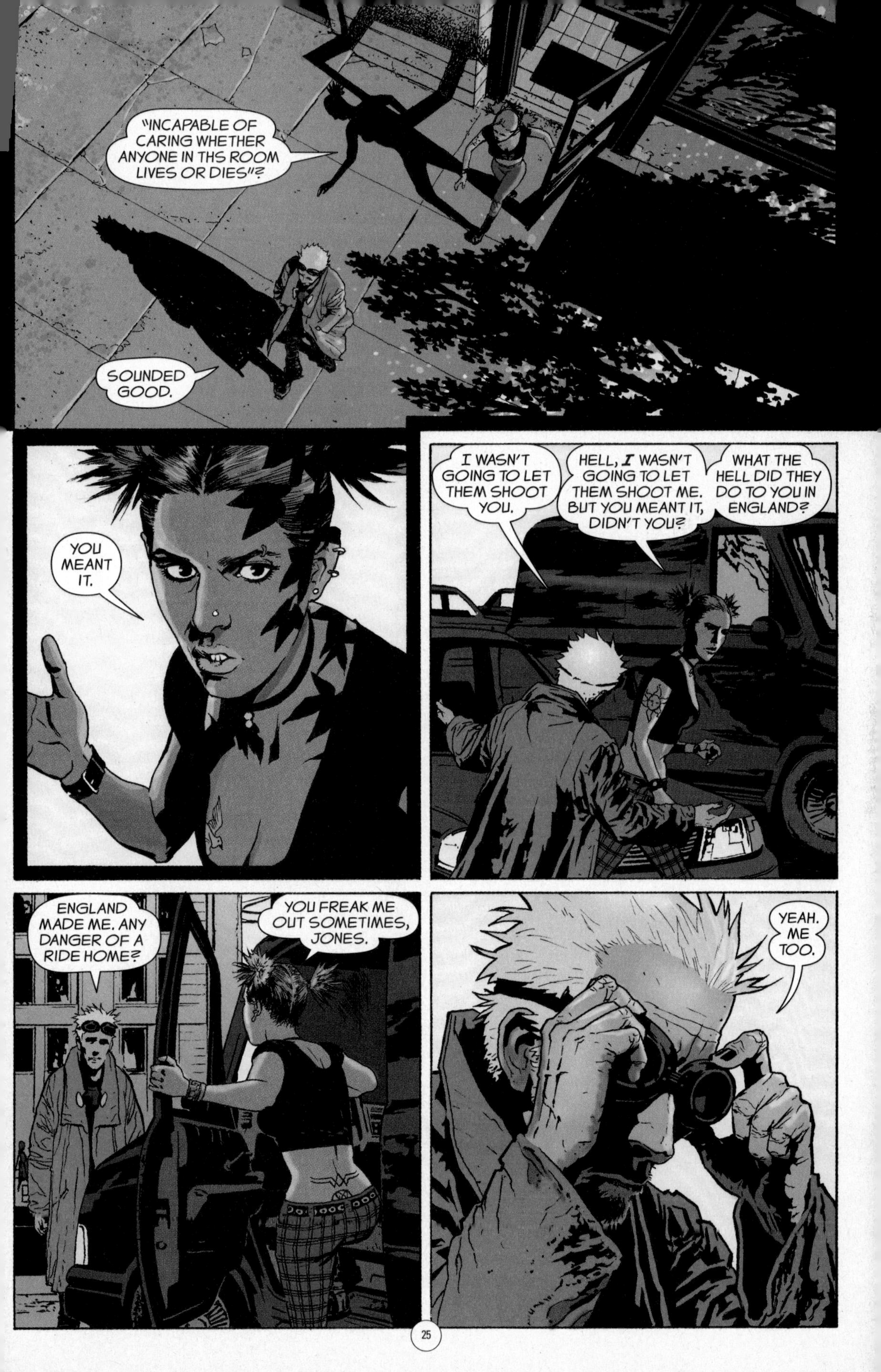
"INCAPABLE OF CARING WHETHER ANYONE IN THS ROOM LIVES OR DIES"?
SOUNDED GOOD.
YOU MEANT IT.
I WASN'T GOING TO LET THEM SHOOT YOU.
HELL, I WASN'T GOING TO LET THEM SHOOT ME. BUT YOU MEANT IT, DIDN'T YOU?
WHAT THE HELL DID THEY DO TO YOU IN ENGLAND?
ENGLAND MADE ME. ANY DANGER OF A RIDE HOME?
YOU FREAK ME OUT SOMETIMES, JONES.
YEAH. ME TOO.

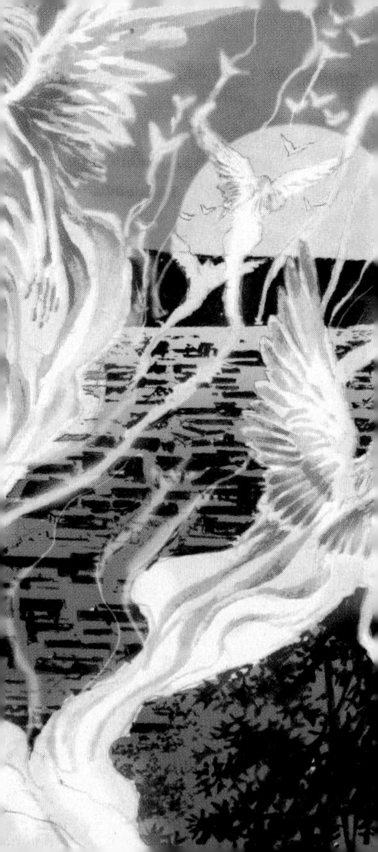

MADE IN ENGLAND PART 2

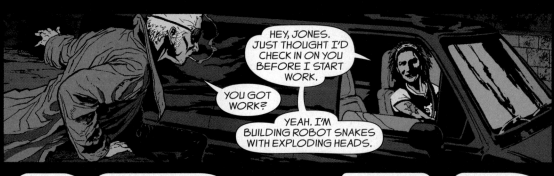

HEY, JONES. JUST THOUGHT I'D CHECK IN ON YOU BEFORE I START WORK.

YOU GOT WORK?

YEAH. I'M BUILDING ROBOT SNAKES WITH EXPLODING HEADS.

HOW THE HELL DO YOU GET THAT KIND OF GIG?

PRIVATE COMMISSION. ACTOR GUY THINKS MRS. ACTOR IS CHEATING ON HIM.

THE SNAKE GOES THROUGH THE A/C INTO THE BEDROOM, CAMS THE SCENE, AND EXPLODES IF SHE'S DOING SOMEONE ELSE.

AND YOU...

...HAVE GOT L.A. PRIVILEGES DUE TO HAVING BEEN SECTIONED OUT OF CIA COUNTER-INSURGENCY.

WHO KNEW A BREAKDOWN AND A LIFETIME SENTENCE TO L.A. WOULD LOOK GOOD ON A RESUMÉ?

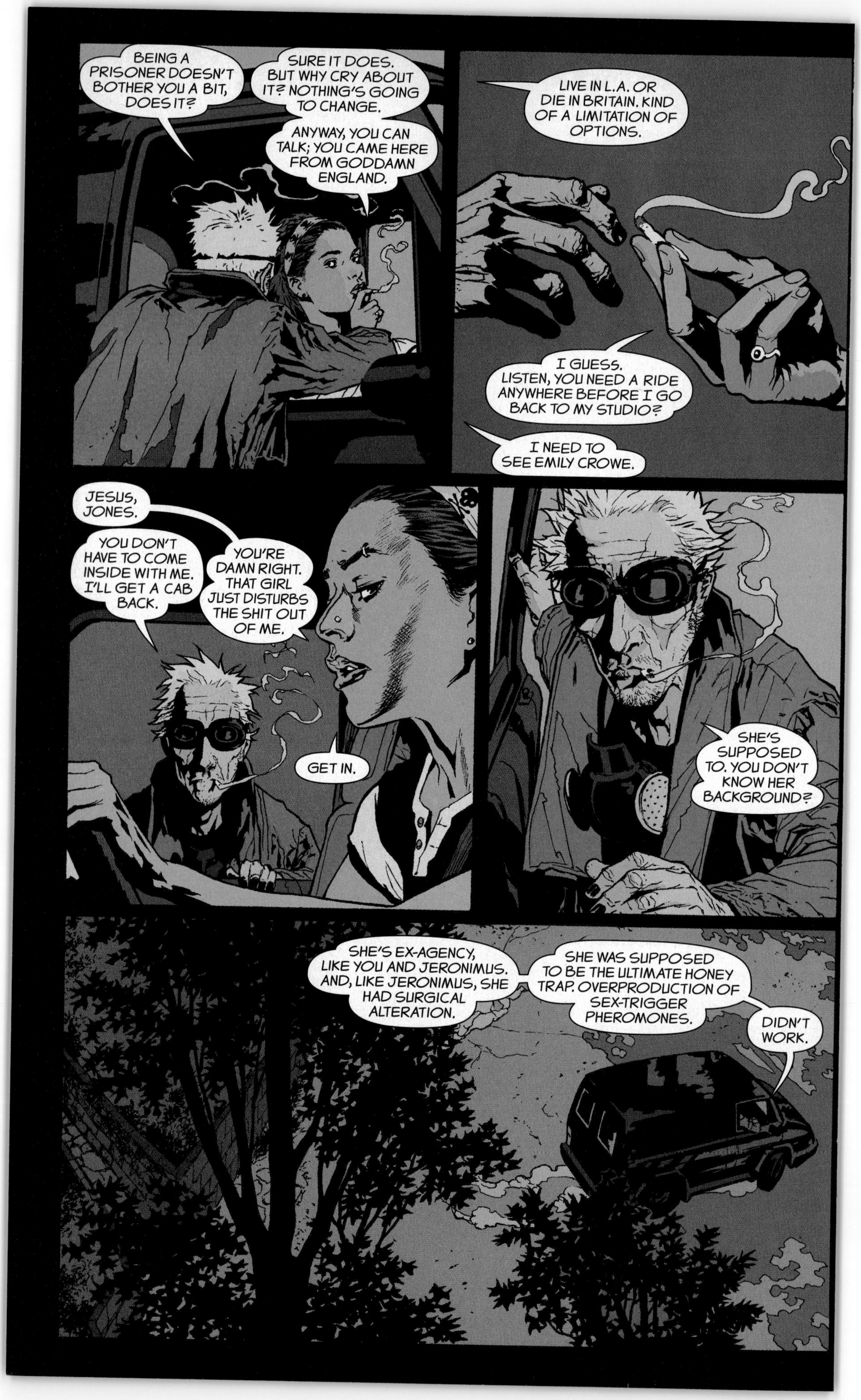
BEING A PRISONER DOESN'T BOTHER YOU A BIT, DOES IT?
SURE IT DOES. BUT WHY CRY ABOUT IT? NOTHING'S GOING TO CHANGE.
ANYWAY, YOU CAN TALK; YOU CAME HERE FROM GODDAMN ENGLAND.
LIVE IN L.A. OR DIE IN BRITAIN. KIND OF A LIMITATION OF OPTIONS.
I GUESS. LISTEN, YOU NEED A RIDE ANYWHERE BEFORE I GO BACK TO MY STUDIO?
I NEED TO SEE EMILY CROWE.
JESUS, JONES.
YOU DON'T HAVE TO COME INSIDE WITH ME. I'LL GET A CAB BACK.
YOU'RE DAMN RIGHT. THAT GIRL JUST DISTURBS THE SHIT OUT OF ME.
GET IN.
SHE'S SUPPOSED TO. YOU DON'T KNOW HER BACKGROUND?
SHE'S EX-AGENCY, LIKE YOU AND JERONIMUS. AND, LIKE JERONIMUS, SHE HAD SURGICAL ALTERATION.
SHE WAS SUPPOSED TO BE THE ULTIMATE HONEY TRAP. OVERPRODUCTION OF SEX-TRIGGER PHEROMONES.
DIDN'T WORK.

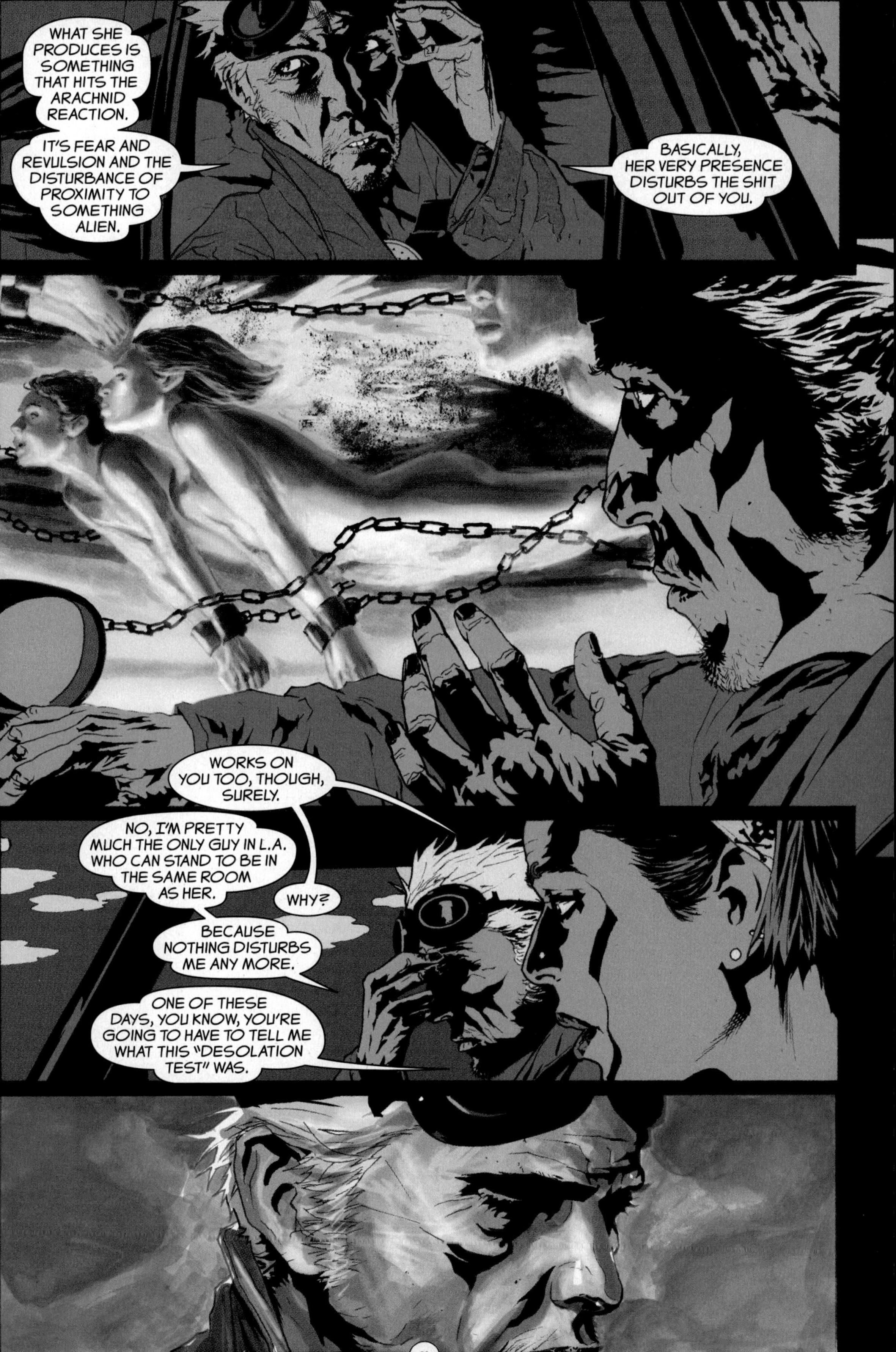
WHAT SHE PRODUCES IS SOMETHING THAT HITS THE ARACHNID REACTION.
IT'S FEAR AND REVULSION AND THE DISTURBANCE OF PROXIMITY TO SOMETHING ALIEN.
BASICALLY, HER VERY PRESENCE DISTURBS THE SHIT OUT OF YOU.
WORKS ON YOU TOO, THOUGH, SURELY.
NO, I'M PRETTY MUCH THE ONLY GUY IN L.A. WHO CAN STAND TO BE IN THE SAME ROOM AS HER.
WHY?
BECAUSE NOTHING DISTURBS ME ANY MORE.
ONE OF THESE DAYS, YOU KNOW, YOU'RE GOING TO HAVE TO TELL ME WHAT THIS "DESOLATION TEST" WAS.

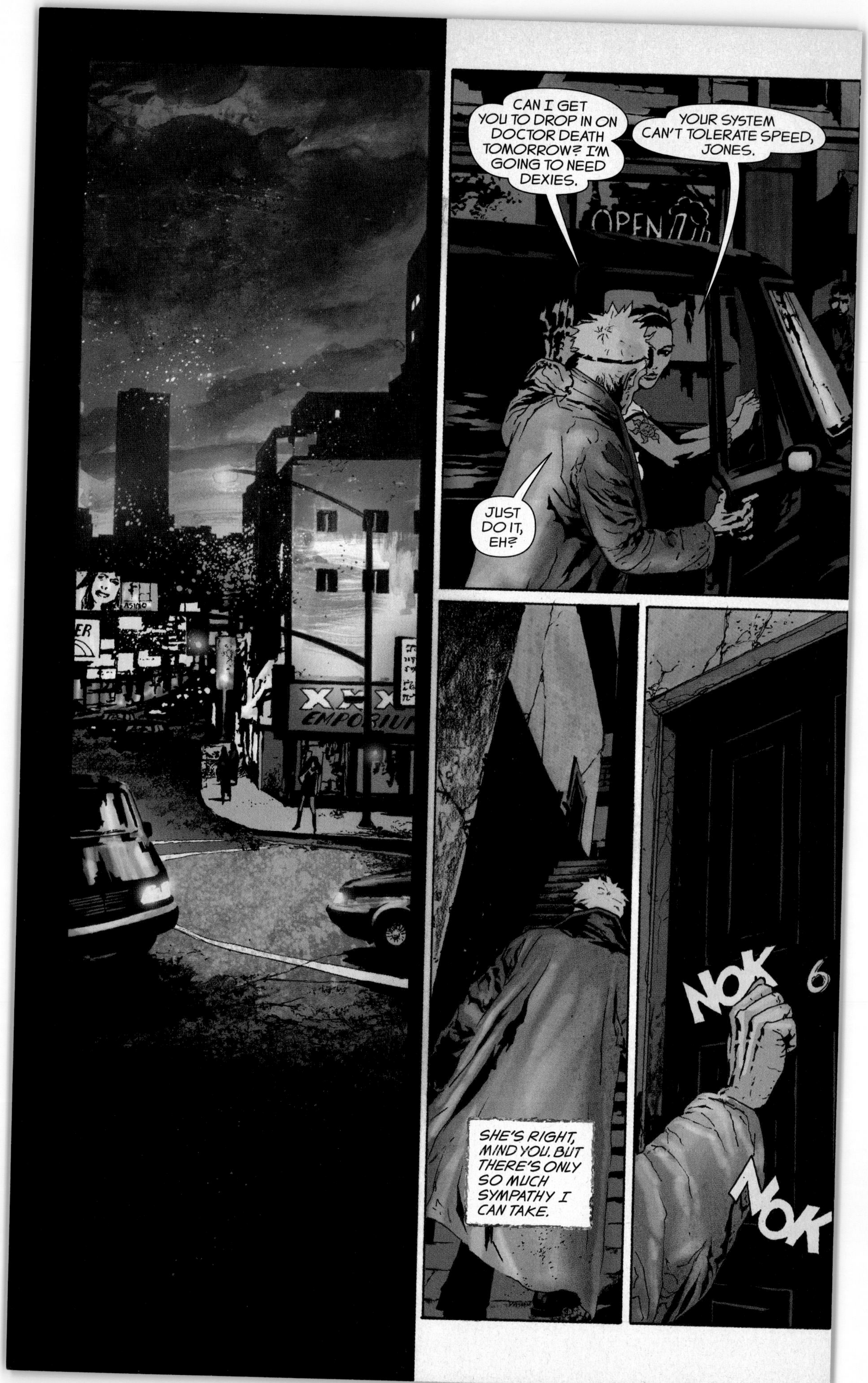

CAN I GET YOU TO DROP IN ON DOCTOR DEATH TOMORROW? I'M GOING TO NEED DEXIES.
YOUR SYSTEM CAN'T TOLERATE SPEED, JONES.
JUST DO IT, EH?
OPEN
XXX EMPORIUM
SHE'S RIGHT, MIND YOU. BUT THERE'S ONLY SO MUCH SYMPATHY I CAN TAKE.
NOK
6
NOK

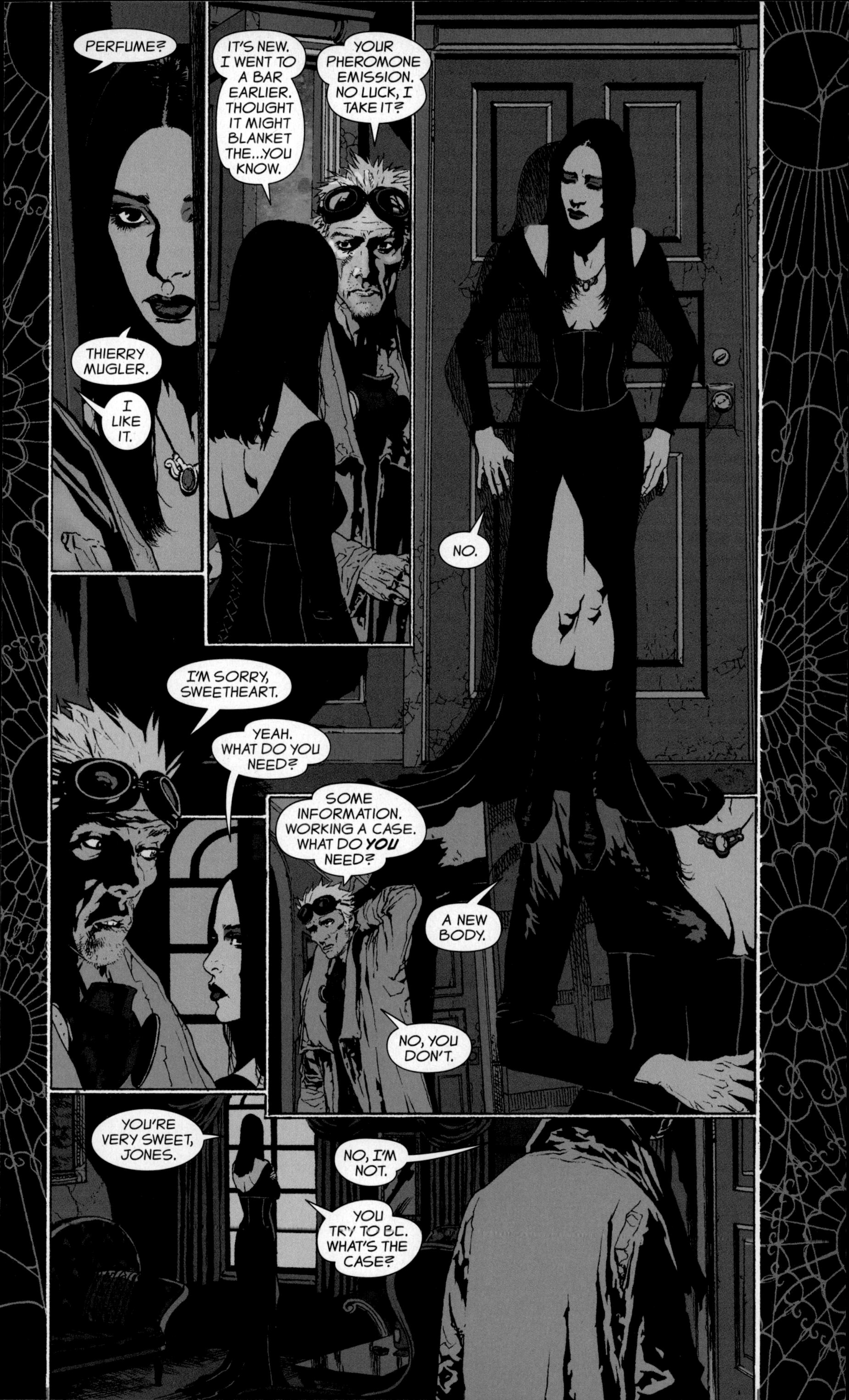
PERFUME?
IT'S NEW. I WENT TO A BAR EARLIER. THOUGHT IT MIGHT BLANKET THE...YOU KNOW.
YOUR PHEROMONE EMISSION. NO LUCK, I TAKE IT?
THIERRY MUGLER.
I LIKE IT.
NO.
I'M SORRY, SWEETHEART.
YEAH. WHAT DO YOU NEED?
SOME INFORMATION. WORKING A CASE. WHAT DO *YOU* NEED?
A NEW BODY.
NO, YOU DON'T.
YOU'RE VERY SWEET, JONES.
NO, I'M NOT.
YOU TRY TO BE. WHAT'S THE CASE?

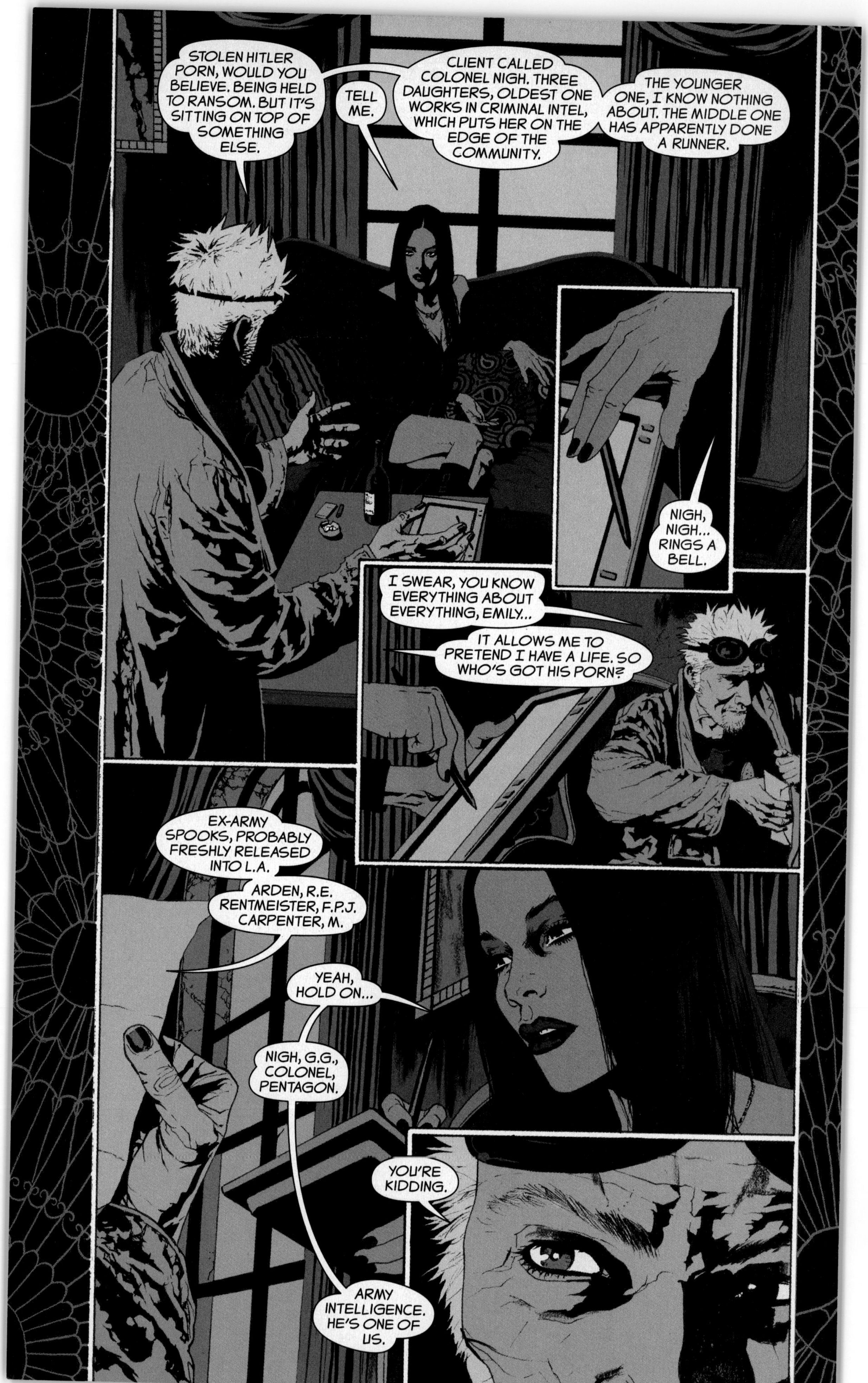
STOLEN HITLER PORN, WOULD YOU BELIEVE. BEING HELD TO RANSOM. BUT IT'S SITTING ON TOP OF SOMETHING ELSE.
TELL ME.
CLIENT CALLED COLONEL NIGH. THREE DAUGHTERS, OLDEST ONE WORKS IN CRIMINAL INTEL, WHICH PUTS HER ON THE EDGE OF THE COMMUNITY.
THE YOUNGER ONE, I KNOW NOTHING ABOUT. THE MIDDLE ONE HAS APPARENTLY DONE A RUNNER.
NIGH, NIGH... RINGS A BELL.
I SWEAR, YOU KNOW EVERYTHING ABOUT EVERYTHING, EMILY...
IT ALLOWS ME TO PRETEND I HAVE A LIFE. SO WHO'S GOT HIS PORN?
EX-ARMY SPOOKS, PROBABLY FRESHLY RELEASED INTO L.A.
ARDEN, R.E. RENTMEISTER, F.P.J. CARPENTER, M.
YEAH, HOLD ON...
NIGH, G.G., COLONEL, PENTAGON.
YOU'RE KIDDING.
ARMY INTELLIGENCE. HE'S ONE OF US.

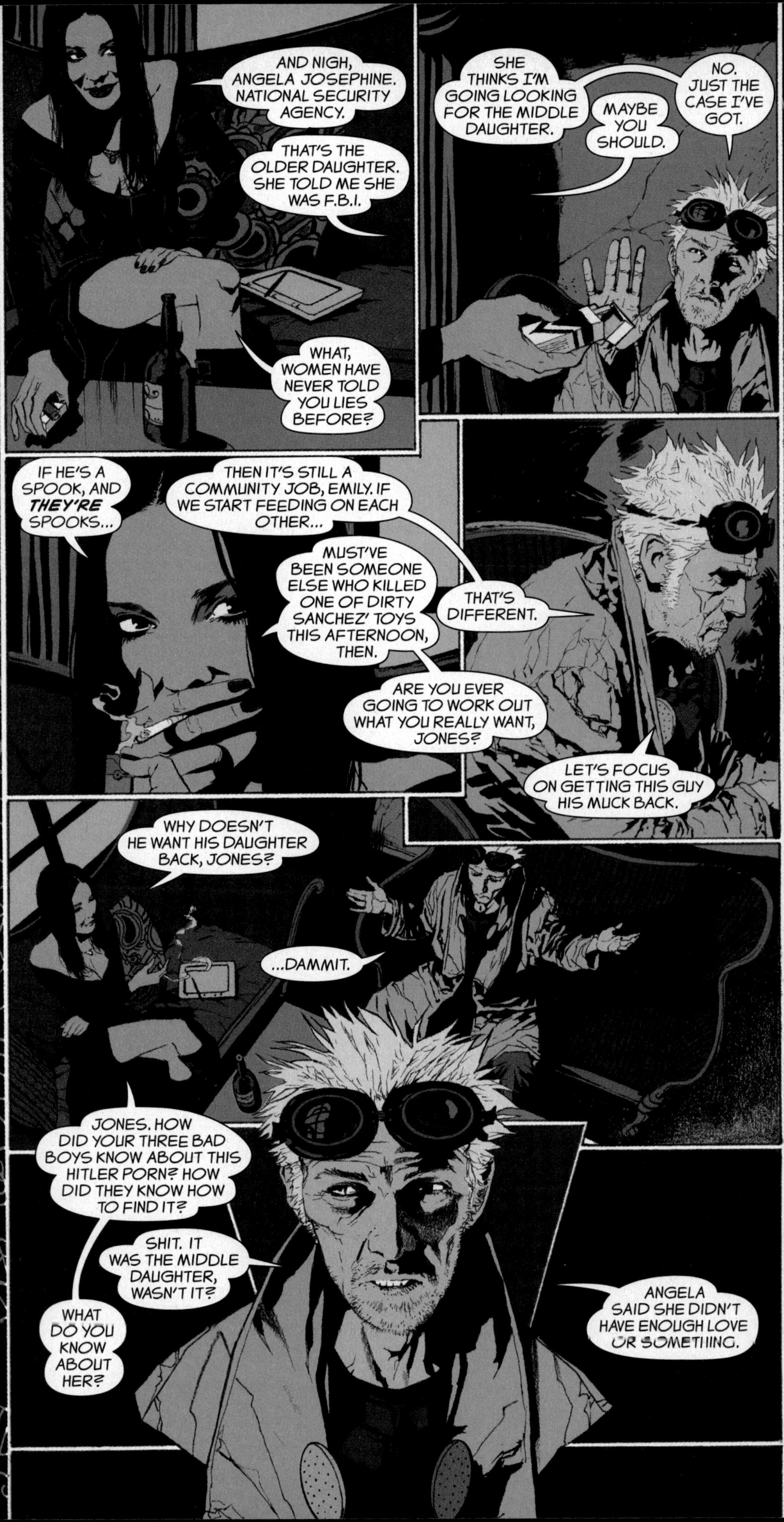
AND NIGH, ANGELA JOSEPHINE. NATIONAL SECURITY AGENCY.
THAT'S THE OLDER DAUGHTER. SHE TOLD ME SHE WAS F.B.I.
WHAT, WOMEN HAVE NEVER TOLD YOU LIES BEFORE?
SHE THINKS I'M GOING LOOKING FOR THE MIDDLE DAUGHTER.
MAYBE YOU SHOULD.
NO. JUST THE CASE I'VE GOT.
IF HE'S A SPOOK, AND THEY'RE SPOOKS...
THEN IT'S STILL A COMMUNITY JOB, EMILY. IF WE START FEEDING ON EACH OTHER...
THAT'S DIFFERENT.
MUST'VE BEEN SOMEONE ELSE WHO KILLED ONE OF DIRTY SANCHEZ' TOYS THIS AFTERNOON, THEN.
ARE YOU EVER GOING TO WORK OUT WHAT YOU REALLY WANT, JONES?
LET'S FOCUS ON GETTING THIS GUY HIS MUCK BACK.
WHY DOESN'T HE WANT HIS DAUGHTER BACK, JONES?
...DAMMIT.
JONES. HOW DID YOUR THREE BAD BOYS KNOW ABOUT THIS HITLER PORN? HOW DID THEY KNOW HOW TO FIND IT?
SHIT. IT WAS THE MIDDLE DAUGHTER, WASN'T IT?
WHAT DO YOU KNOW ABOUT HER?
ANGELA SAID SHE DIDN'T HAVE ENOUGH LOVE OR SOMETHING.

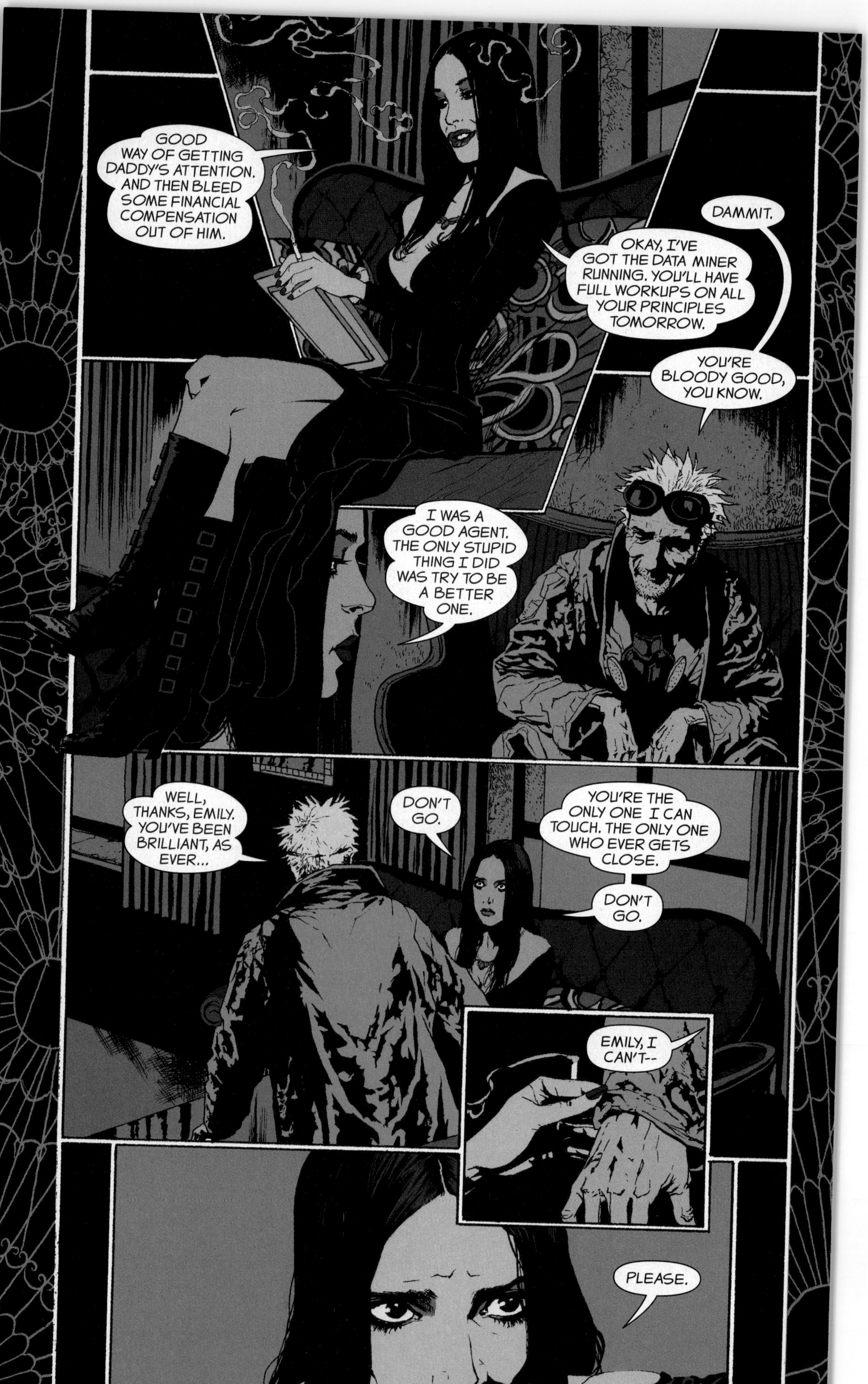
GOOD WAY OF GETTING DADDY'S ATTENTION. AND THEN BLEED SOME FINANCIAL COMPENSATION OUT OF HIM.
DAMMIT.
OKAY, I'VE GOT THE DATA MINER RUNNING. YOU'LL HAVE FULL WORKUPS ON ALL YOUR PRINCIPLES TOMORROW.
YOU'RE BLOODY GOOD, YOU KNOW.
I WAS A GOOD AGENT. THE ONLY STUPID THING I DID WAS TRY TO BE A BETTER ONE.
WELL, THANKS, EMILY. YOU'VE BEEN BRILLIANT, AS EVER...
DON'T GO.
YOU'RE THE ONLY ONE I CAN TOUCH. THE ONLY ONE WHO EVER GETS CLOSE.
DON'T GO.
EMILY, I CAN'T--
PLEASE.

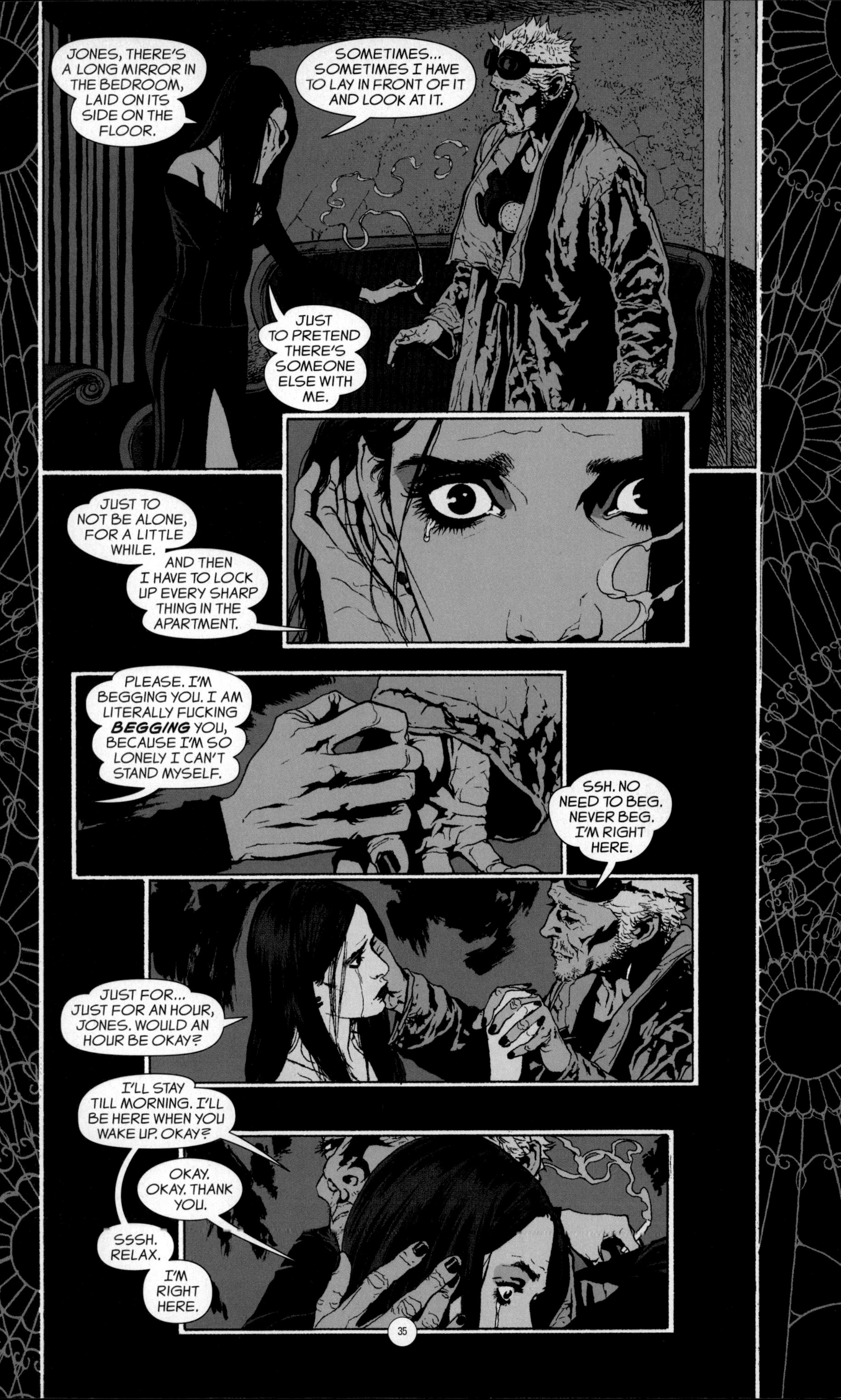
JONES, THERE'S A LONG MIRROR IN THE BEDROOM, LAID ON ITS SIDE ON THE FLOOR.
SOMETIMES... SOMETIMES I HAVE TO LAY IN FRONT OF IT AND LOOK AT IT.
JUST TO PRETEND THERE'S SOMEONE ELSE WITH ME.
JUST TO NOT BE ALONE, FOR A LITTLE WHILE.
AND THEN I HAVE TO LOCK UP EVERY SHARP THING IN THE APARTMENT.
PLEASE. I'M BEGGING YOU. I AM LITERALLY FUCKING **BEGGING** YOU, BECAUSE I'M SO LONELY I CAN'T STAND MYSELF.
SSH. NO NEED TO BEG. NEVER BEG. I'M RIGHT HERE.
JUST FOR... JUST FOR AN HOUR, JONES. WOULD AN HOUR BE OKAY?
I'LL STAY TILL MORNING. I'LL BE HERE WHEN YOU WAKE UP. OKAY?
OKAY. OKAY. THANK YOU.
SSSH. RELAX.
I'M RIGHT HERE.

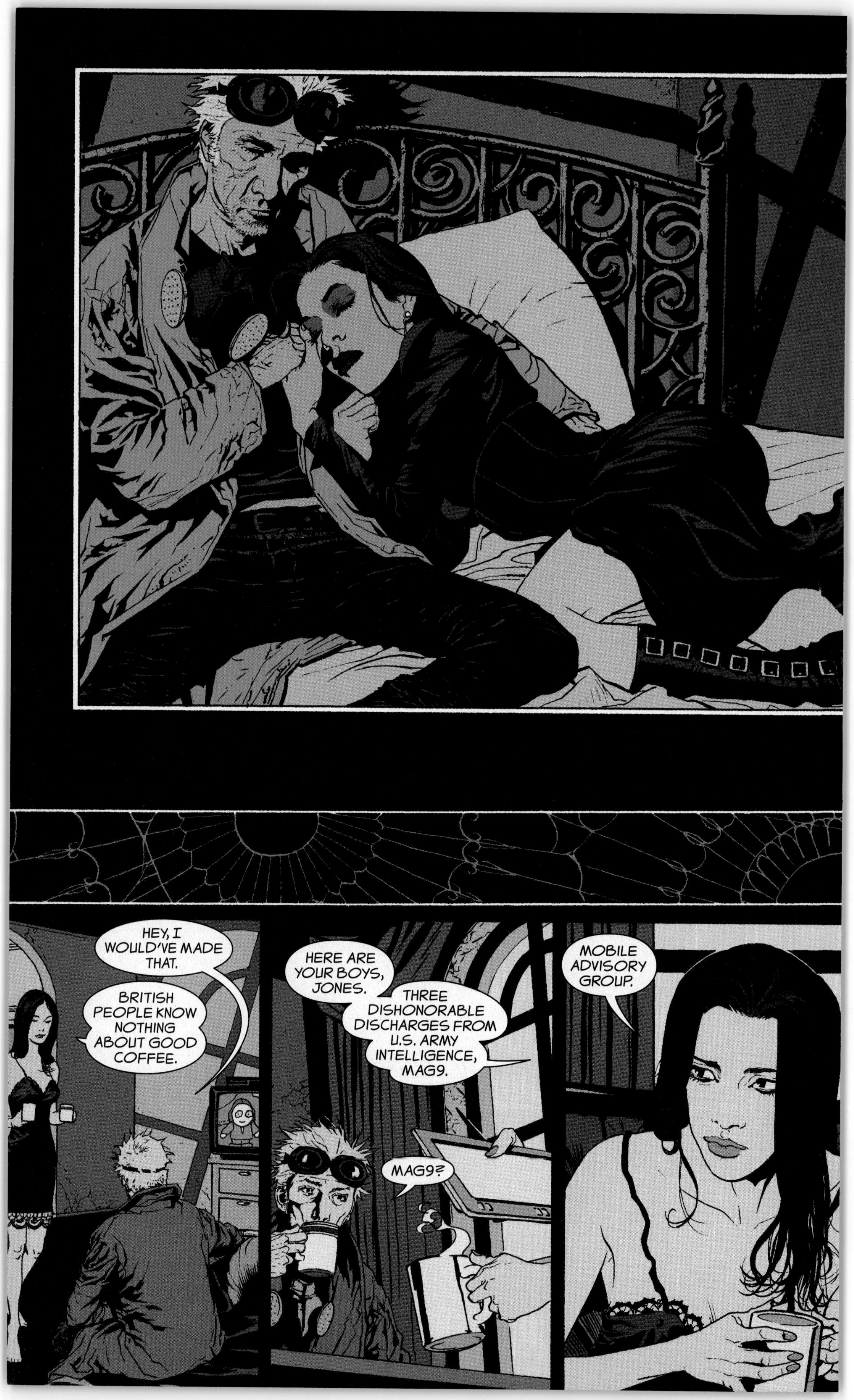
HEY, I WOULD'VE MADE THAT.
BRITISH PEOPLE KNOW NOTHING ABOUT GOOD COFFEE.
HERE ARE YOUR BOYS, JONES.
THREE DISHONORABLE DISCHARGES FROM U.S. ARMY INTELLIGENCE, MAG9.
MAG9?
MOBILE ADVISORY GROUP.

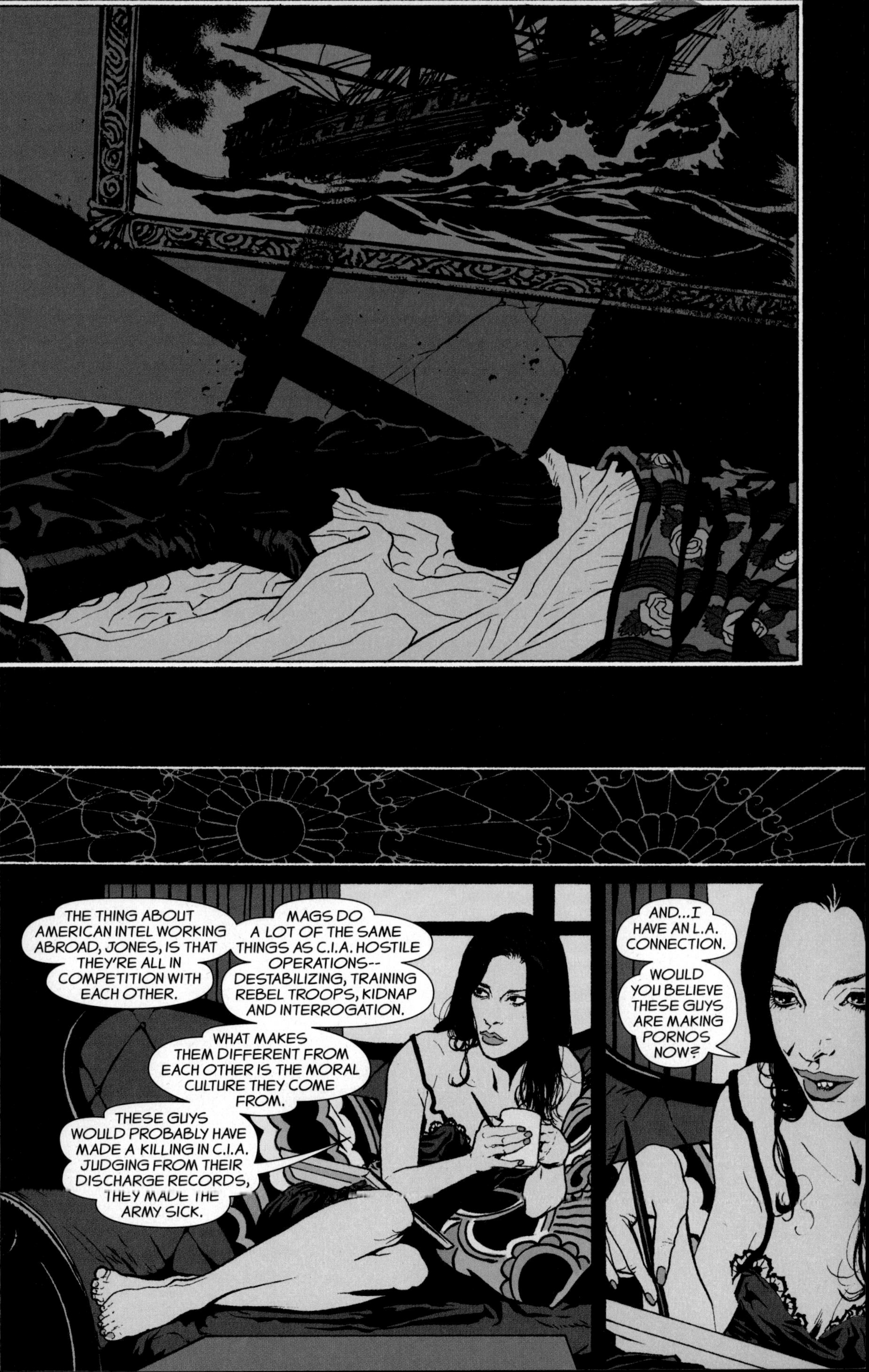
THE THING ABOUT AMERICAN INTEL WORKING ABROAD, JONES, IS THAT THEY'RE ALL IN COMPETITION WITH EACH OTHER.
MAGS DO A LOT OF THE SAME THINGS AS C.I.A. HOSTILE OPERATIONS--DESTABILIZING, TRAINING REBEL TROOPS, KIDNAP AND INTERROGATION.
WHAT MAKES THEM DIFFERENT FROM EACH OTHER IS THE MORAL CULTURE THEY COME FROM.
THESE GUYS WOULD PROBABLY HAVE MADE A KILLING IN C.I.A. JUDGING FROM THEIR DISCHARGE RECORDS, THEY MADE THE ARMY SICK.
AND...I HAVE AN L.A. CONNECTION.
WOULD YOU BELIEVE THESE GUYS ARE MAKING PORNOS NOW?

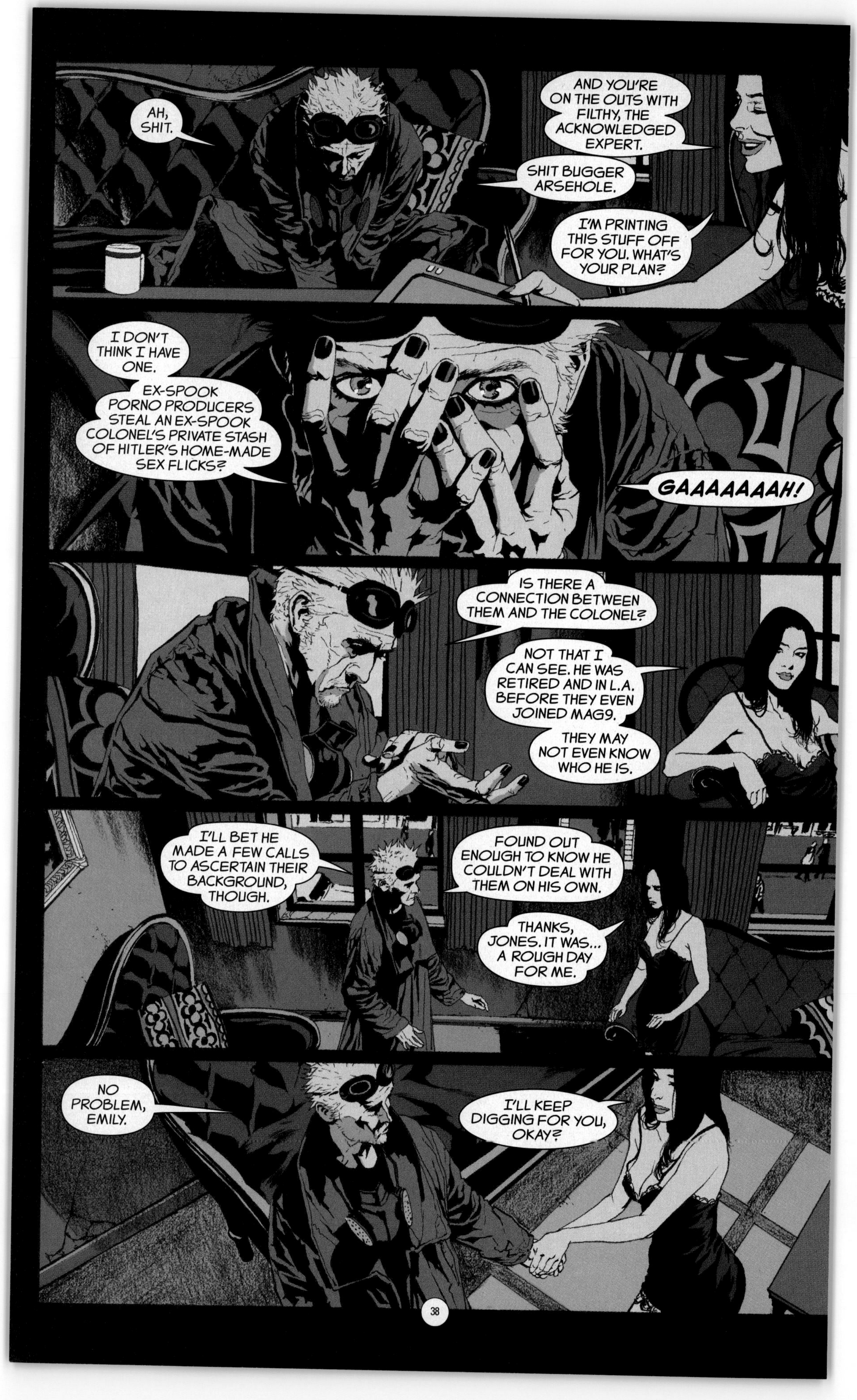
AH, SHIT.
AND YOU'RE ON THE OUTS WITH FILTHY, THE ACKNOWLEDGED EXPERT.
SHIT BUGGER ARSEHOLE.
I'M PRINTING THIS STUFF OFF FOR YOU. WHAT'S YOUR PLAN?
I DON'T THINK I HAVE ONE.
EX-SPOOK PORNO PRODUCERS STEAL AN EX-SPOOK COLONEL'S PRIVATE STASH OF HITLER'S HOME-MADE SEX FLICKS?
GAAAAAAAH!
IS THERE A CONNECTION BETWEEN THEM AND THE COLONEL?
NOT THAT I CAN SEE. HE WAS RETIRED AND IN L.A. BEFORE THEY EVEN JOINED MAG9.
THEY MAY NOT EVEN KNOW WHO HE IS.
I'LL BET HE MADE A FEW CALLS TO ASCERTAIN THEIR BACKGROUND, THOUGH.
FOUND OUT ENOUGH TO KNOW HE COULDN'T DEAL WITH THEM ON HIS OWN.
THANKS, JONES. IT WAS... A ROUGH DAY FOR ME.
NO PROBLEM, EMILY.
I'LL KEEP DIGGING FOR YOU, OKAY?

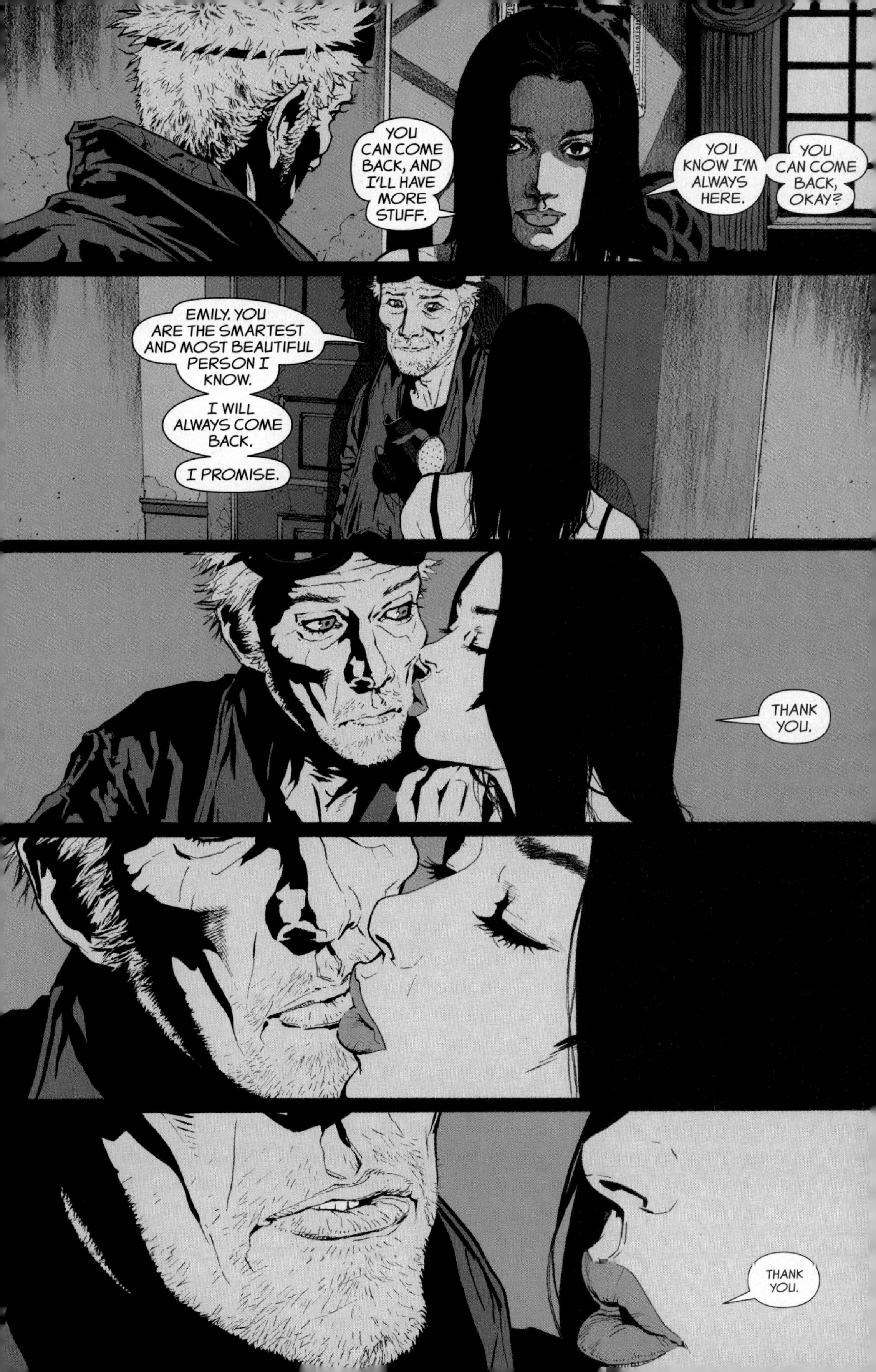
YOU CAN COME BACK, AND I'LL HAVE MORE STUFF.
YOU KNOW I'M ALWAYS HERE.
YOU CAN COME BACK, OKAY?
EMILY. YOU ARE THE SMARTEST AND MOST BEAUTIFUL PERSON I KNOW.
I WILL ALWAYS COME BACK.
I PROMISE.
THANK YOU.
THANK YOU.

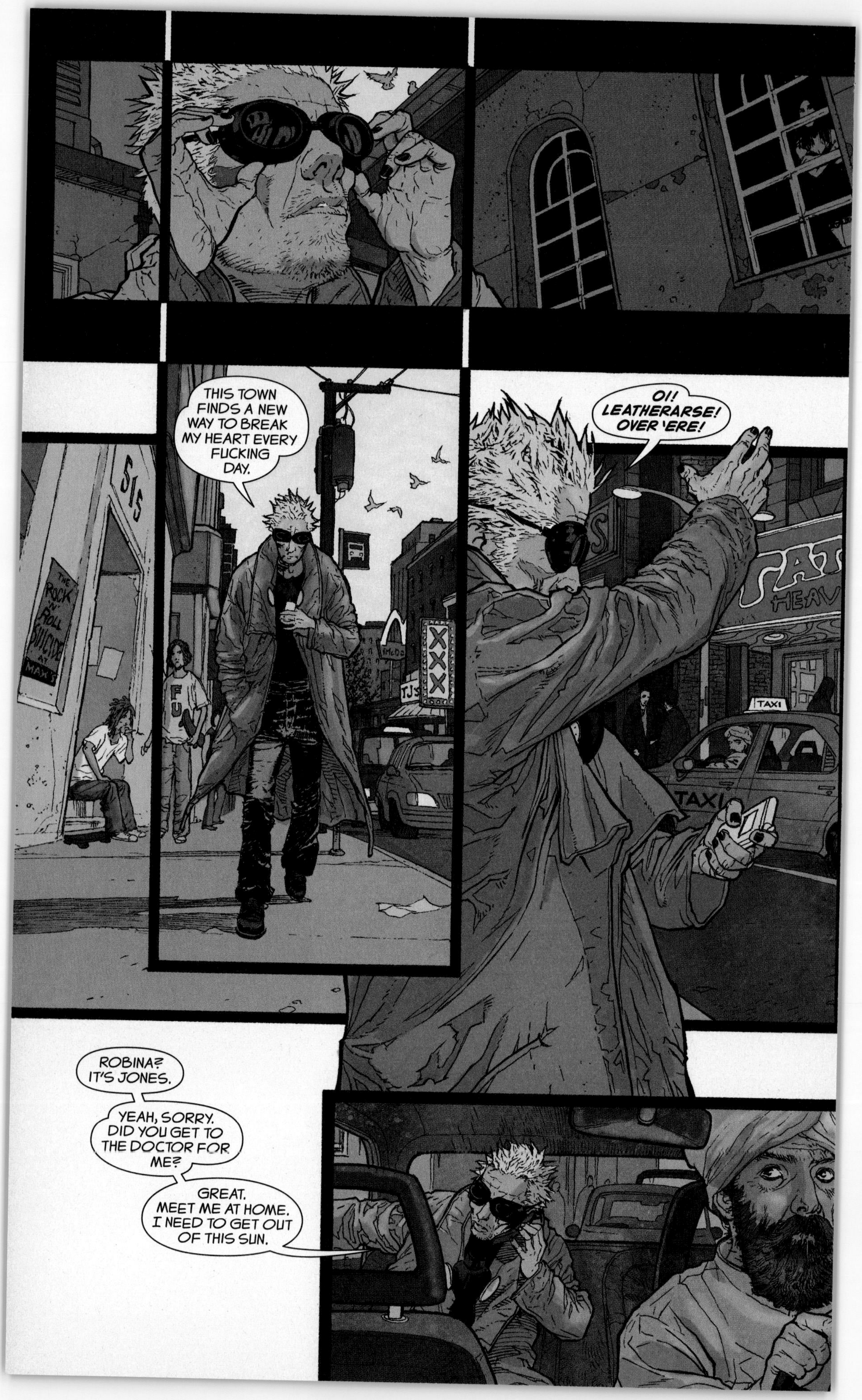
THIS TOWN FINDS A NEW WAY TO BREAK MY HEART EVERY FUCKING DAY.
OI! LEATHERARSE! OVER 'ERE!
TAXI
TAXI
ROBINA? IT'S JONES.
YEAH, SORRY. DID YOU GET TO THE DOCTOR FOR ME?
GREAT. MEET ME AT HOME. I NEED TO GET OUT OF THIS SUN.

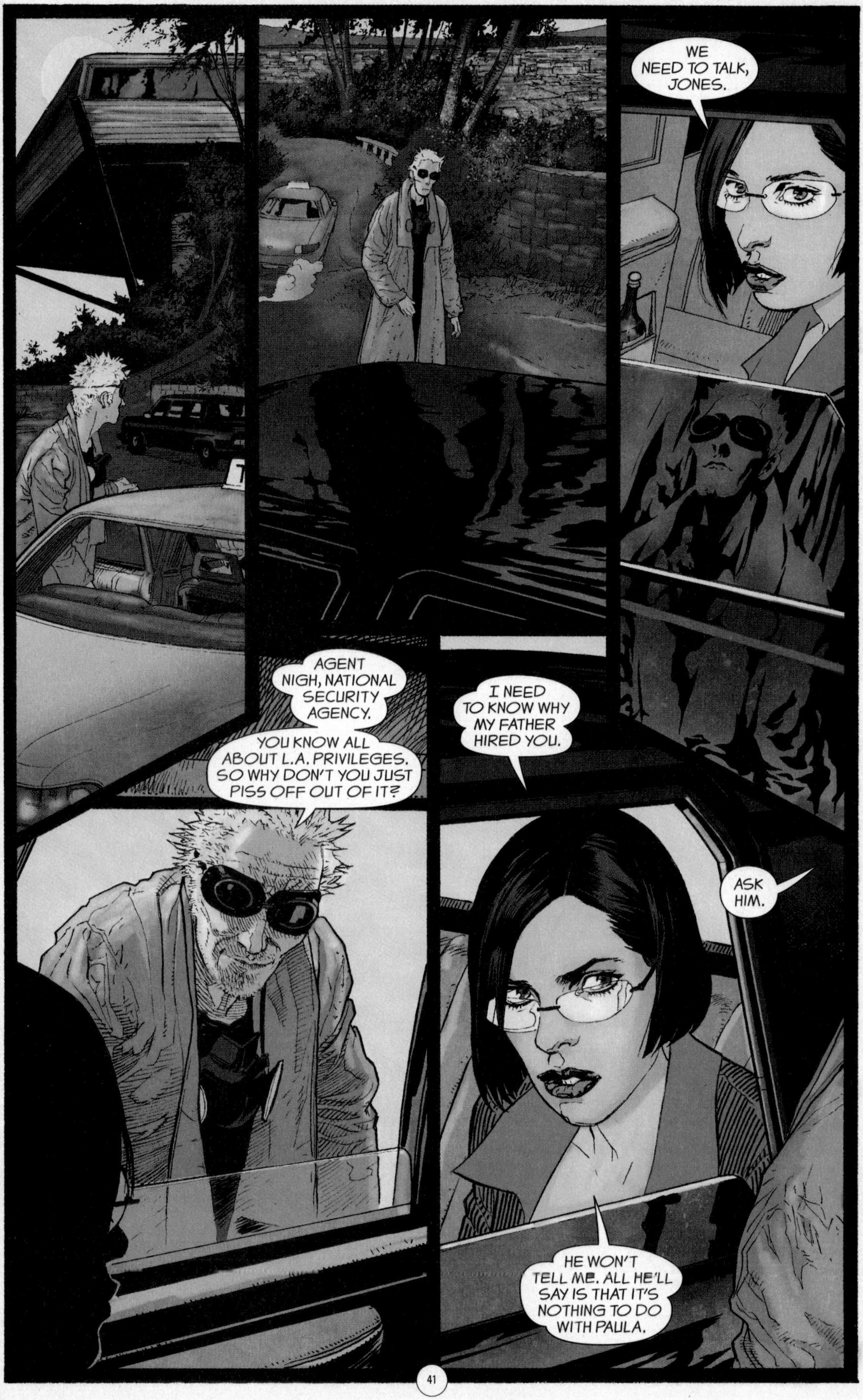
WE NEED TO TALK, JONES.
AGENT NIGH, NATIONAL SECURITY AGENCY.
YOU KNOW ALL ABOUT L.A. PRIVILEGES. SO WHY DON'T YOU JUST PISS OFF OUT OF IT?
I NEED TO KNOW WHY MY FATHER HIRED YOU.
ASK HIM.
HE WON'T TELL ME. ALL HE'LL SAY IS THAT IT'S NOTHING TO DO WITH PAULA.

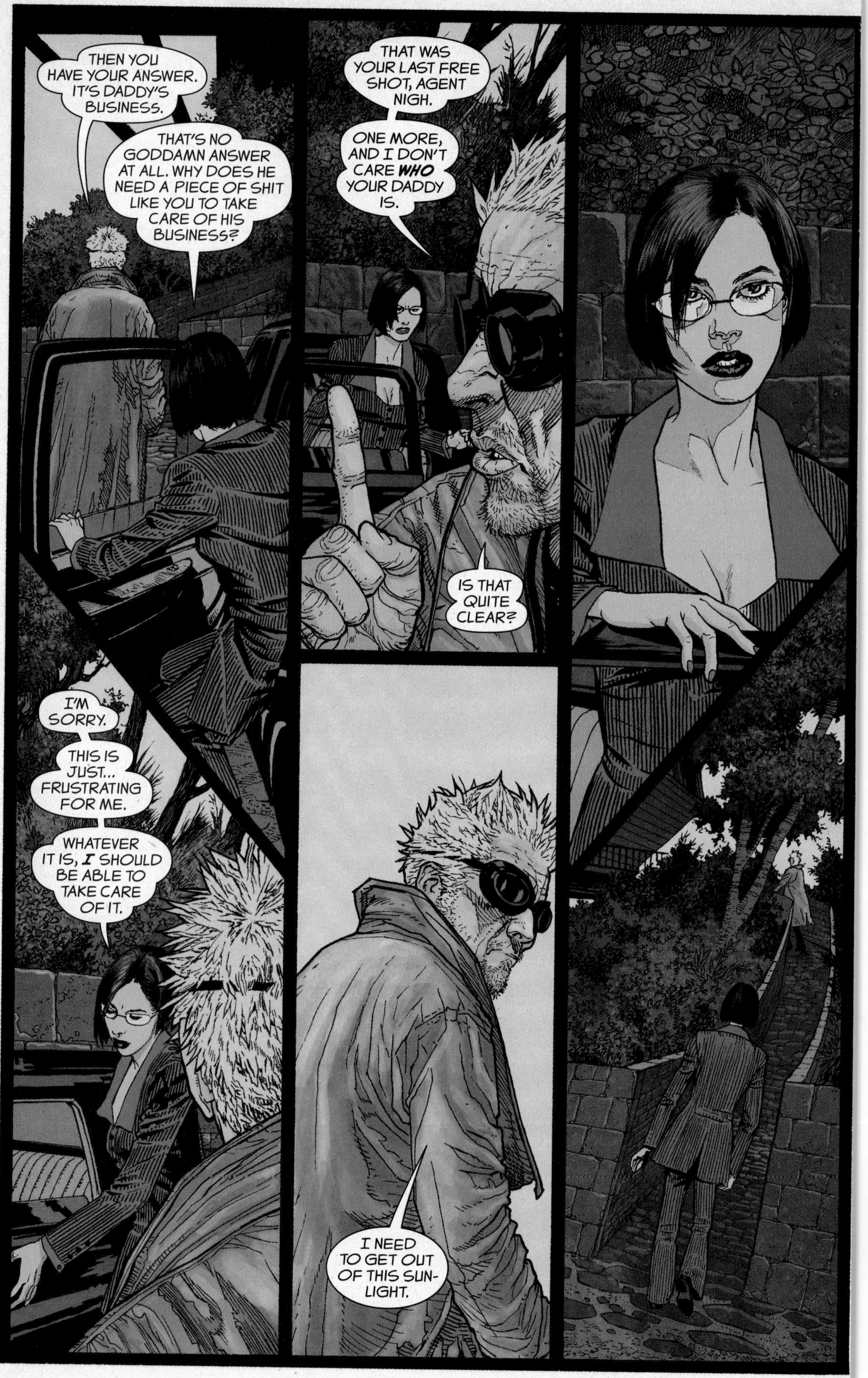

THEN YOU HAVE YOUR ANSWER. IT'S DADDY'S BUSINESS.
THAT'S NO GODDAMN ANSWER AT ALL. WHY DOES HE NEED A PIECE OF SHIT LIKE YOU TO TAKE CARE OF HIS BUSINESS?
THAT WAS YOUR LAST FREE SHOT, AGENT NIGH.
ONE MORE, AND I DON'T CARE WHO YOUR DADDY IS.
IS THAT QUITE CLEAR?
I'M SORRY.
THIS IS JUST... FRUSTRATING FOR ME.
WHATEVER IT IS, I SHOULD BE ABLE TO TAKE CARE OF IT.
I NEED TO GET OUT OF THIS SUN-LIGHT.

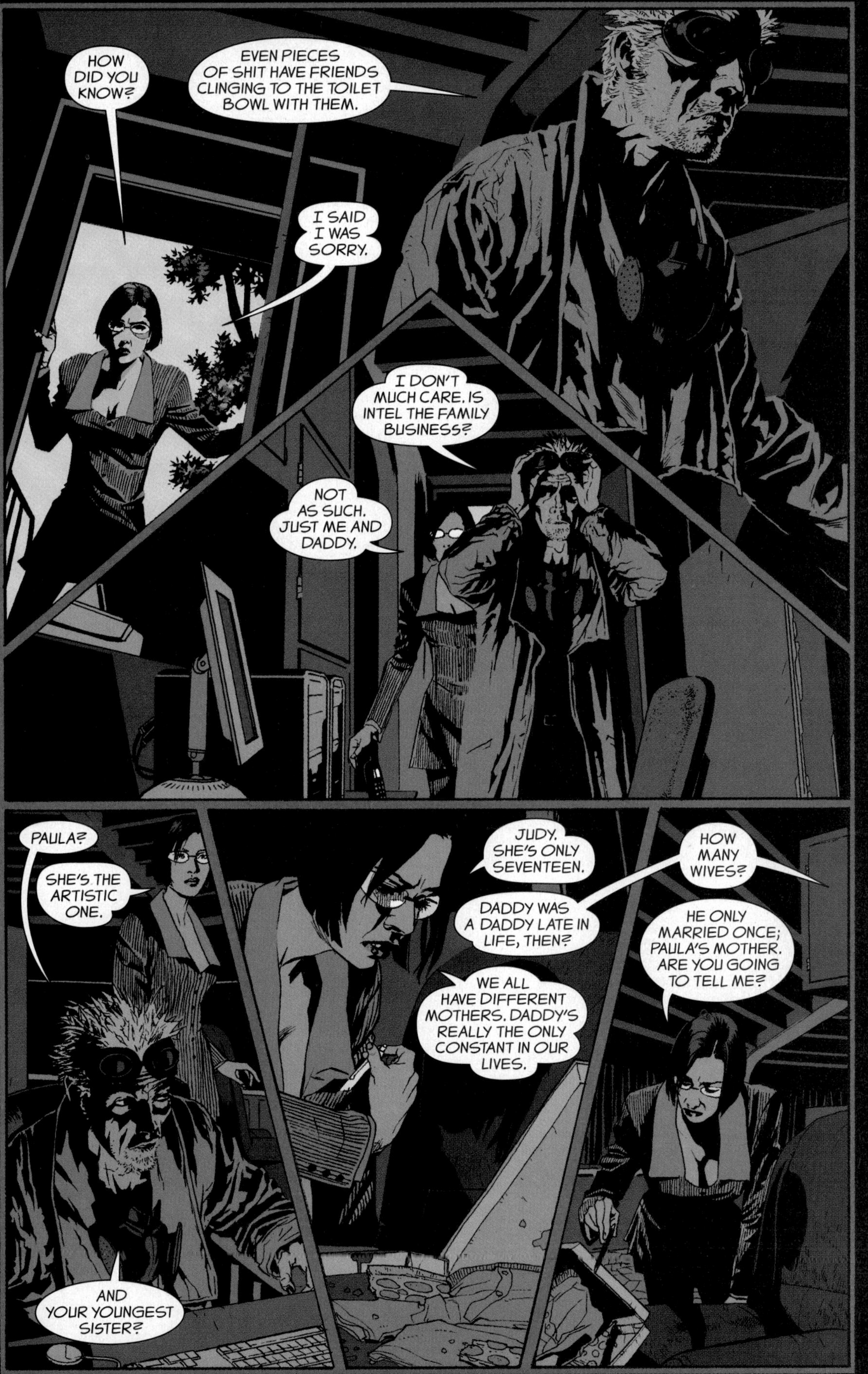
HOW DID YOU KNOW?
EVEN PIECES OF SHIT HAVE FRIENDS CLINGING TO THE TOILET BOWL WITH THEM.
I SAID I WAS SORRY.
I DON'T MUCH CARE. IS INTEL THE FAMILY BUSINESS?
NOT AS SUCH. JUST ME AND DADDY.
PAULA?
SHE'S THE ARTISTIC ONE.
AND YOUR YOUNGEST SISTER?
JUDY. SHE'S ONLY SEVENTEEN.
DADDY WAS A DADDY LATE IN LIFE, THEN?
WE ALL HAVE DIFFERENT MOTHERS. DADDY'S REALLY THE ONLY CONSTANT IN OUR LIVES.
HOW MANY WIVES?
HE ONLY MARRIED ONCE; PAULA'S MOTHER. ARE YOU GOING TO TELL ME?

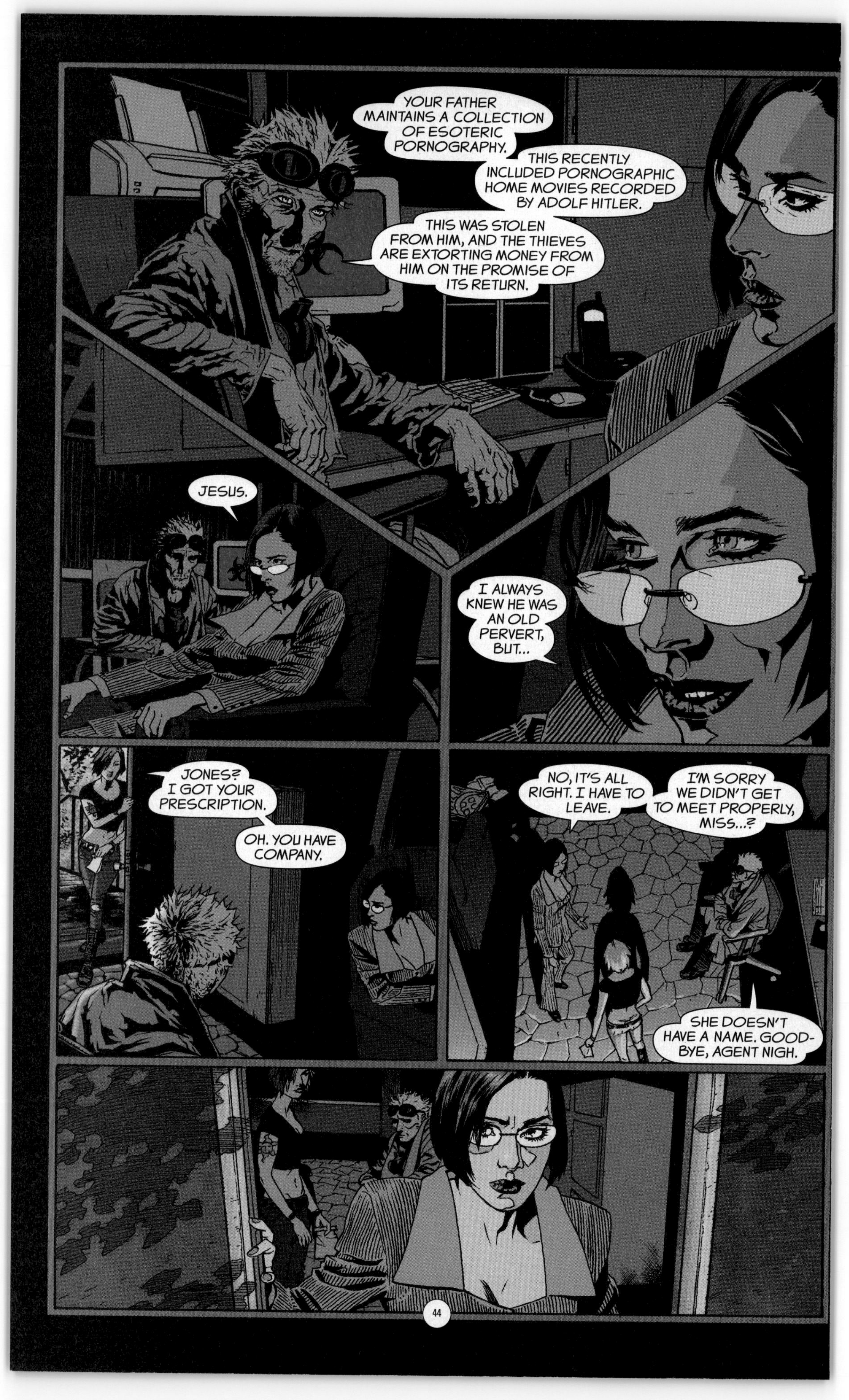
YOUR FATHER MAINTAINS A COLLECTION OF ESOTERIC PORNOGRAPHY.
THIS RECENTLY INCLUDED PORNOGRAPHIC HOME MOVIES RECORDED BY ADOLF HITLER.
THIS WAS STOLEN FROM HIM, AND THE THIEVES ARE EXTORTING MONEY FROM HIM ON THE PROMISE OF ITS RETURN.
JESUS.
I ALWAYS KNEW HE WAS AN OLD PERVERT, BUT...
JONES? I GOT YOUR PRESCRIPTION.
OH. YOU HAVE COMPANY.
NO, IT'S ALL RIGHT. I HAVE TO LEAVE.
I'M SORRY WE DIDN'T GET TO MEET PROPERLY, MISS...?
SHE DOESN'T HAVE A NAME. GOOD-BYE, AGENT NIGH.

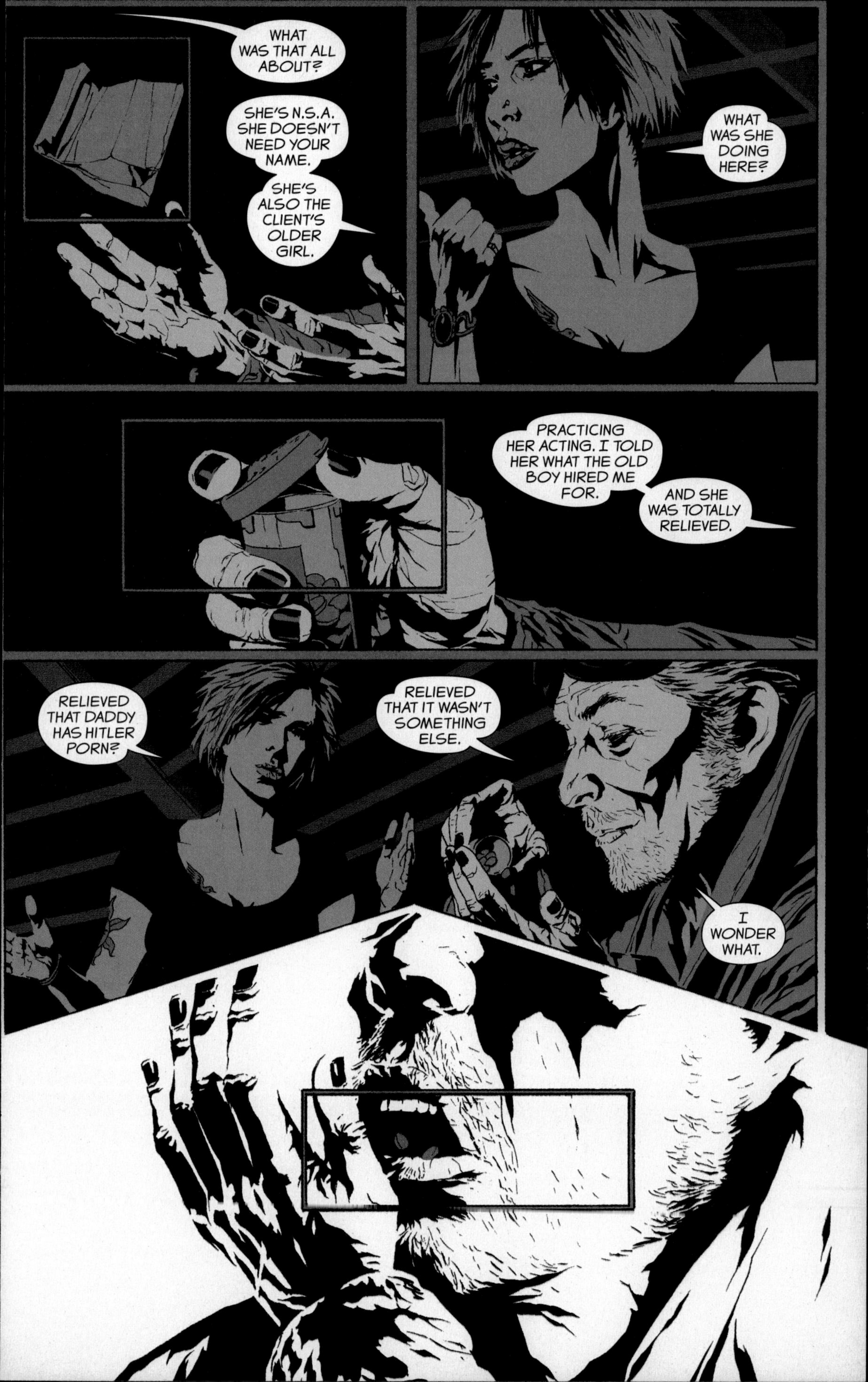
WHAT WAS THAT ALL ABOUT?
SHE'S N.S.A. SHE DOESN'T NEED YOUR NAME.
SHE'S ALSO THE CLIENT'S OLDER GIRL.
WHAT WAS SHE DOING HERE?
PRACTICING HER ACTING. I TOLD HER WHAT THE OLD BOY HIRED ME FOR.
AND SHE WAS TOTALLY RELIEVED.
RELIEVED THAT DADDY HAS HITLER PORN?
RELIEVED THAT IT WASN'T SOMETHING ELSE.
I WONDER WHAT.

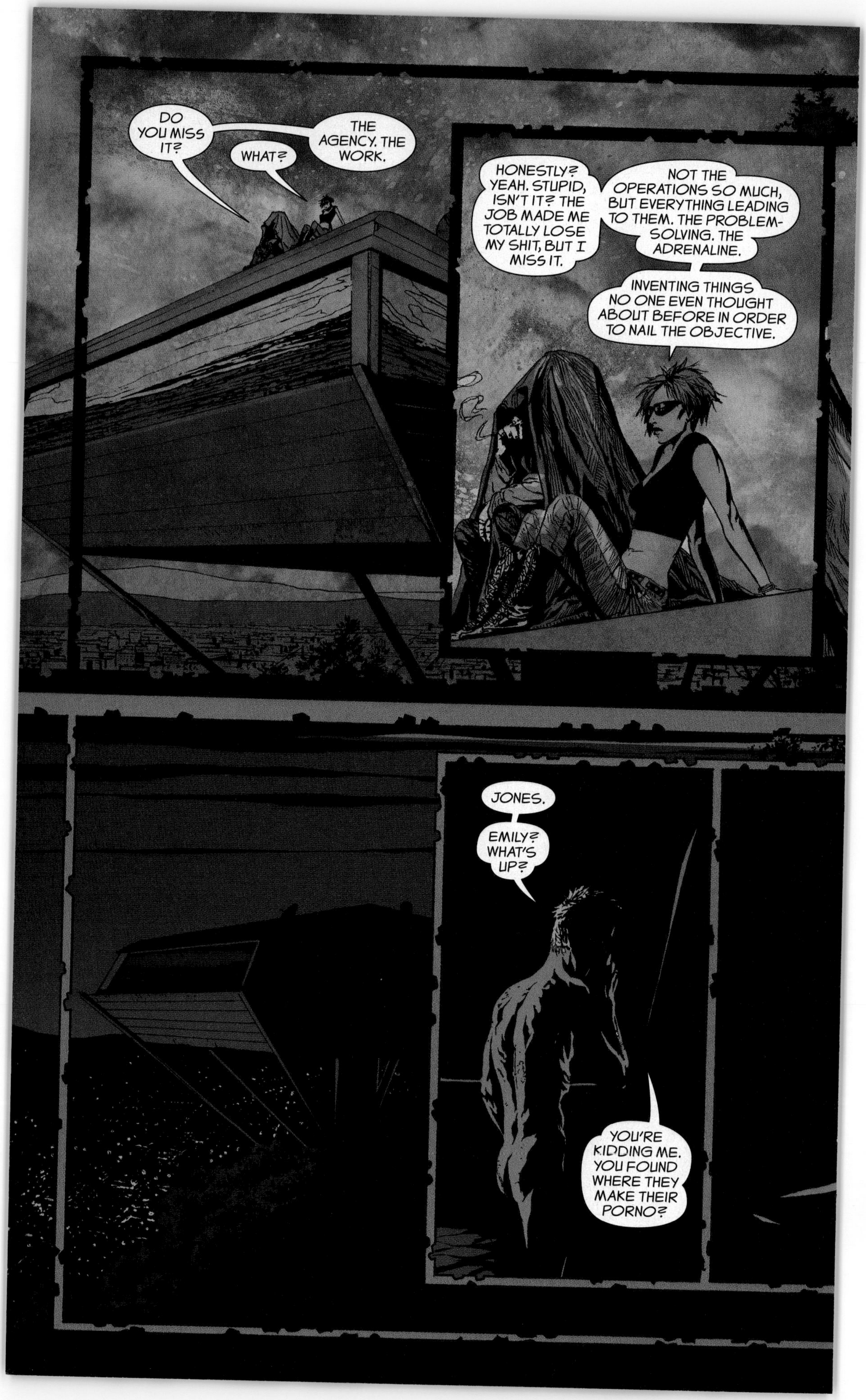

DO YOU MISS IT?
WHAT?
THE AGENCY. THE WORK.
HONESTLY? YEAH. STUPID, ISN'T IT? THE JOB MADE ME TOTALLY LOSE MY SHIT, BUT I MISS IT.
NOT THE OPERATIONS SO MUCH, BUT EVERYTHING LEADING TO THEM. THE PROBLEM-SOLVING. THE ADRENALINE.
INVENTING THINGS NO ONE EVEN THOUGHT ABOUT BEFORE IN ORDER TO NAIL THE OBJECTIVE.
JONES.
EMILY? WHAT'S UP?
YOU'RE KIDDING ME. YOU FOUND WHERE THEY MAKE THEIR PORNO?

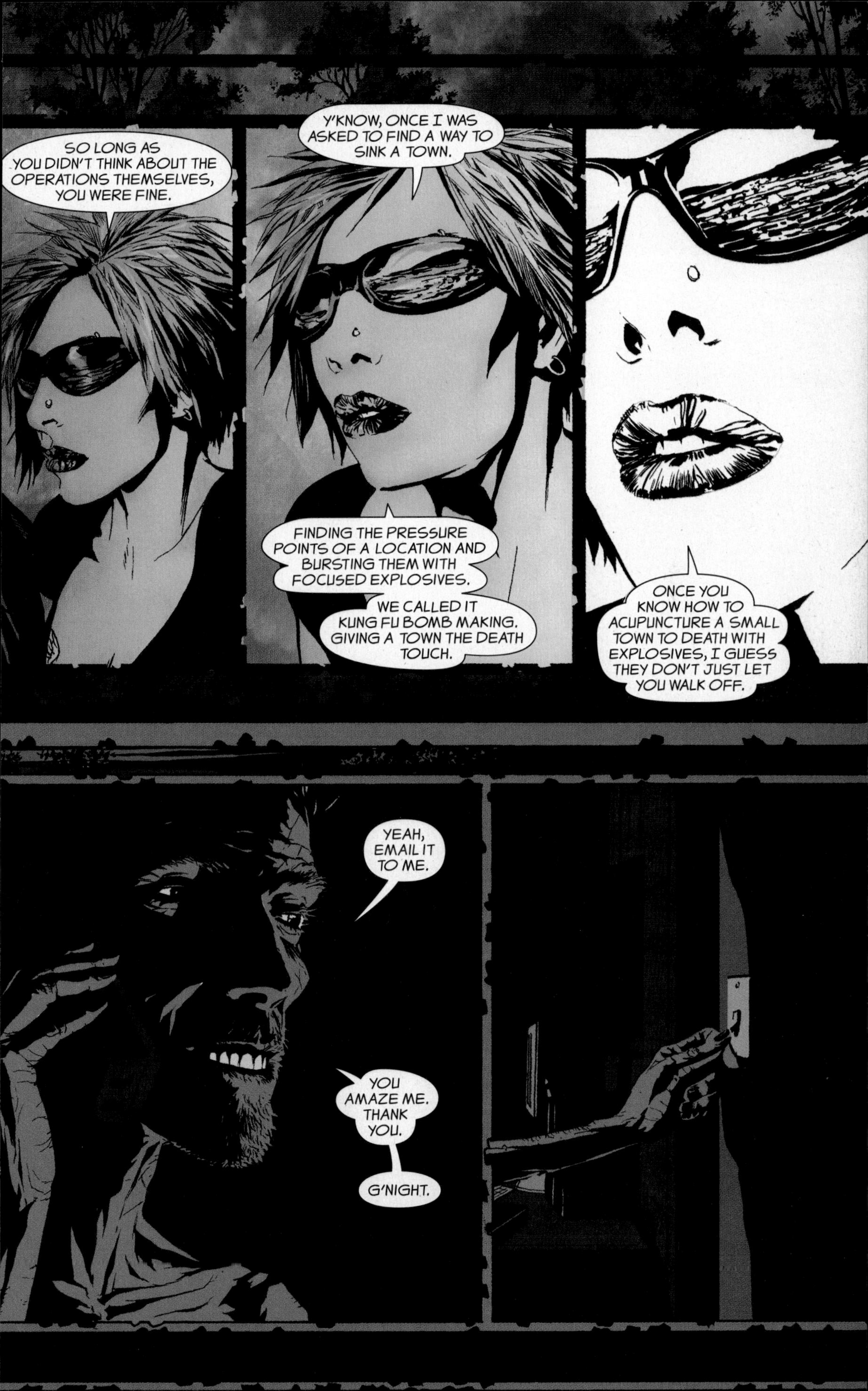
SO LONG AS YOU DIDN'T THINK ABOUT THE OPERATIONS THEMSELVES, YOU WERE FINE.
Y'KNOW, ONCE I WAS ASKED TO FIND A WAY TO SINK A TOWN.
FINDING THE PRESSURE POINTS OF A LOCATION AND BURSTING THEM WITH FOCUSED EXPLOSIVES.
WE CALLED IT KUNG FU BOMB MAKING. GIVING A TOWN THE DEATH TOUCH.
ONCE YOU KNOW HOW TO ACUPUNCTURE A SMALL TOWN TO DEATH WITH EXPLOSIVES, I GUESS THEY DON'T JUST LET YOU WALK OFF.
YEAH, EMAIL IT TO ME.
YOU AMAZE ME. THANK YOU.
G'NIGHT.

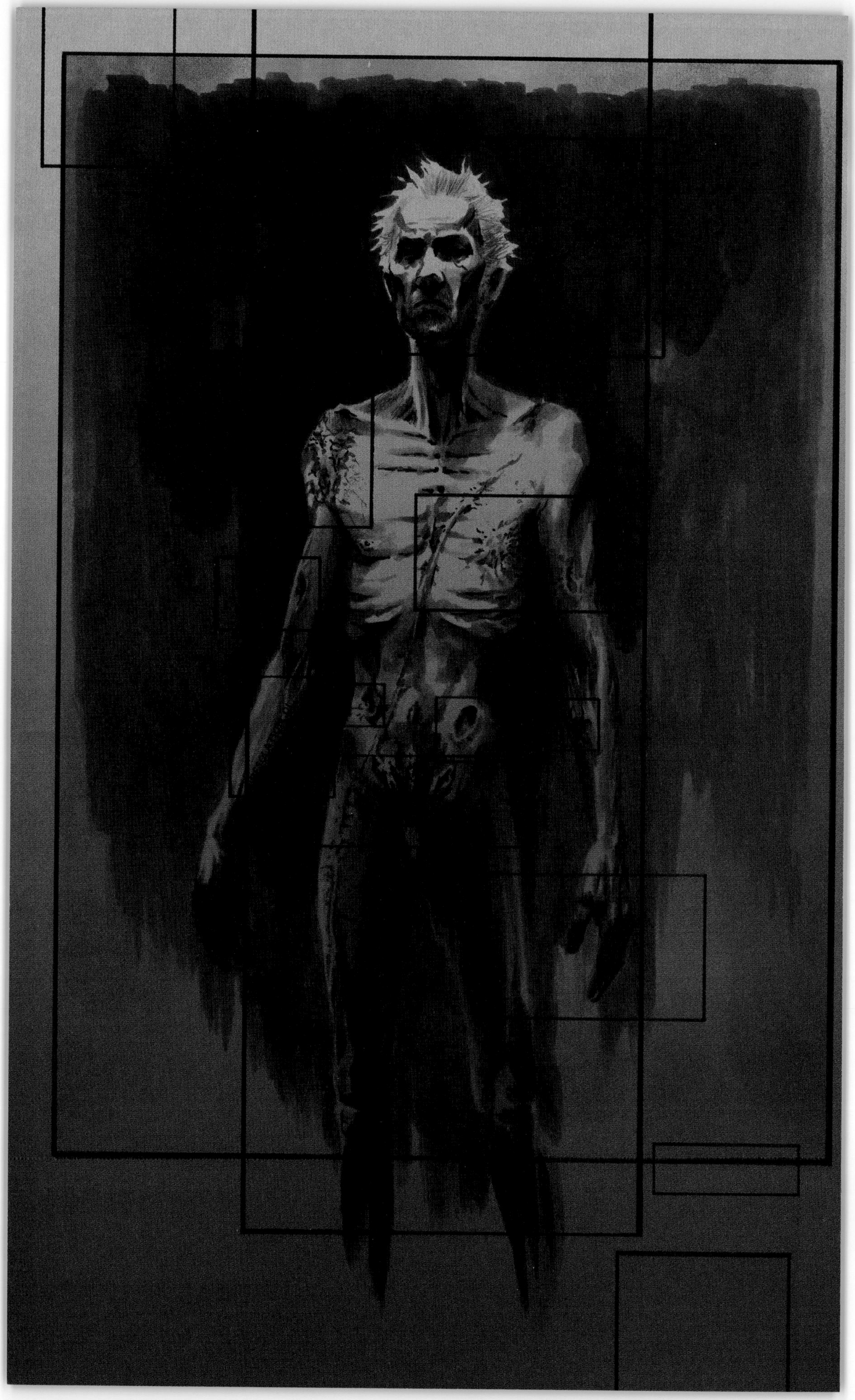

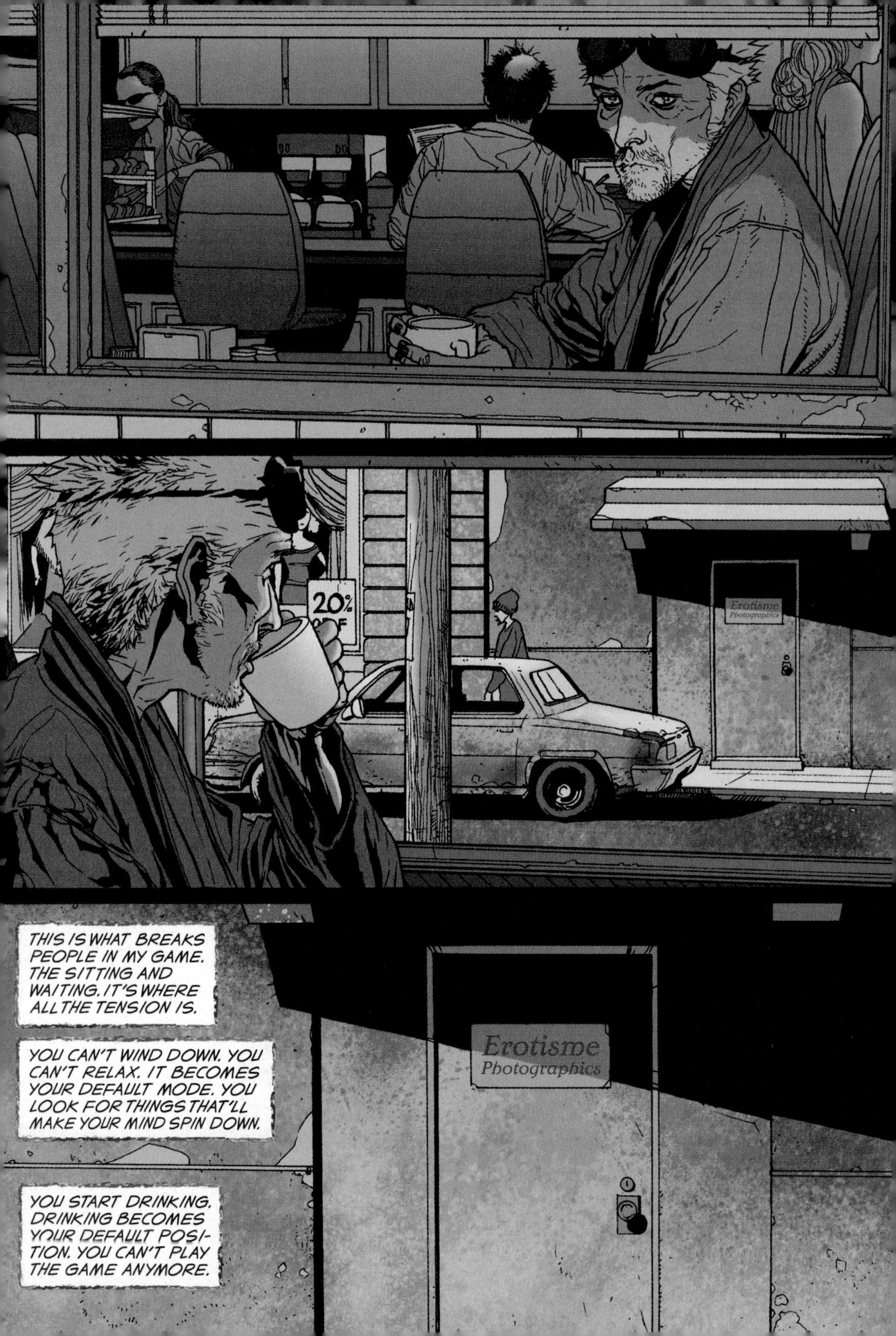

20% OFF
Erotisme Photographics
THIS IS WHAT BREAKS PEOPLE IN MY GAME. THE SITTING AND WAITING. IT'S WHERE ALL THE TENSION IS.
YOU CAN'T WIND DOWN. YOU CAN'T RELAX. IT BECOMES YOUR DEFAULT MODE. YOU LOOK FOR THINGS THAT'LL MAKE YOUR MIND SPIN DOWN.
YOU START DRINKING. DRINKING BECOMES YOUR DEFAULT POSITION. YOU CAN'T PLAY THE GAME ANYMORE.
Erotisme Photographics

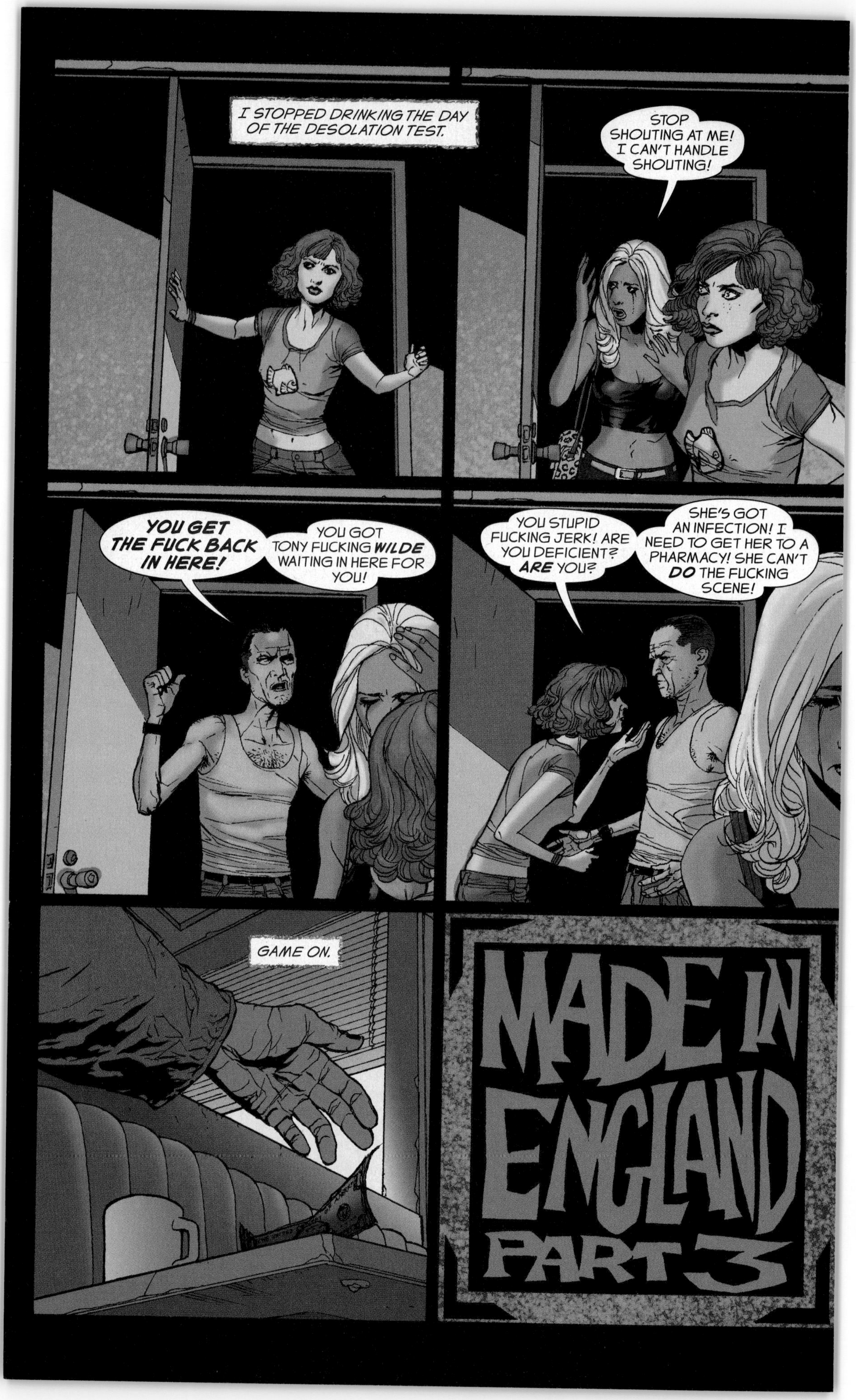

I STOPPED DRINKING THE DAY OF THE DESOLATION TEST.
STOP SHOUTING AT ME! I CAN'T HANDLE SHOUTING!
YOU GET THE FUCK BACK IN HERE!
YOU GOT TONY FUCKING WILDE WAITING IN HERE FOR YOU!
YOU STUPID FUCKING JERK! ARE YOU DEFICIENT? ARE YOU?
SHE'S GOT AN INFECTION! I NEED TO GET HER TO A PHARMACY! SHE CAN'T DO THE FUCKING SCENE!
GAME ON.
MADE IN ENGLAND
PART 3

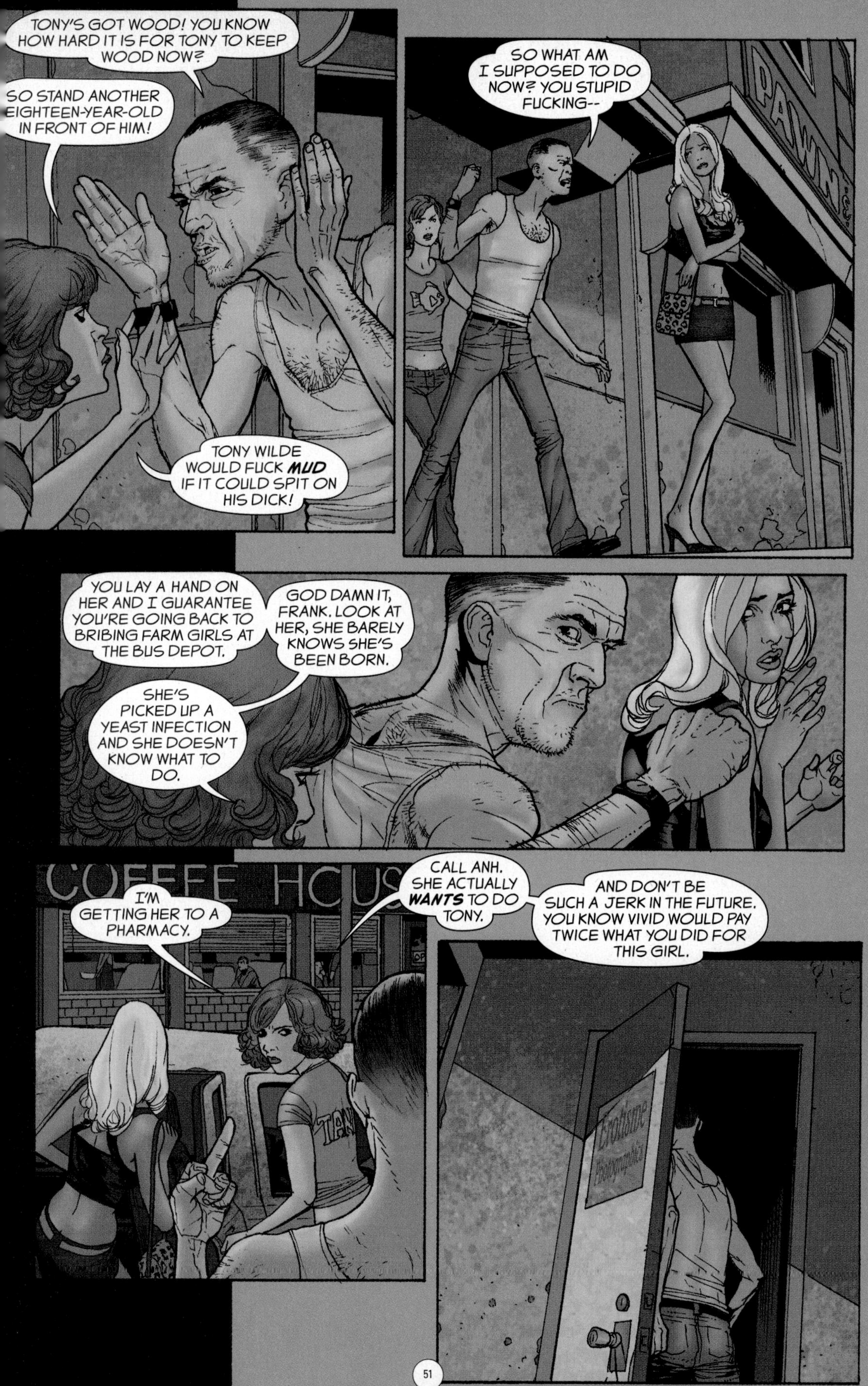
TONY'S GOT WOOD! YOU KNOW HOW HARD IT IS FOR TONY TO KEEP WOOD NOW?
SO STAND ANOTHER EIGHTEEN-YEAR-OLD IN FRONT OF HIM!
TONY WILDE WOULD FUCK MUD IF IT COULD SPIT ON HIS DICK!
SO WHAT AM I SUPPOSED TO DO NOW? YOU STUPID FUCKING--
PAWN
YOU LAY A HAND ON HER AND I GUARANTEE YOU'RE GOING BACK TO BRIBING FARM GIRLS AT THE BUS DEPOT.
GOD DAMN IT, FRANK. LOOK AT HER, SHE BARELY KNOWS SHE'S BEEN BORN.
SHE'S PICKED UP A YEAST INFECTION AND SHE DOESN'T KNOW WHAT TO DO.
COFFEE HOUS
I'M GETTING HER TO A PHARMACY.
CALL ANH. SHE ACTUALLY WANTS TO DO TONY.
AND DON'T BE SUCH A JERK IN THE FUTURE. YOU KNOW VIVID WOULD PAY TWICE WHAT YOU DID FOR THIS GIRL.

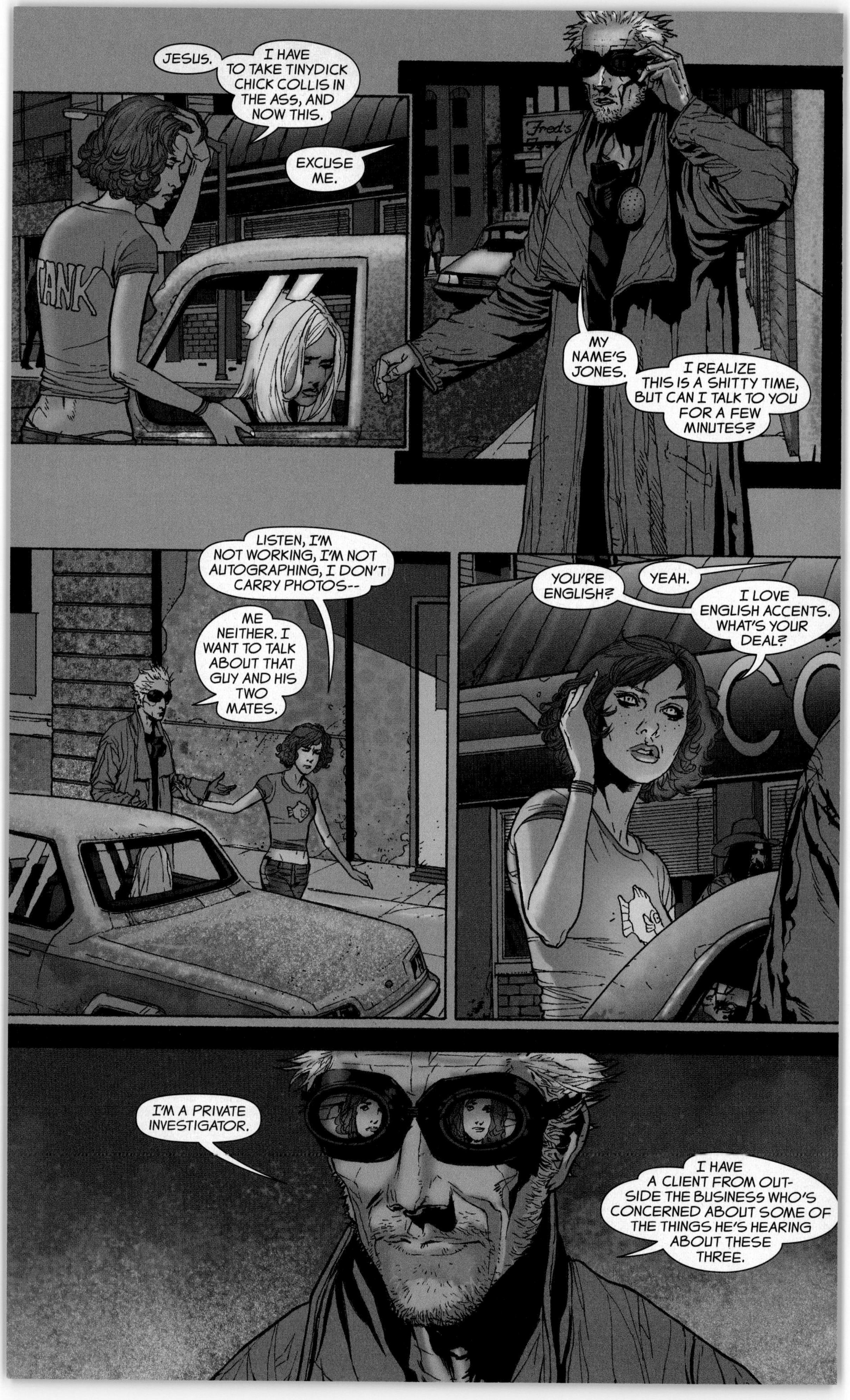
JESUS.
I HAVE TO TAKE TINYDICK CHICK COLLIS IN THE ASS, AND NOW THIS.
EXCUSE ME.
TANK
Fred's
MY NAME'S JONES.
I REALIZE THIS IS A SHITTY TIME, BUT CAN I TALK TO YOU FOR A FEW MINUTES?
LISTEN, I'M NOT WORKING, I'M NOT AUTOGRAPHING, I DON'T CARRY PHOTOS--
ME NEITHER. I WANT TO TALK ABOUT THAT GUY AND HIS TWO MATES.
YOU'RE ENGLISH?
YEAH.
I LOVE ENGLISH ACCENTS. WHAT'S YOUR DEAL?
I'M A PRIVATE INVESTIGATOR.
I HAVE A CLIENT FROM OUT-SIDE THE BUSINESS WHO'S CONCERNED ABOUT SOME OF THE THINGS HE'S HEARING ABOUT THESE THREE.

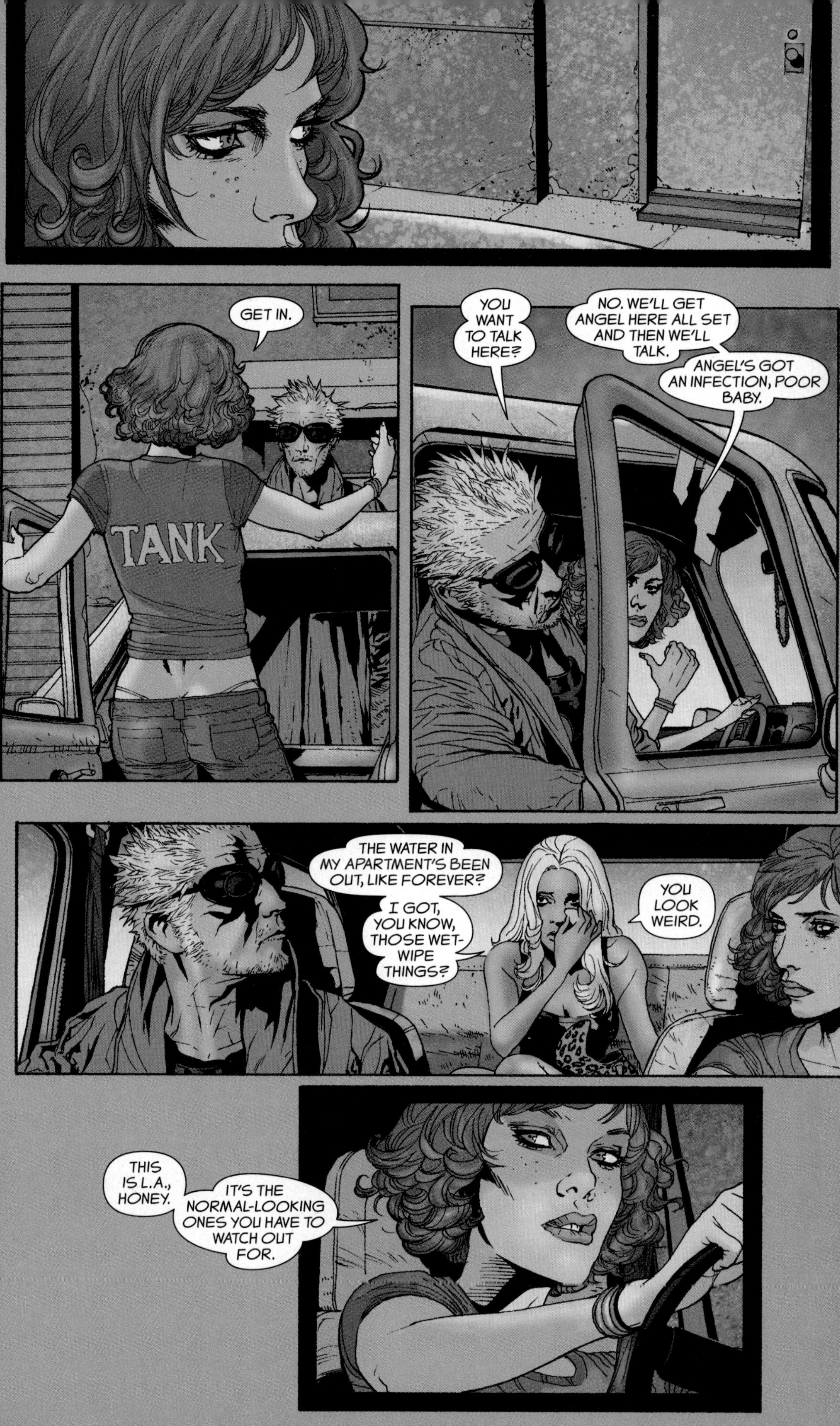
GET IN.
YOU WANT TO TALK HERE?
NO. WE'LL GET ANGEL HERE ALL SET AND THEN WE'LL TALK.
ANGEL'S GOT AN INFECTION, POOR BABY.
TANK
THE WATER IN MY APARTMENT'S BEEN OUT, LIKE FOREVER?
I GOT, YOU KNOW, THOSE WET-WIPE THINGS?
YOU LOOK WEIRD.
THIS IS L.A., HONEY.
IT'S THE NORMAL-LOOKING ONES YOU HAVE TO WATCH OUT FOR.

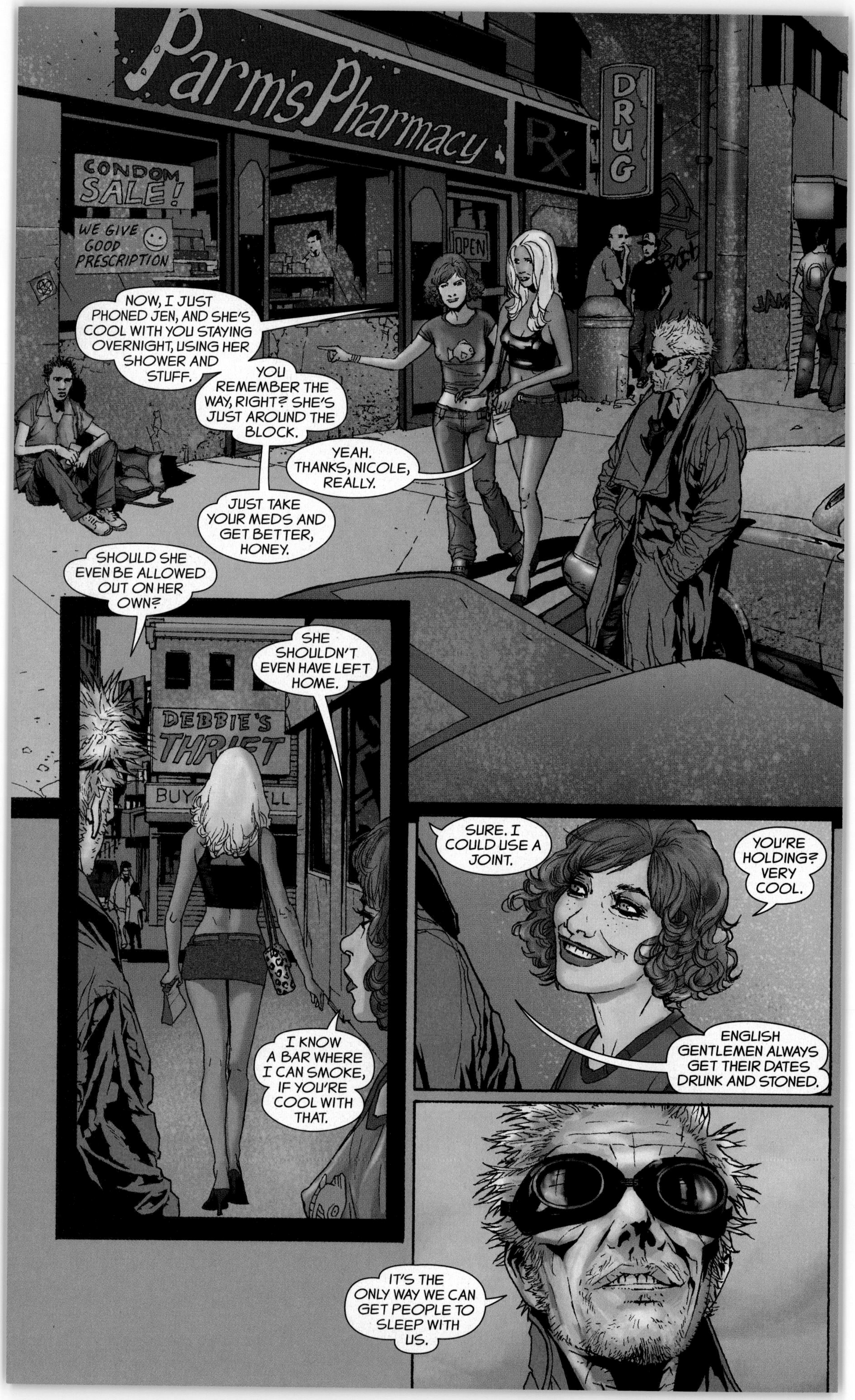
Parm's Pharmacy
RX
DRUG
CONDOM SALE!
WE GIVE GOOD PRESCRIPTION
OPEN
NOW, I JUST PHONED JEN, AND SHE'S COOL WITH YOU STAYING OVERNIGHT, USING HER SHOWER AND STUFF.
YOU REMEMBER THE WAY, RIGHT? SHE'S JUST AROUND THE BLOCK.
YEAH. THANKS, NICOLE, REALLY.
JUST TAKE YOUR MEDS AND GET BETTER, HONEY.
SHOULD SHE EVEN BE ALLOWED OUT ON HER OWN?
SHE SHOULDN'T EVEN HAVE LEFT HOME.
DEBBIE'S THRIFT
I KNOW A BAR WHERE I CAN SMOKE, IF YOU'RE COOL WITH THAT.
SURE. I COULD USE A JOINT.
YOU'RE HOLDING? VERY COOL.
ENGLISH GENTLEMEN ALWAYS GET THEIR DATES DRUNK AND STONED.
IT'S THE ONLY WAY WE CAN GET PEOPLE TO SLEEP WITH US.

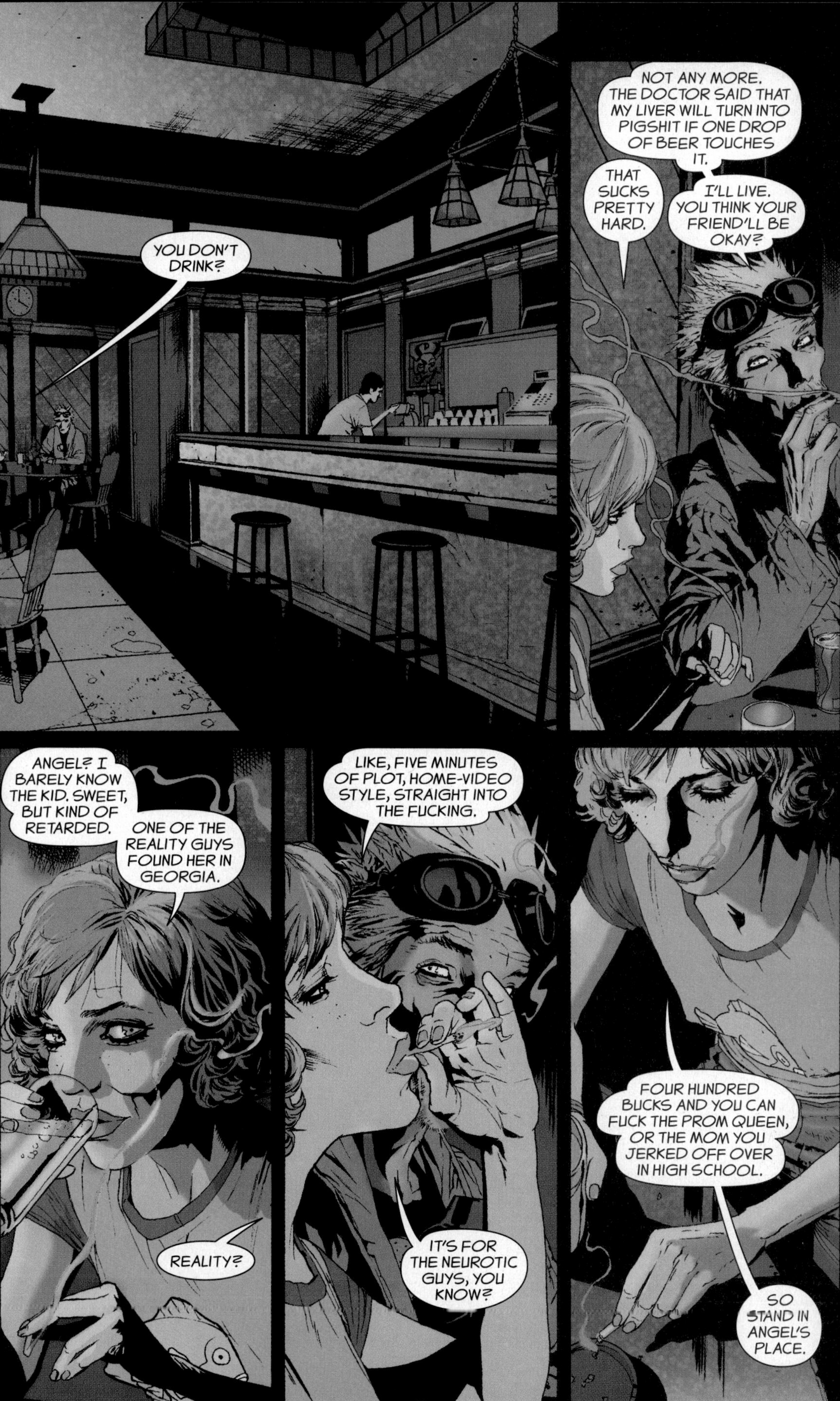
YOU DON'T DRINK?
NOT ANY MORE. THE DOCTOR SAID THAT MY LIVER WILL TURN INTO PIGSHIT IF ONE DROP OF BEER TOUCHES IT.
THAT SUCKS PRETTY HARD.
I'LL LIVE. YOU THINK YOUR FRIEND'LL BE OKAY?
ANGEL? I BARELY KNOW THE KID. SWEET, BUT KIND OF RETARDED.
ONE OF THE REALITY GUYS FOUND HER IN GEORGIA.
REALITY?
LIKE, FIVE MINUTES OF PLOT, HOME-VIDEO STYLE, STRAIGHT INTO THE FUCKING.
IT'S FOR THE NEUROTIC GUYS, YOU KNOW?
FOUR HUNDRED BUCKS AND YOU CAN FUCK THE PROM QUEEN, OR THE MOM YOU JERKED OFF OVER IN HIGH SCHOOL.
SO STAND IN ANGEL'S PLACE.

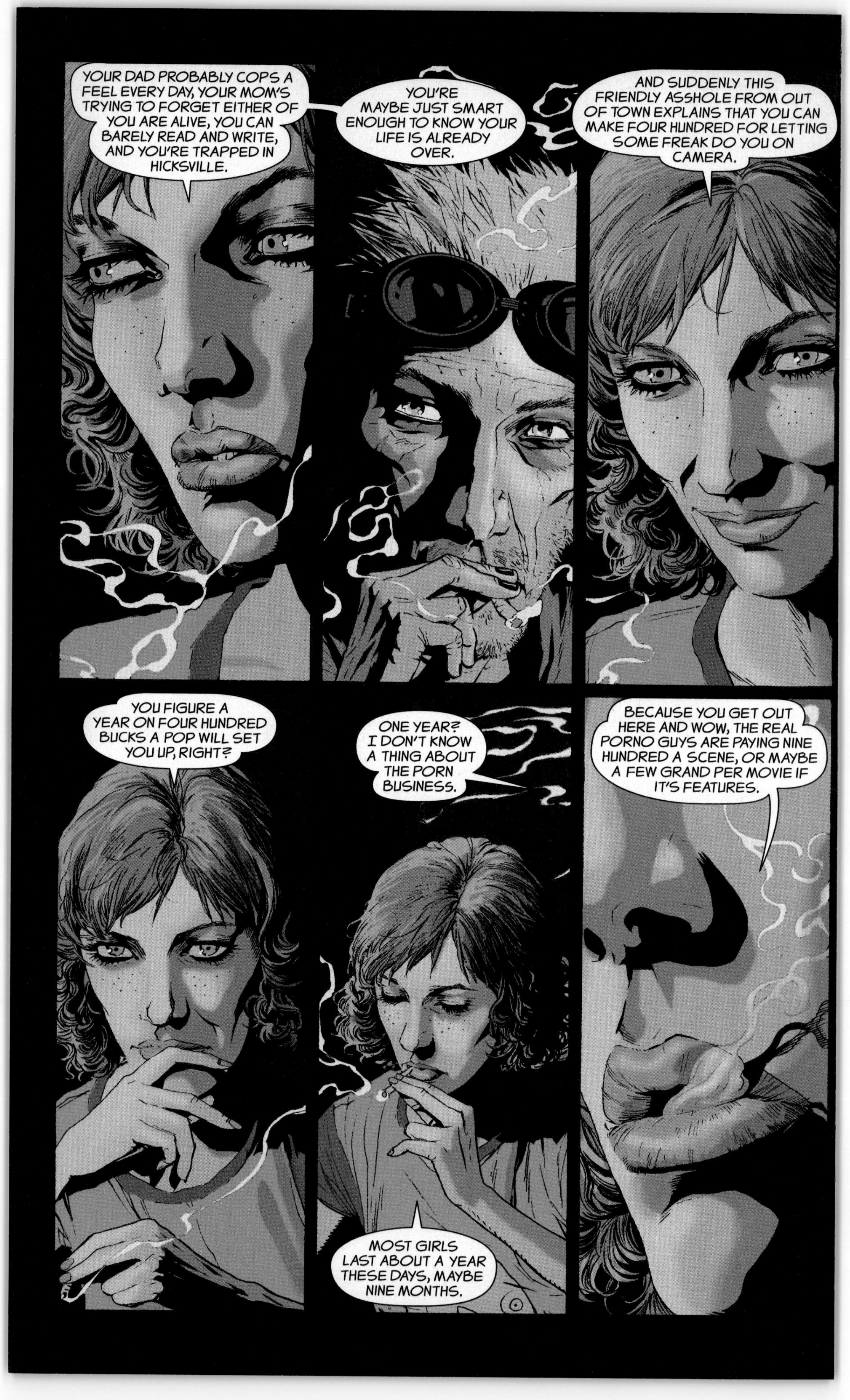

YOUR DAD PROBABLY COPS A FEEL EVERY DAY, YOUR MOM'S TRYING TO FORGET EITHER OF YOU ARE ALIVE, YOU CAN BARELY READ AND WRITE, AND YOU'RE TRAPPED IN HICKSVILLE.
YOU'RE MAYBE JUST SMART ENOUGH TO KNOW YOUR LIFE IS ALREADY OVER.
AND SUDDENLY THIS FRIENDLY ASSHOLE FROM OUT OF TOWN EXPLAINS THAT YOU CAN MAKE FOUR HUNDRED FOR LETTING SOME FREAK DO YOU ON CAMERA.
YOU FIGURE A YEAR ON FOUR HUNDRED BUCKS A POP WILL SET YOU UP, RIGHT?
ONE YEAR? I DON'T KNOW A THING ABOUT THE PORN BUSINESS.
MOST GIRLS LAST ABOUT A YEAR THESE DAYS, MAYBE NINE MONTHS.
BECAUSE YOU GET OUT HERE AND WOW, THE REAL PORNO GUYS ARE PAYING NINE HUNDRED A SCENE, OR MAYBE A FEW GRAND PER MOVIE IF IT'S FEATURES.

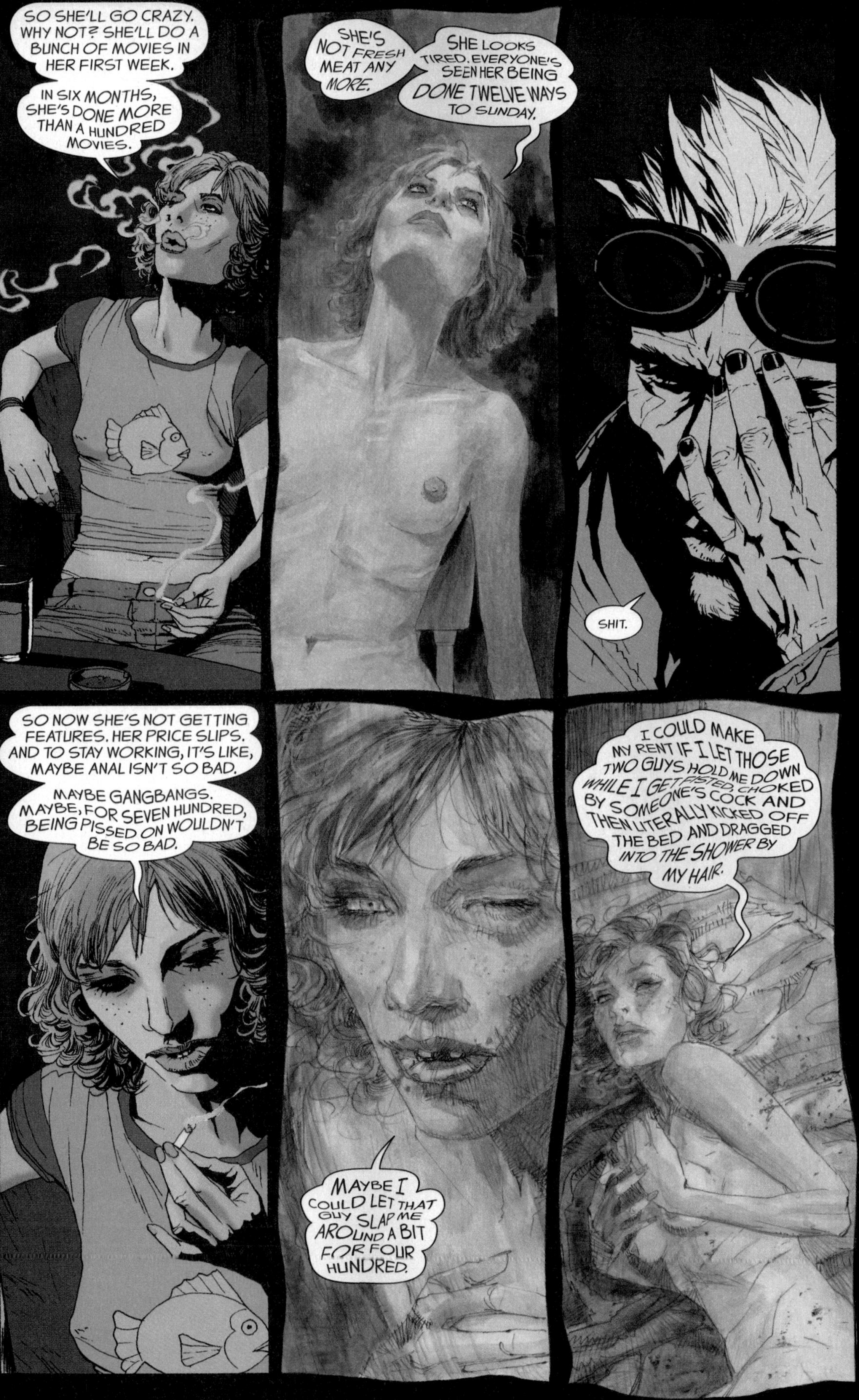
SO SHE'LL GO CRAZY. WHY NOT? SHE'LL DO A BUNCH OF MOVIES IN HER FIRST WEEK.
IN SIX MONTHS, SHE'S DONE MORE THAN A HUNDRED MOVIES.
SHE'S NOT FRESH MEAT ANY MORE.
SHE LOOKS TIRED. EVERYONE'S SEEN HER BEING DONE TWELVE WAYS TO SUNDAY.
SHIT.
SO NOW SHE'S NOT GETTING FEATURES. HER PRICE SLIPS. AND TO STAY WORKING, IT'S LIKE, MAYBE ANAL ISN'T SO BAD.
MAYBE GANGBANGS. MAYBE, FOR SEVEN HUNDRED, BEING PISSED ON WOULDN'T BE SO BAD.
MAYBE I COULD LET THAT GUY SLAP ME AROUND A BIT FOR FOUR HUNDRED.
I COULD MAKE MY RENT IF I LET THOSE TWO GUYS HOLD ME DOWN WHILE I GET FISTED, CHOKED BY SOMEONE'S COCK AND THEN LITERALLY KICKED OFF THE BED AND DRAGGED INTO THE SHOWER BY MY HAIR.

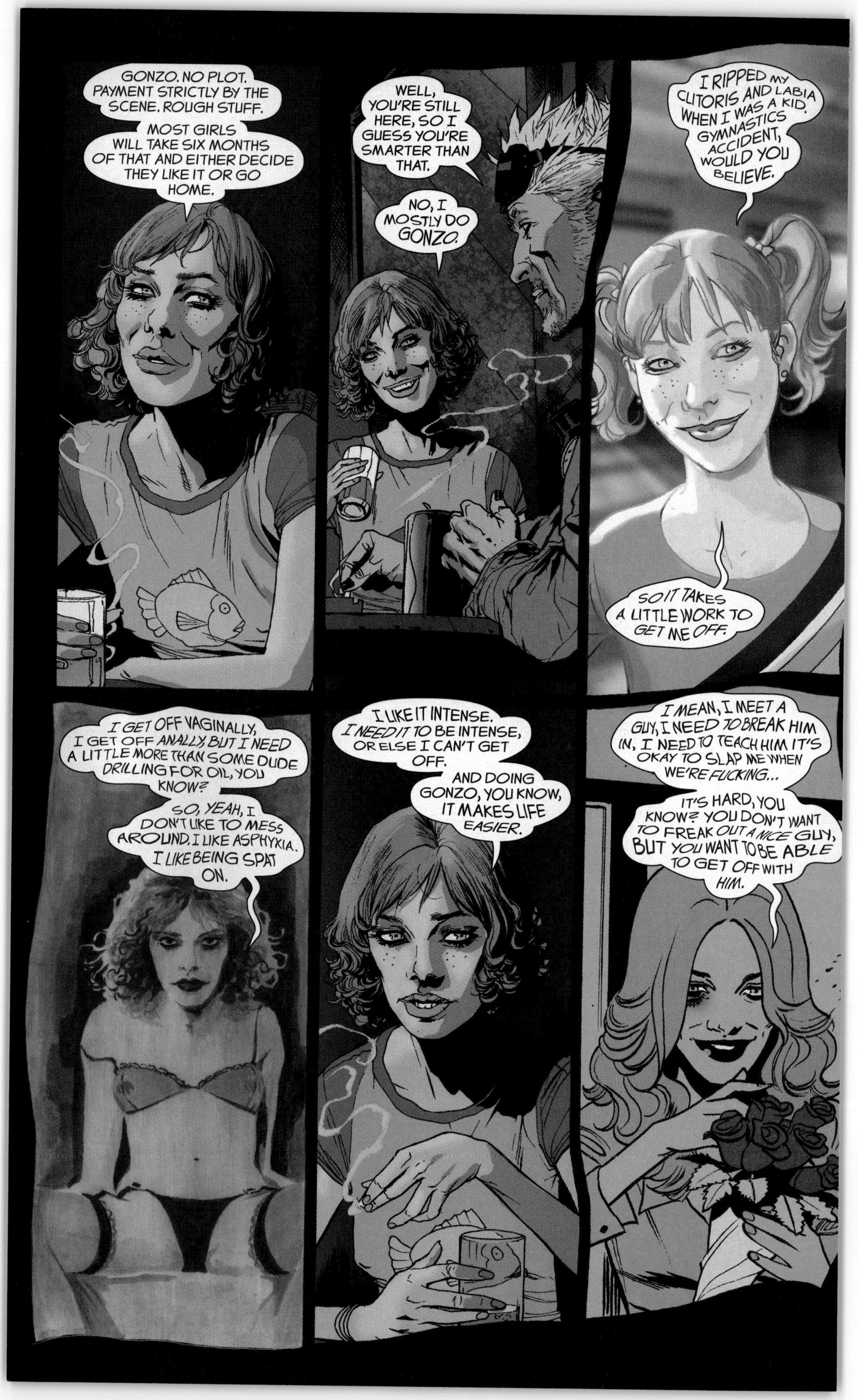
GONZO. NO PLOT. PAYMENT STRICTLY BY THE SCENE. ROUGH STUFF.
MOST GIRLS WILL TAKE SIX MONTHS OF THAT AND EITHER DECIDE THEY LIKE IT OR GO HOME.
WELL, YOU'RE STILL HERE, SO I GUESS YOU'RE SMARTER THAN THAT.
NO, I MOSTLY DO GONZO.
I RIPPED MY CLITORIS AND LABIA WHEN I WAS A KID. GYMNASTICS ACCIDENT, WOULD YOU BELIEVE.
SO IT TAKES A LITTLE WORK TO GET ME OFF.
I GET OFF VAGINALLY, I GET OFF ANALLY, BUT I NEED A LITTLE MORE THAN SOME DUDE DRILLING FOR OIL, YOU KNOW?
SO, YEAH, I DON'T LIKE TO MESS AROUND. I LIKE ASPHYXIA. I LIKE BEING SPAT ON.
I LIKE IT INTENSE. I NEED IT TO BE INTENSE, OR ELSE I CAN'T GET OFF.
AND DOING GONZO, YOU KNOW, IT MAKES LIFE EASIER.
I MEAN, I MEET A GUY, I NEED TO BREAK HIM IN, I NEED TO TEACH HIM IT'S OKAY TO SLAP ME WHEN WE'RE FUCKING...
IT'S HARD, YOU KNOW? YOU DON'T WANT TO FREAK OUT A NICE GUY, BUT YOU WANT TO BE ABLE TO GET OFF WITH HIM.

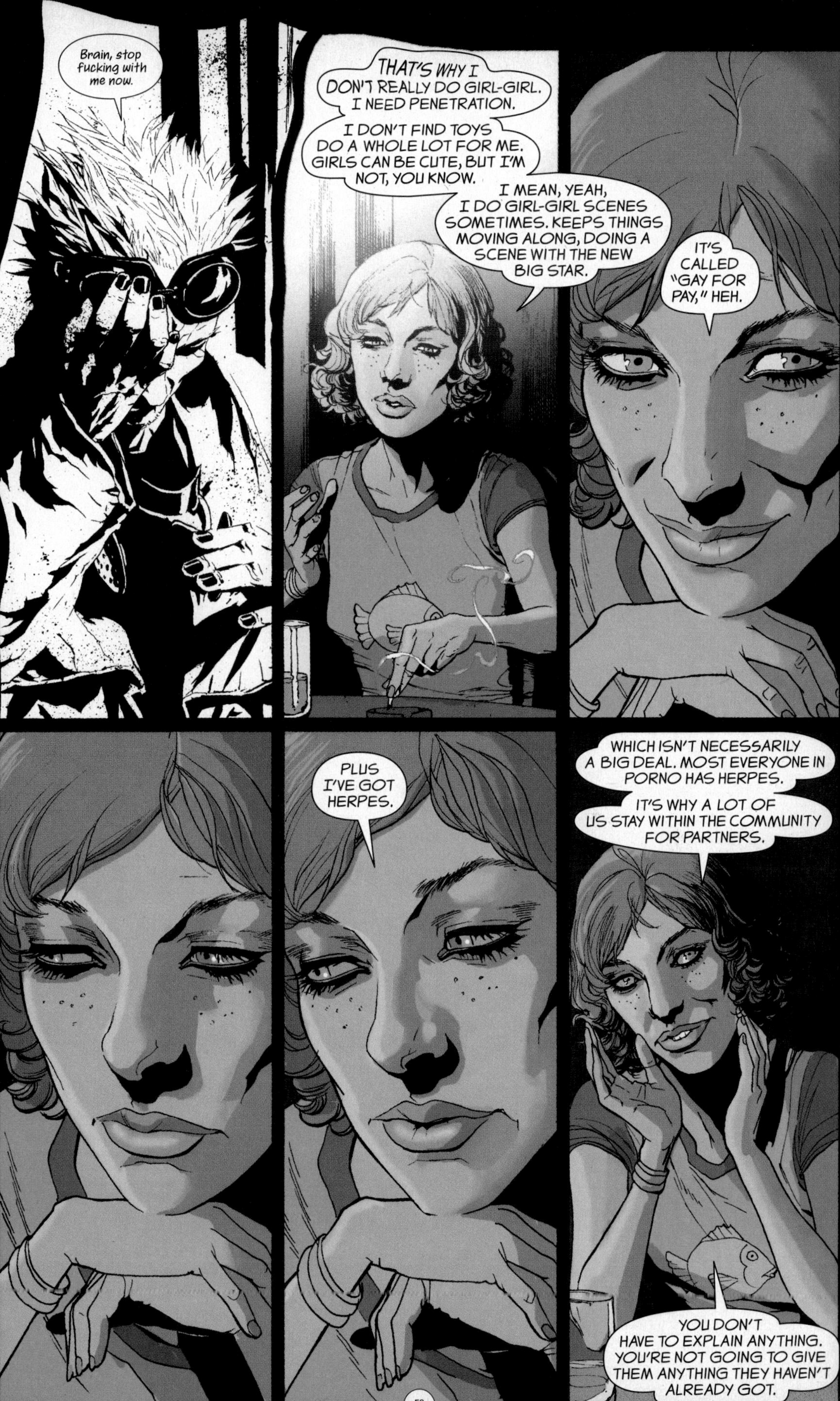

Brain, stop fucking with me now.
THAT'S WHY I DON'T REALLY DO GIRL-GIRL. I NEED PENETRATION.
I DON'T FIND TOYS DO A WHOLE LOT FOR ME. GIRLS CAN BE CUTE, BUT I'M NOT, YOU KNOW.
I MEAN, YEAH, I DO GIRL-GIRL SCENES SOMETIMES. KEEPS THINGS MOVING ALONG, DOING A SCENE WITH THE NEW BIG STAR.
IT'S CALLED "GAY FOR PAY," HEH.
PLUS I'VE GOT HERPES.
WHICH ISN'T NECESSARILY A BIG DEAL. MOST EVERYONE IN PORNO HAS HERPES.
IT'S WHY A LOT OF US STAY WITHIN THE COMMUNITY FOR PARTNERS.
YOU DON'T HAVE TO EXPLAIN ANYTHING. YOU'RE NOT GOING TO GIVE THEM ANYTHING THEY HAVEN'T ALREADY GOT.

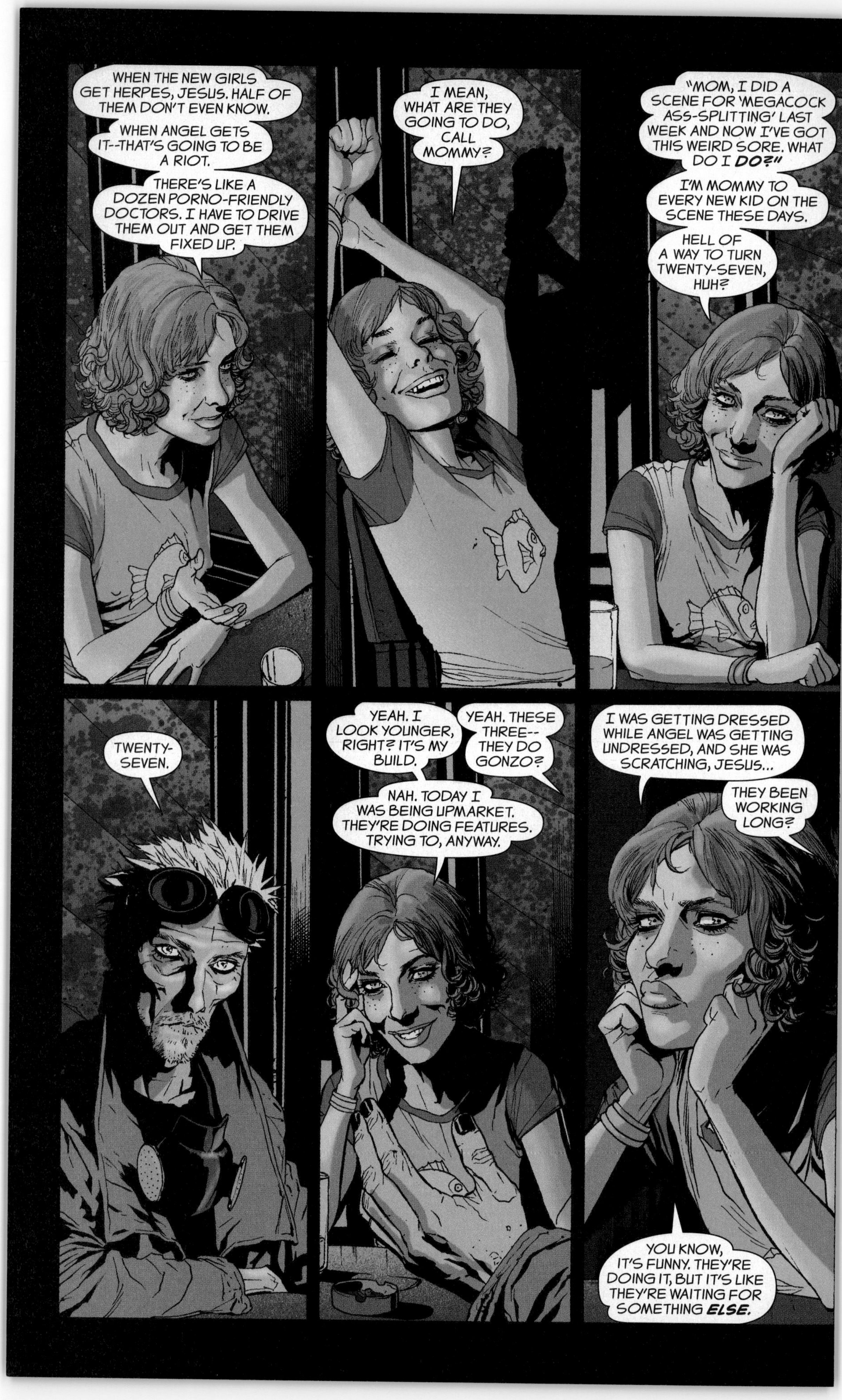
WHEN THE NEW GIRLS GET HERPES, JESUS. HALF OF THEM DON'T EVEN KNOW.
WHEN ANGEL GETS IT--THAT'S GOING TO BE A RIOT.
THERE'S LIKE A DOZEN PORNO-FRIENDLY DOCTORS. I HAVE TO DRIVE THEM OUT AND GET THEM FIXED UP.
I MEAN, WHAT ARE THEY GOING TO DO, CALL MOMMY?
"MOM, I DID A SCENE FOR 'MEGACOCK ASS-SPLITTING' LAST WEEK AND NOW I'VE GOT THIS WEIRD SORE. WHAT DO I DO?"
I'M MOMMY TO EVERY NEW KID ON THE SCENE THESE DAYS.
HELL OF A WAY TO TURN TWENTY-SEVEN, HUH?
TWENTY-SEVEN.
YEAH. I LOOK YOUNGER, RIGHT? IT'S MY BUILD.
YEAH. THESE THREE--THEY DO GONZO?
NAH. TODAY I WAS BEING UPMARKET. THEY'RE DOING FEATURES. TRYING TO, ANYWAY.
I WAS GETTING DRESSED WHILE ANGEL WAS GETTING UNDRESSED, AND SHE WAS SCRATCHING, JESUS...
THEY BEEN WORKING LONG?
YOU KNOW, IT'S FUNNY. THEY'RE DOING IT, BUT IT'S LIKE THEY'RE WAITING FOR SOMETHING ELSE.

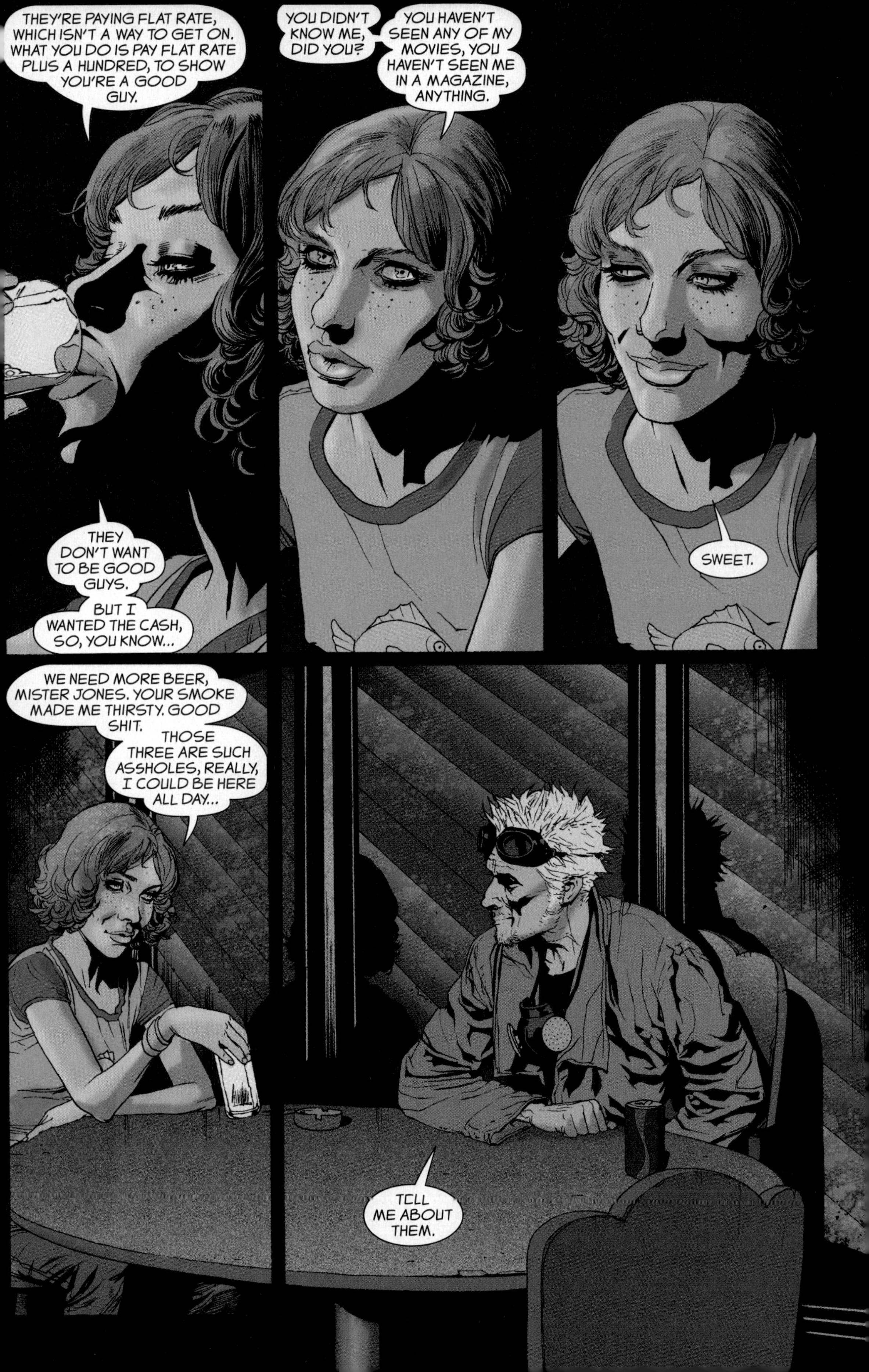
THEY'RE PAYING FLAT RATE, WHICH ISN'T A WAY TO GET ON. WHAT YOU DO IS PAY FLAT RATE PLUS A HUNDRED, TO SHOW YOU'RE A GOOD GUY.
THEY DON'T WANT TO BE GOOD GUYS.
BUT I WANTED THE CASH, SO, YOU KNOW...
YOU DIDN'T KNOW ME, DID YOU?
YOU HAVEN'T SEEN ANY OF MY MOVIES, YOU HAVEN'T SEEN ME IN A MAGAZINE, ANYTHING.
SWEET.
WE NEED MORE BEER, MISTER JONES. YOUR SMOKE MADE ME THIRSTY. GOOD SHIT.
THOSE THREE ARE SUCH ASSHOLES, REALLY, I COULD BE HERE ALL DAY...
TELL ME ABOUT THEM.

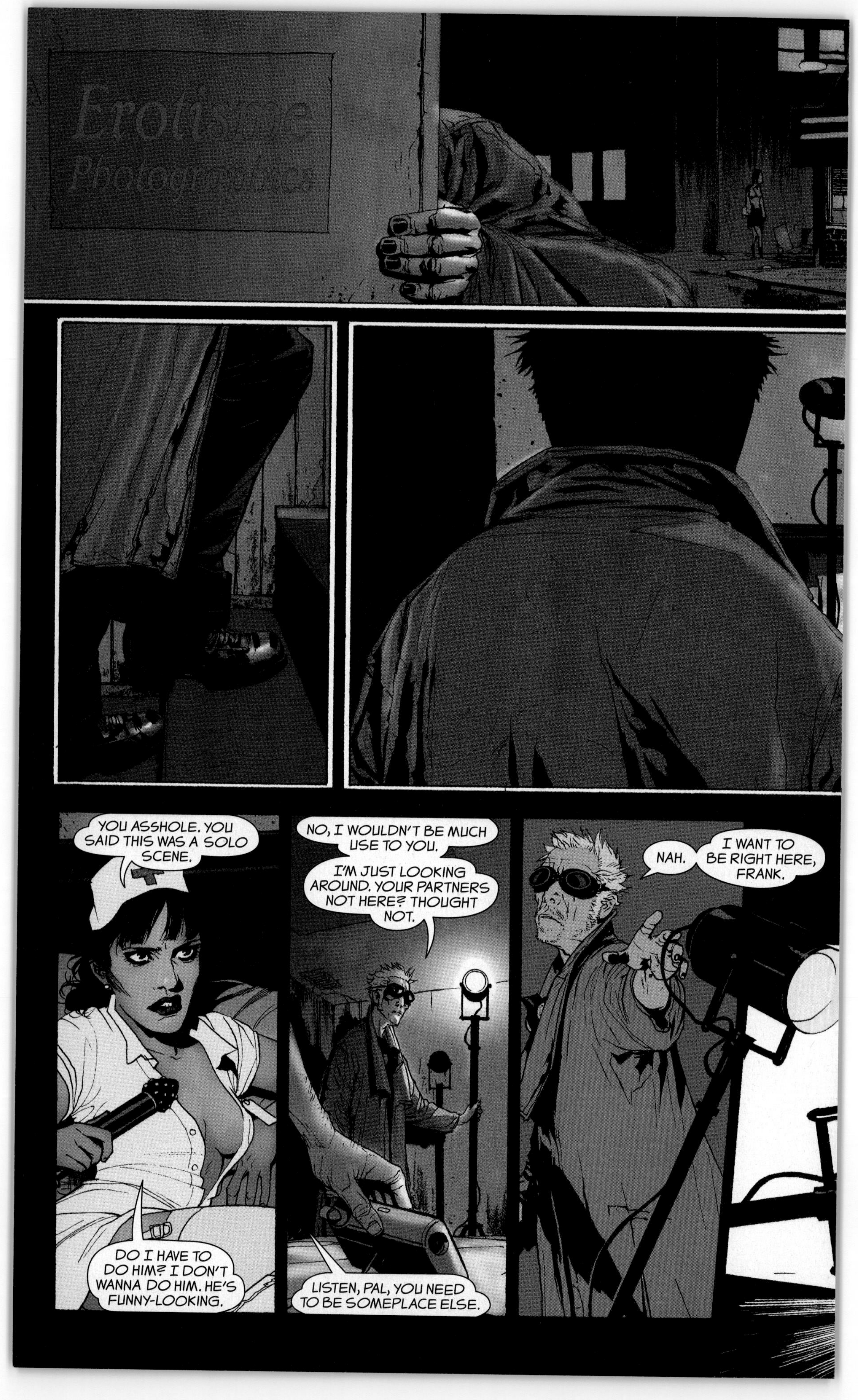
Erotisme
Photographics
YOU ASSHOLE. YOU SAID THIS WAS A SOLO SCENE.
DO I HAVE TO DO HIM? I DON'T WANNA DO HIM. HE'S FUNNY-LOOKING.
NO, I WOULDN'T BE MUCH USE TO YOU.
I'M JUST LOOKING AROUND. YOUR PARTNERS NOT HERE? THOUGHT NOT.
LISTEN, PAL, YOU NEED TO BE SOMEPLACE ELSE.
NAH.
I WANT TO BE RIGHT HERE, FRANK.

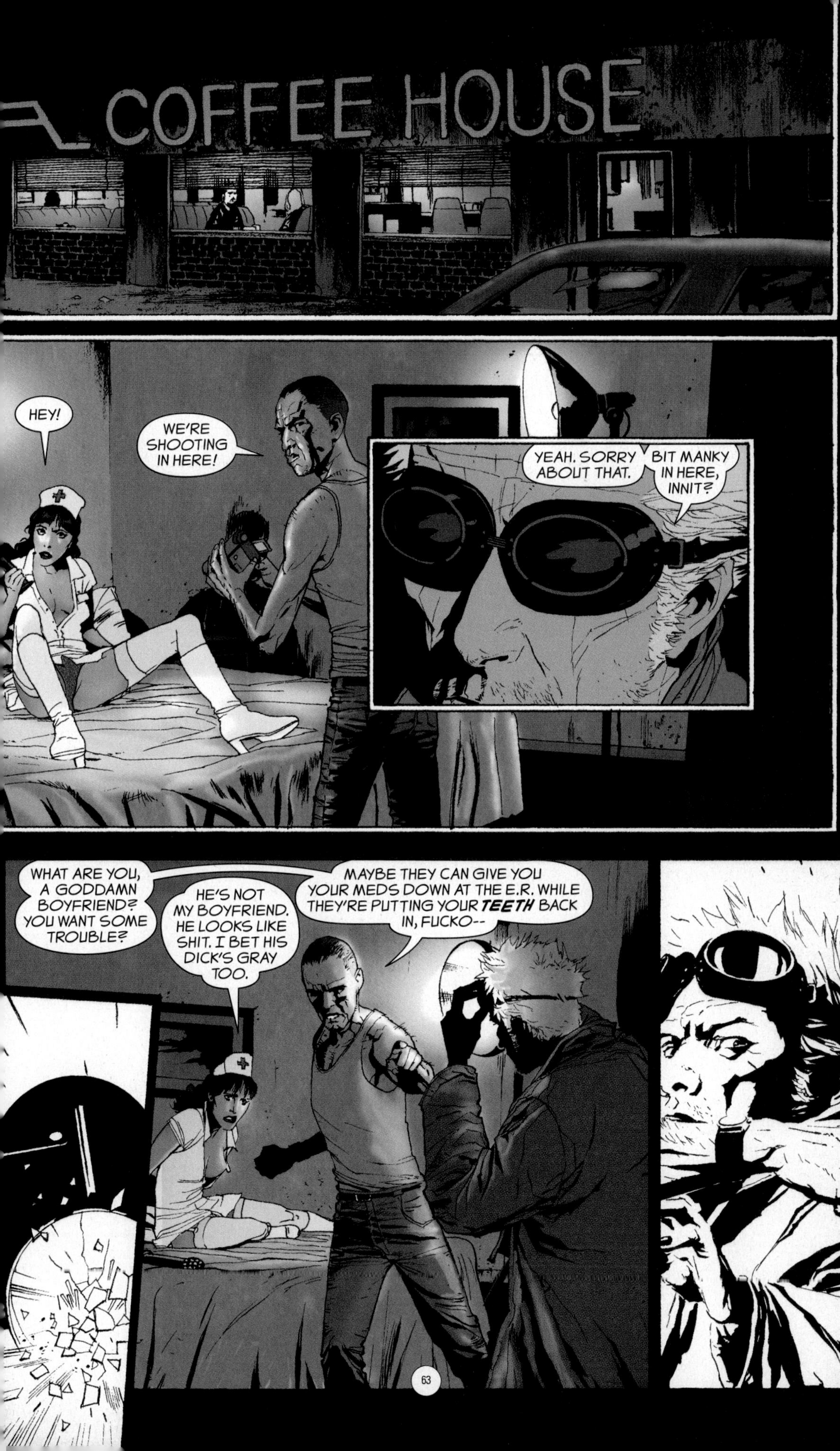

COFFEE HOUSE
HEY!
WE'RE SHOOTING IN HERE!
YEAH. SORRY ABOUT THAT.
BIT MANKY IN HERE, INNIT?
WHAT ARE YOU, A GODDAMN BOYFRIEND? YOU WANT SOME TROUBLE?
HE'S NOT MY BOYFRIEND. HE LOOKS LIKE SHIT. I BET HIS DICK'S GRAY TOO.
MAYBE THEY CAN GIVE YOU YOUR MEDS DOWN AT THE E.R. WHILE THEY'RE PUTTING YOUR **TEETH** BACK IN, FUCKO--

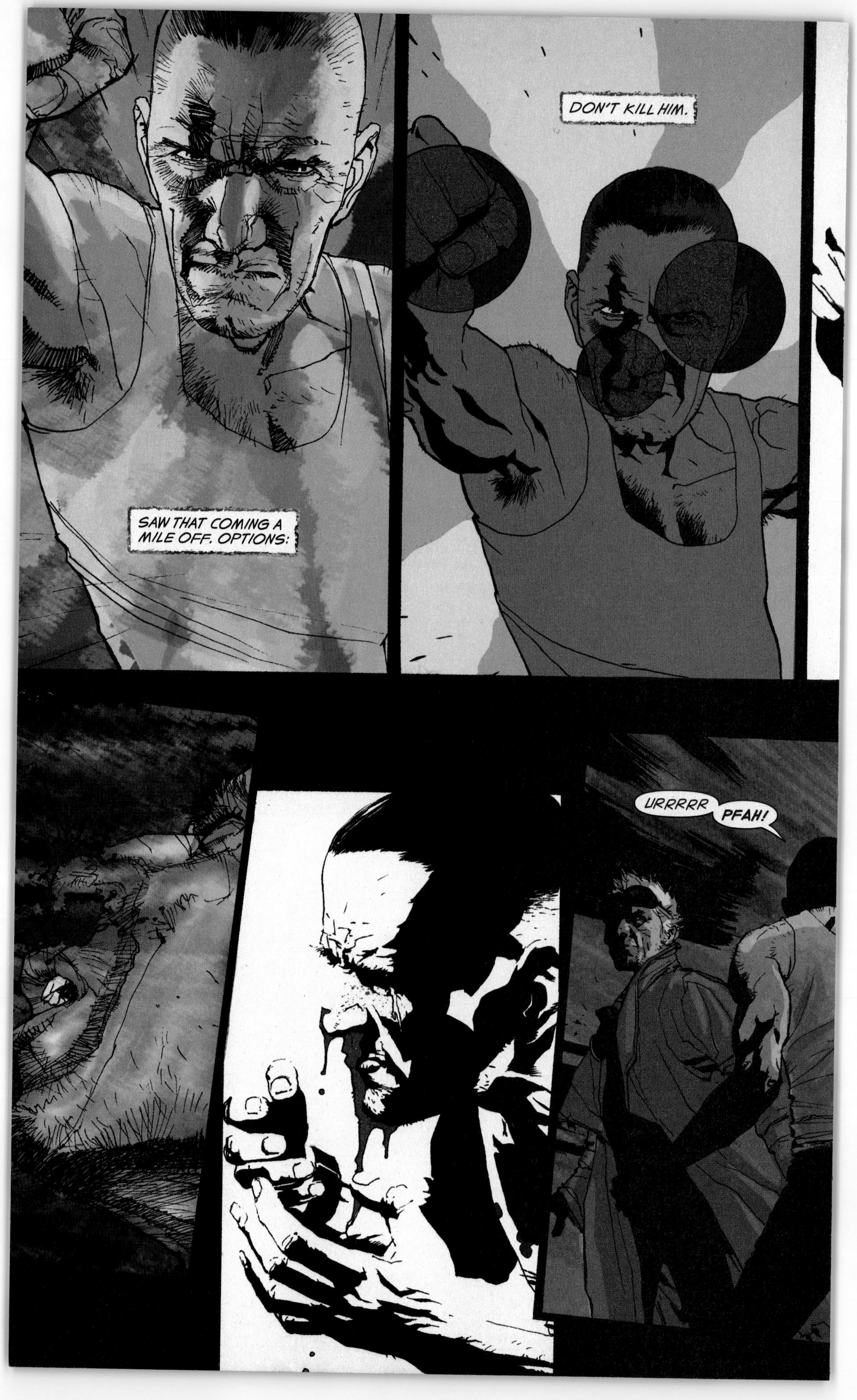
SAW THAT COMING A MILE OFF. OPTIONS:
DON'T KILL HIM.
URRRRR
PFAH!

DON'T LET HIM MAKE THE SECOND STRIKE. DON'T GET CLEVER.
STOP HIM MAKING THE PUNCH.
SHUT HIM DOWN.
AAAAAAA!!
I GOT TO TELL YOU: FOR AN EX-MAG TOUGH GUY, YOU'RE A BIT CRAP.

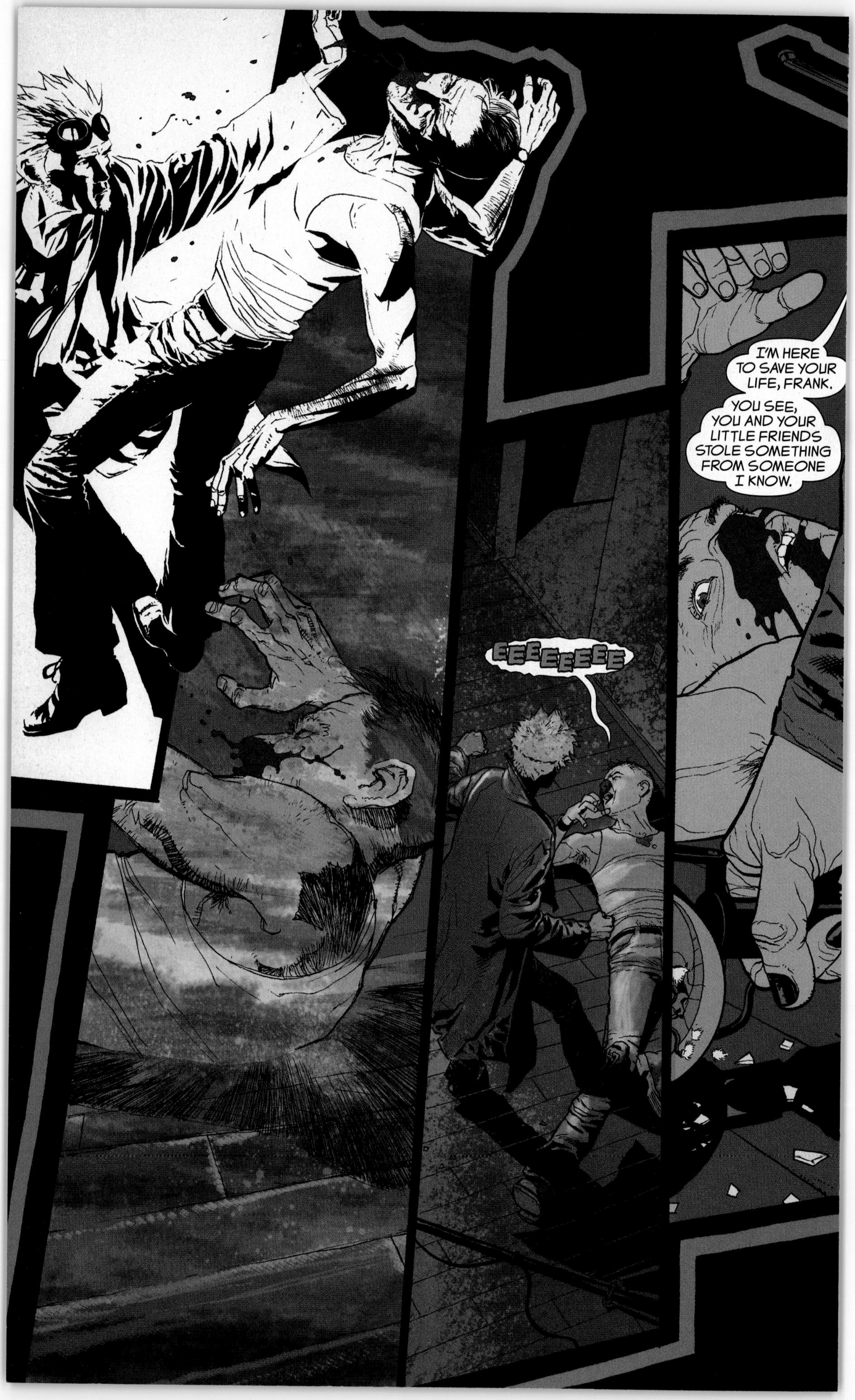
I'M HERE TO SAVE YOUR LIFE, FRANK.
YOU SEE, YOU AND YOUR LITTLE FRIENDS STOLE SOMETHING FROM SOMEONE I KNOW.
EEEEEEEE

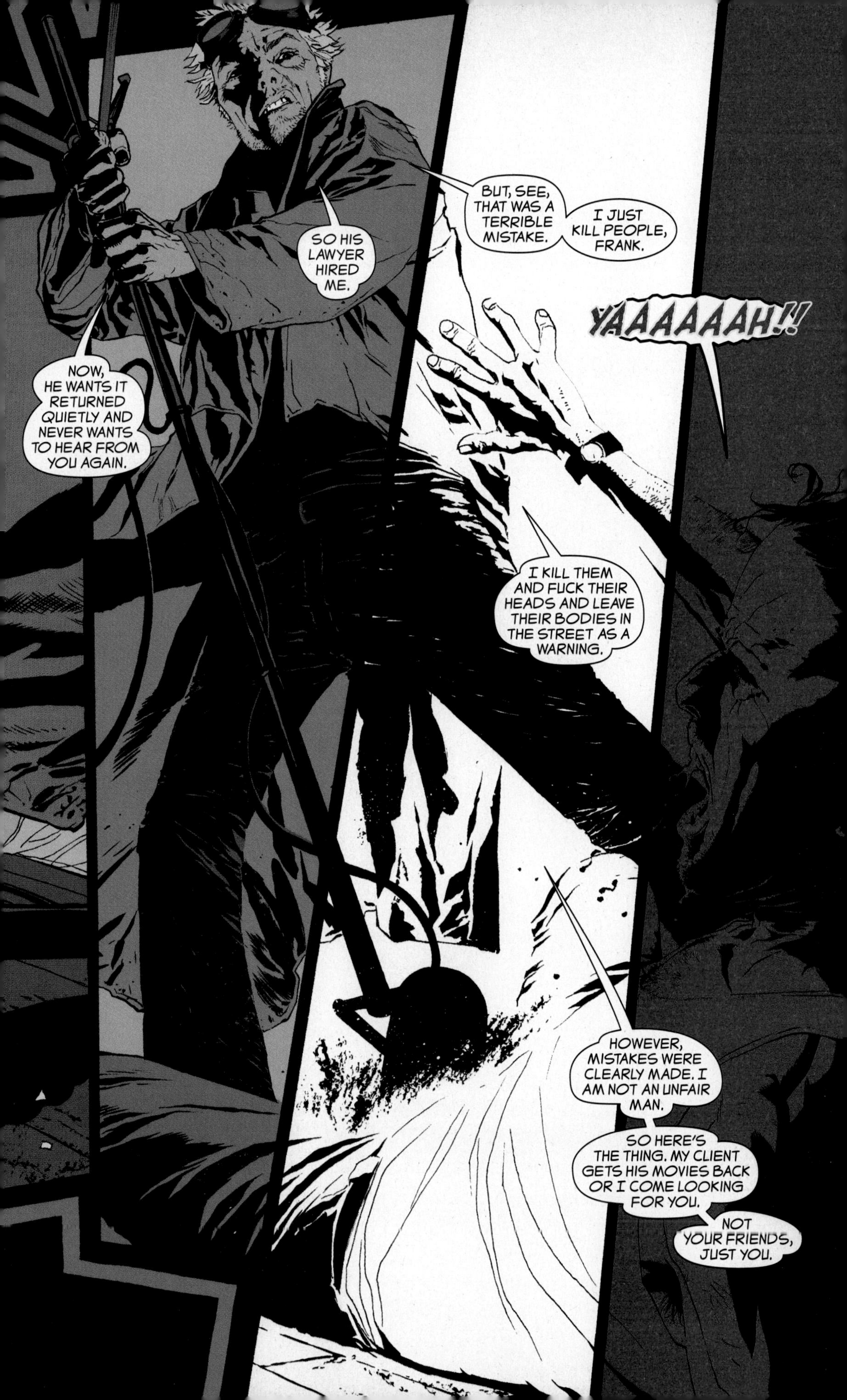
SO HIS LAWYER HIRED ME.
NOW, HE WANTS IT RETURNED QUIETLY AND NEVER WANTS TO HEAR FROM YOU AGAIN.
BUT, SEE, THAT WAS A TERRIBLE MISTAKE.
I JUST KILL PEOPLE, FRANK.
YAAAAAAH!!
I KILL THEM AND FUCK THEIR HEADS AND LEAVE THEIR BODIES IN THE STREET AS A WARNING.
HOWEVER, MISTAKES WERE CLEARLY MADE. I AM NOT AN UNFAIR MAN.
SO HERE'S THE THING. MY CLIENT GETS HIS MOVIES BACK OR I COME LOOKING FOR YOU.
NOT YOUR FRIENDS, JUST YOU.

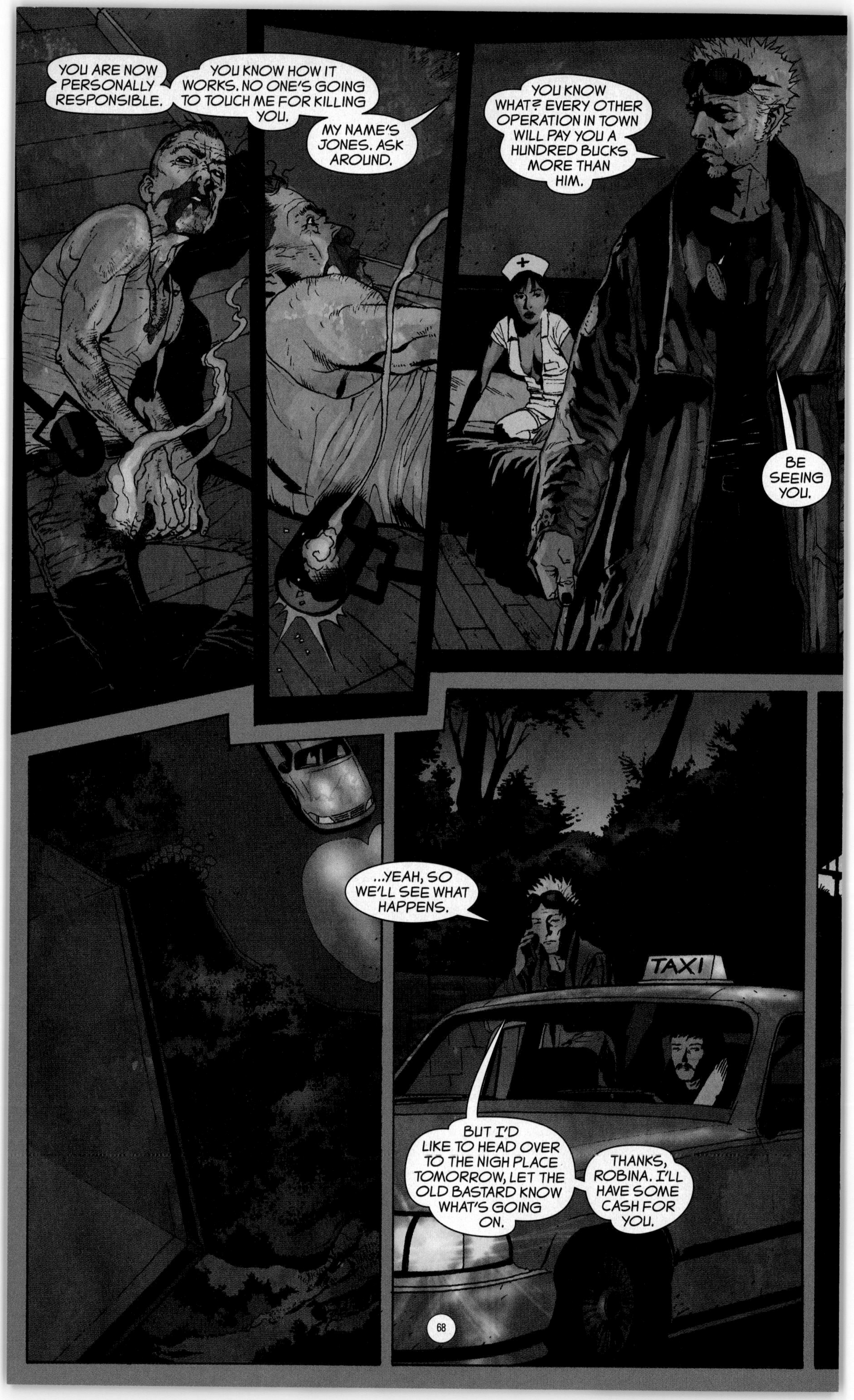
YOU ARE NOW PERSONALLY RESPONSIBLE.
YOU KNOW HOW IT WORKS. NO ONE'S GOING TO TOUCH ME FOR KILLING YOU.
MY NAME'S JONES. ASK AROUND.
YOU KNOW WHAT? EVERY OTHER OPERATION IN TOWN WILL PAY YOU A HUNDRED BUCKS MORE THAN HIM.
BE SEEING YOU.
...YEAH, SO WE'LL SEE WHAT HAPPENS.
TAXI
BUT I'D LIKE TO HEAD OVER TO THE NIGH PLACE TOMORROW, LET THE OLD BASTARD KNOW WHAT'S GOING ON.
THANKS, ROBINA. I'LL HAVE SOME CASH FOR YOU.

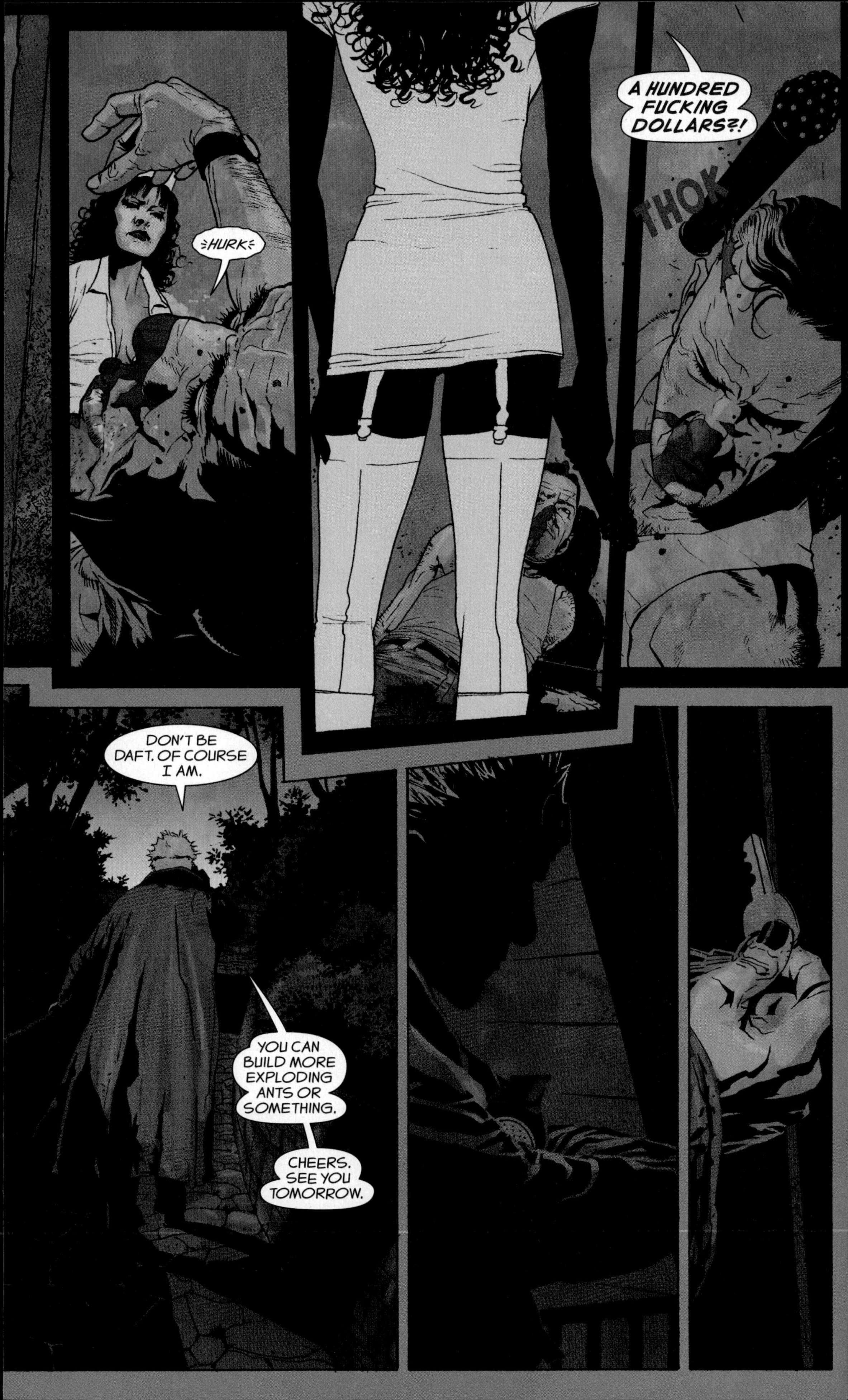
HURK
A HUNDRED FUCKING DOLLARS?!
THOK
DON'T BE DAFT. OF COURSE I AM.
YOU CAN BUILD MORE EXPLODING ANTS OR SOMETHING.
CHEERS. SEE YOU TOMORROW.

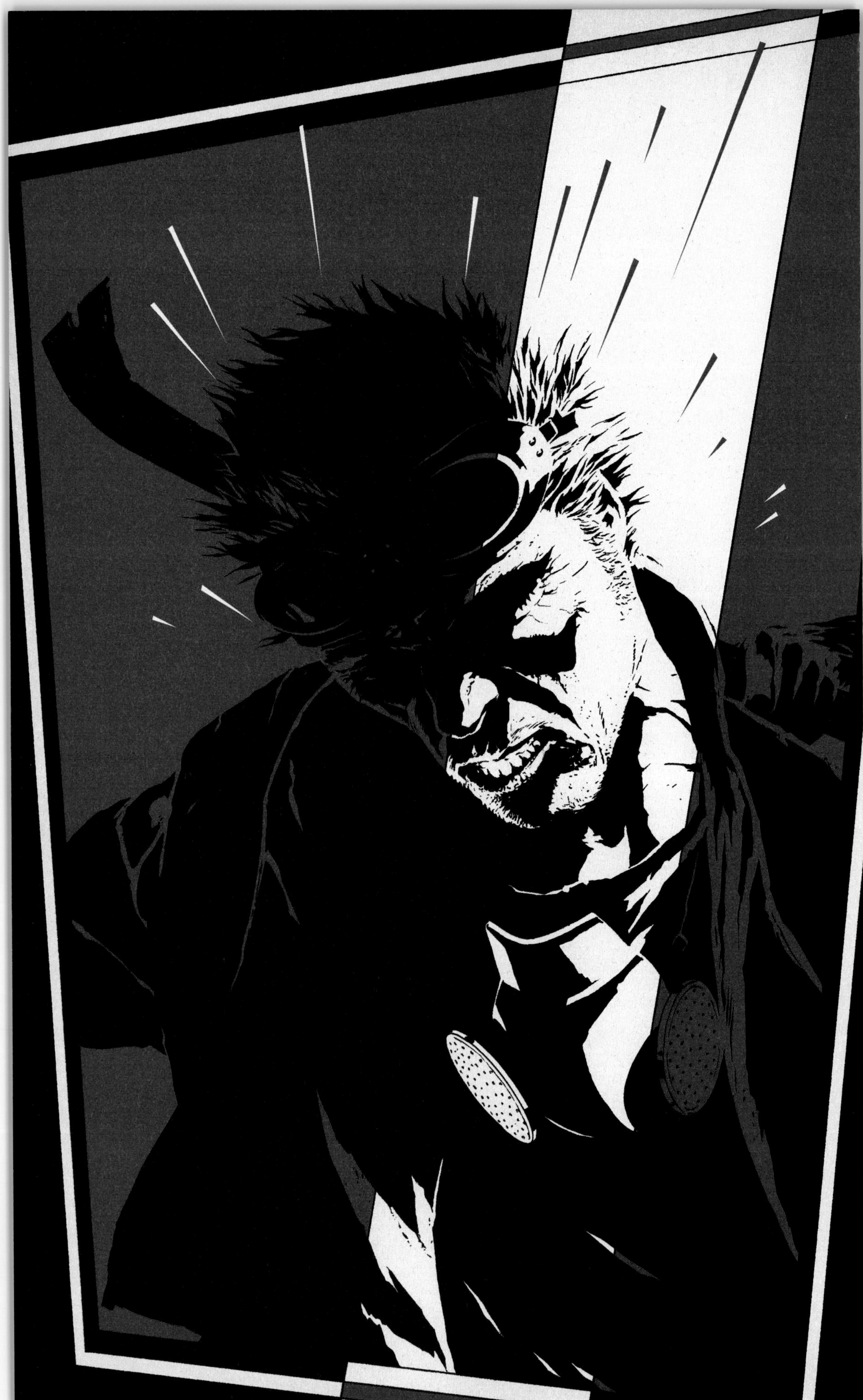

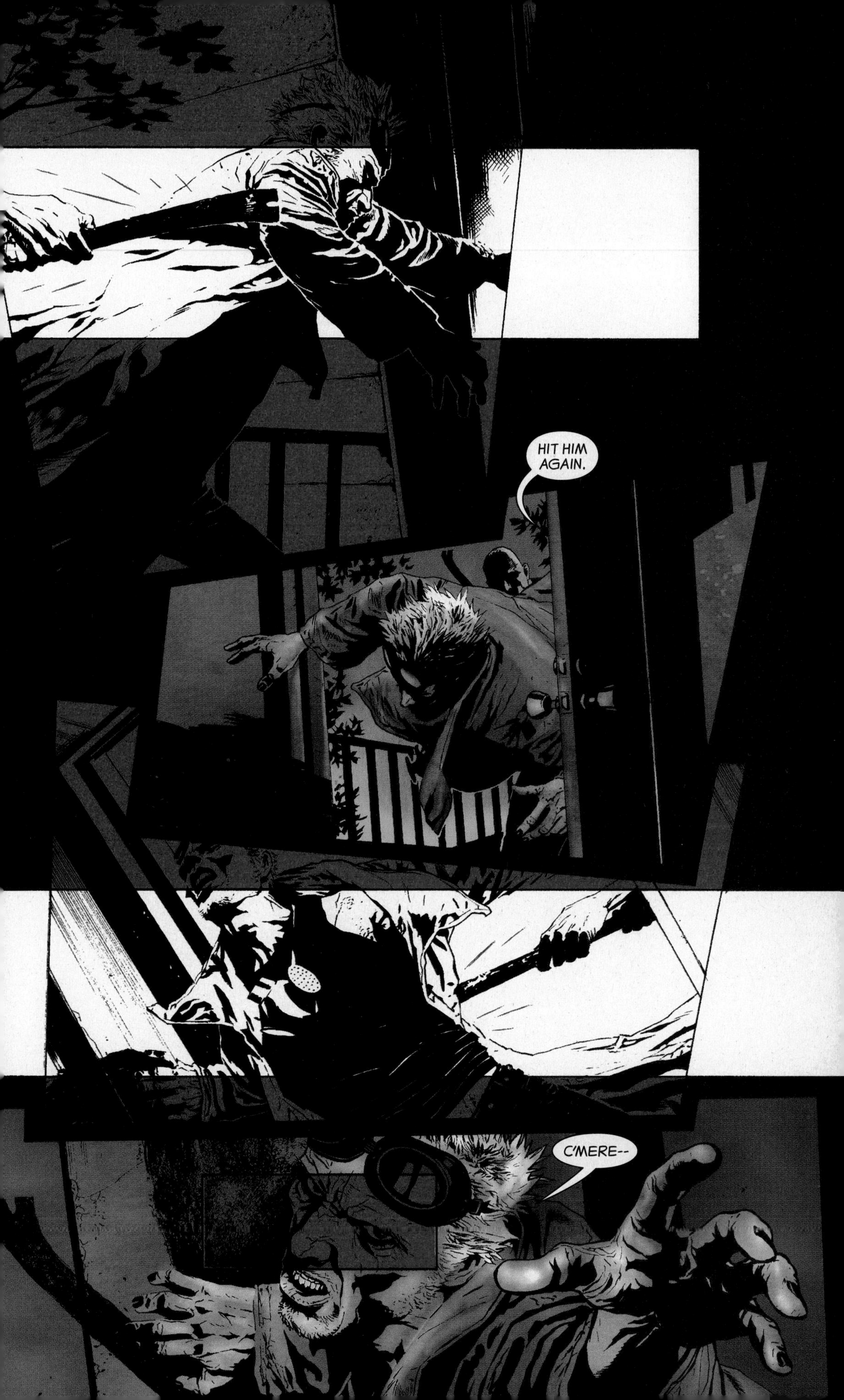
HIT HIM AGAIN.
C'MERE--

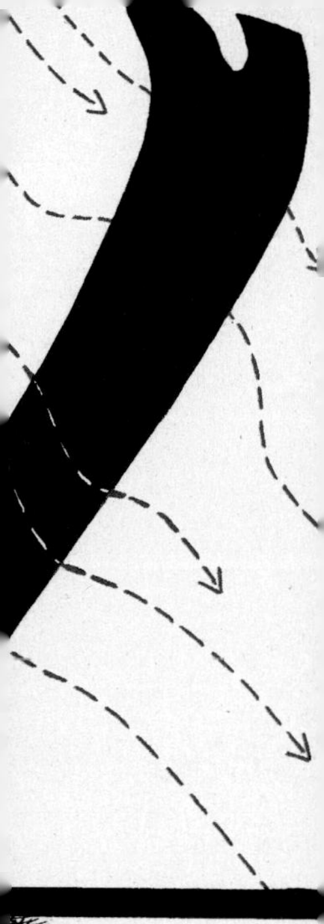

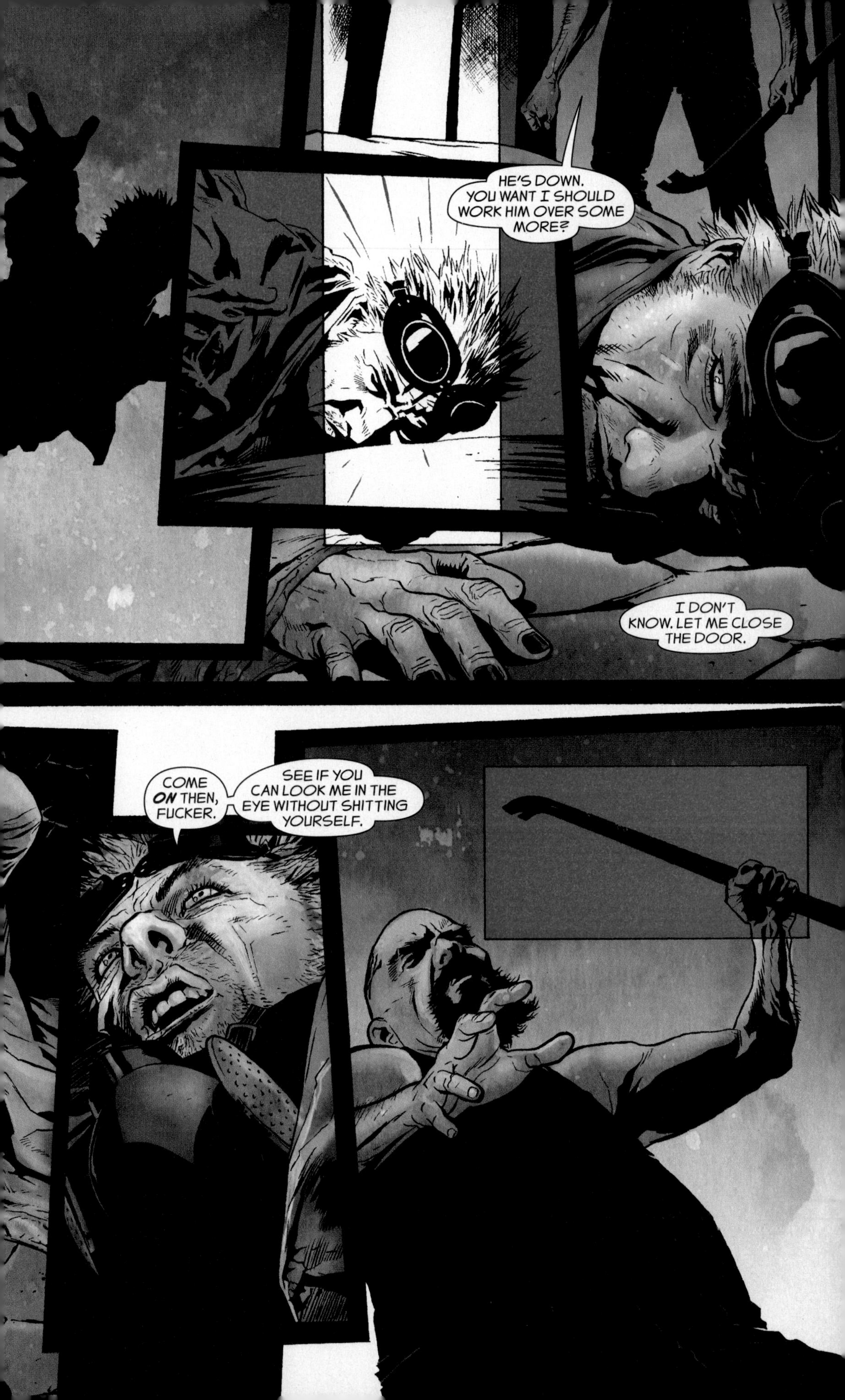
HE'S DOWN. YOU WANT I SHOULD WORK HIM OVER SOME MORE?
I DON'T KNOW. LET ME CLOSE THE DOOR.
COME ON THEN, FUCKER.
SEE IF YOU CAN LOOK ME IN THE EYE WITHOUT SHITTING YOURSELF.

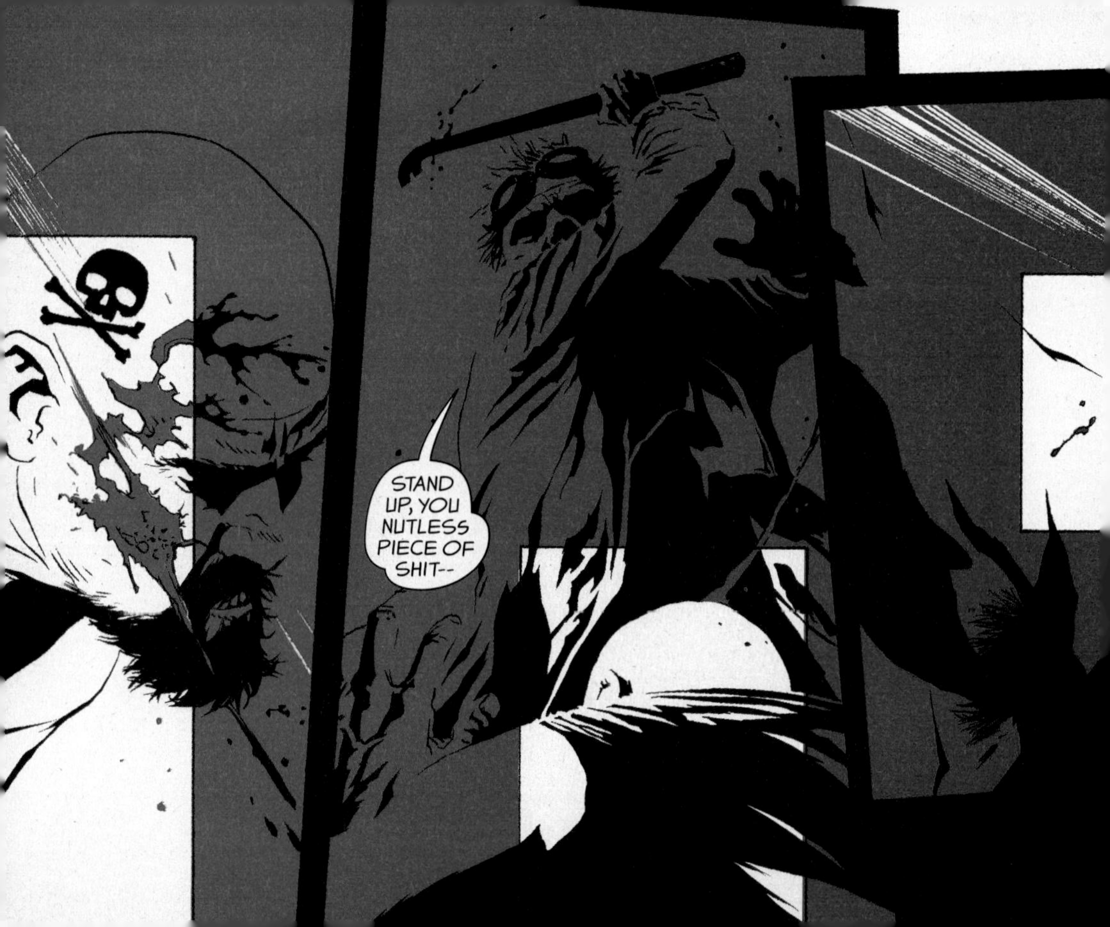
STAND UP, YOU NUTLESS PIECE OF SHIT--

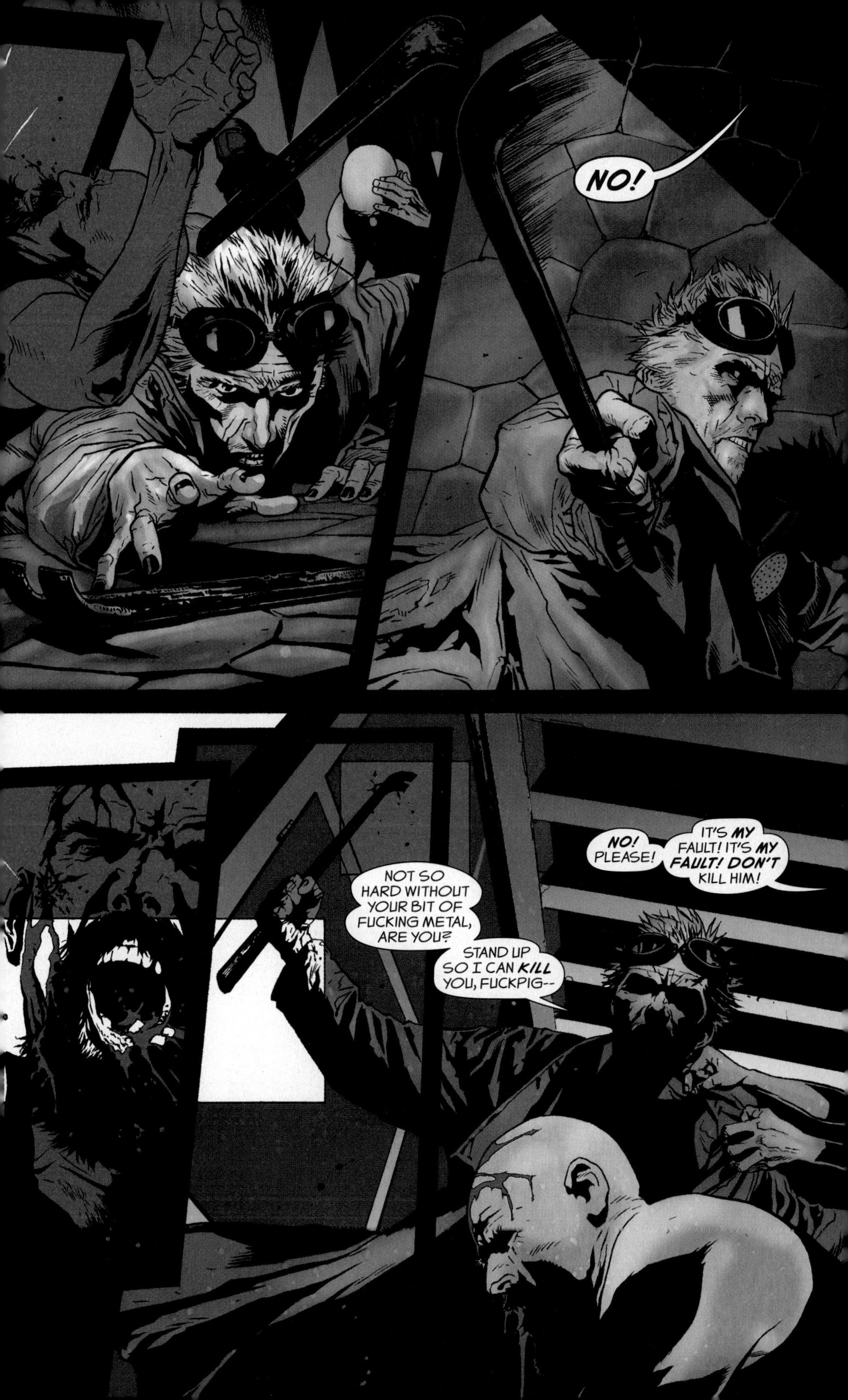
NO!
NOT SO HARD WITHOUT YOUR BIT OF FUCKING METAL, ARE YOU?
STAND UP SO I CAN KILL YOU, FUCKPIG--
NO! PLEASE!
IT'S MY FAULT! IT'S MY FAULT! DON'T KILL HIM!

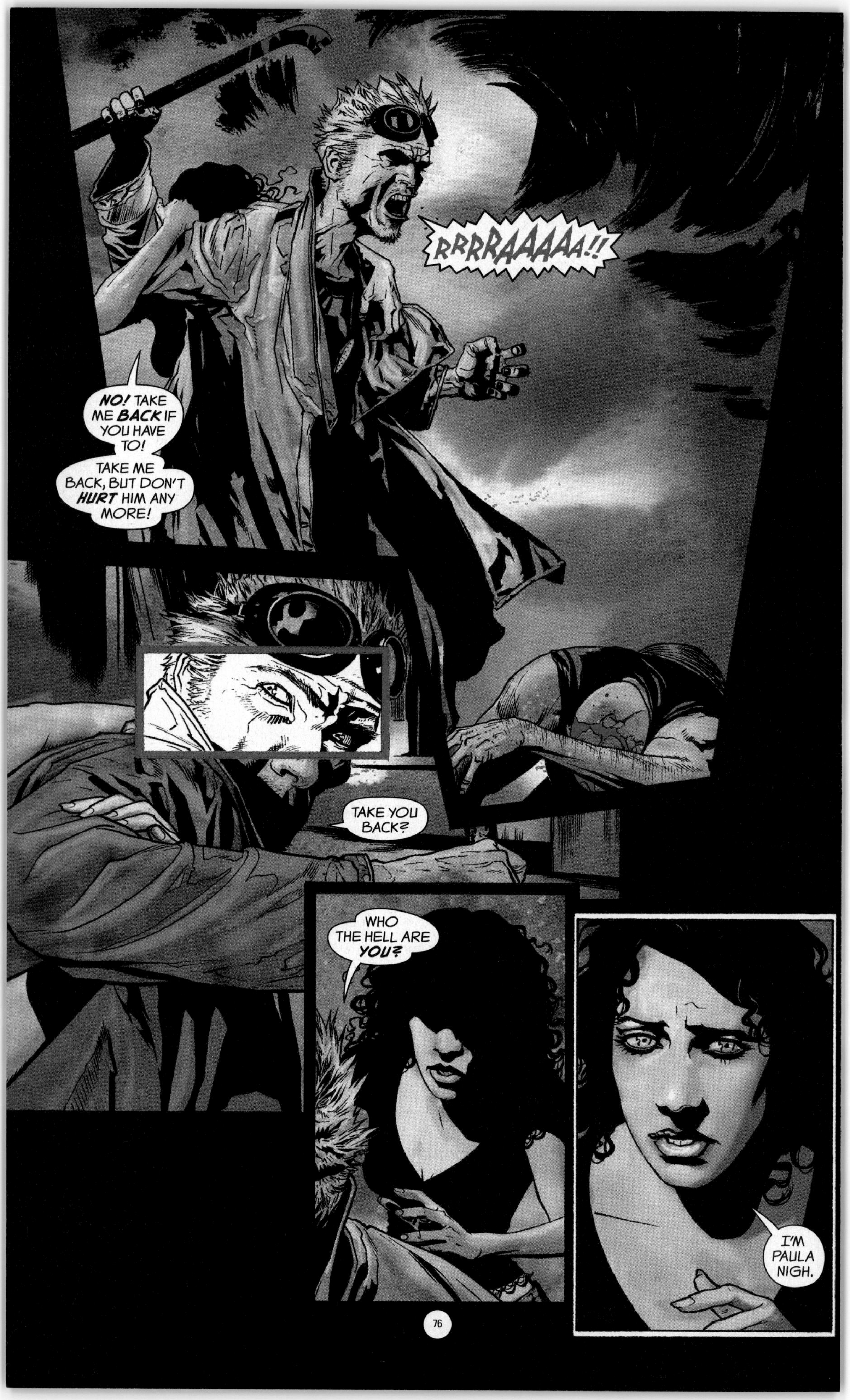

RRRRAAAAAA!!
NO! TAKE ME BACK IF YOU HAVE TO!
TAKE ME BACK, BUT DON'T HURT HIM ANY MORE!
TAKE YOU BACK?
WHO THE HELL ARE YOU?
I'M PAULA NIGH.

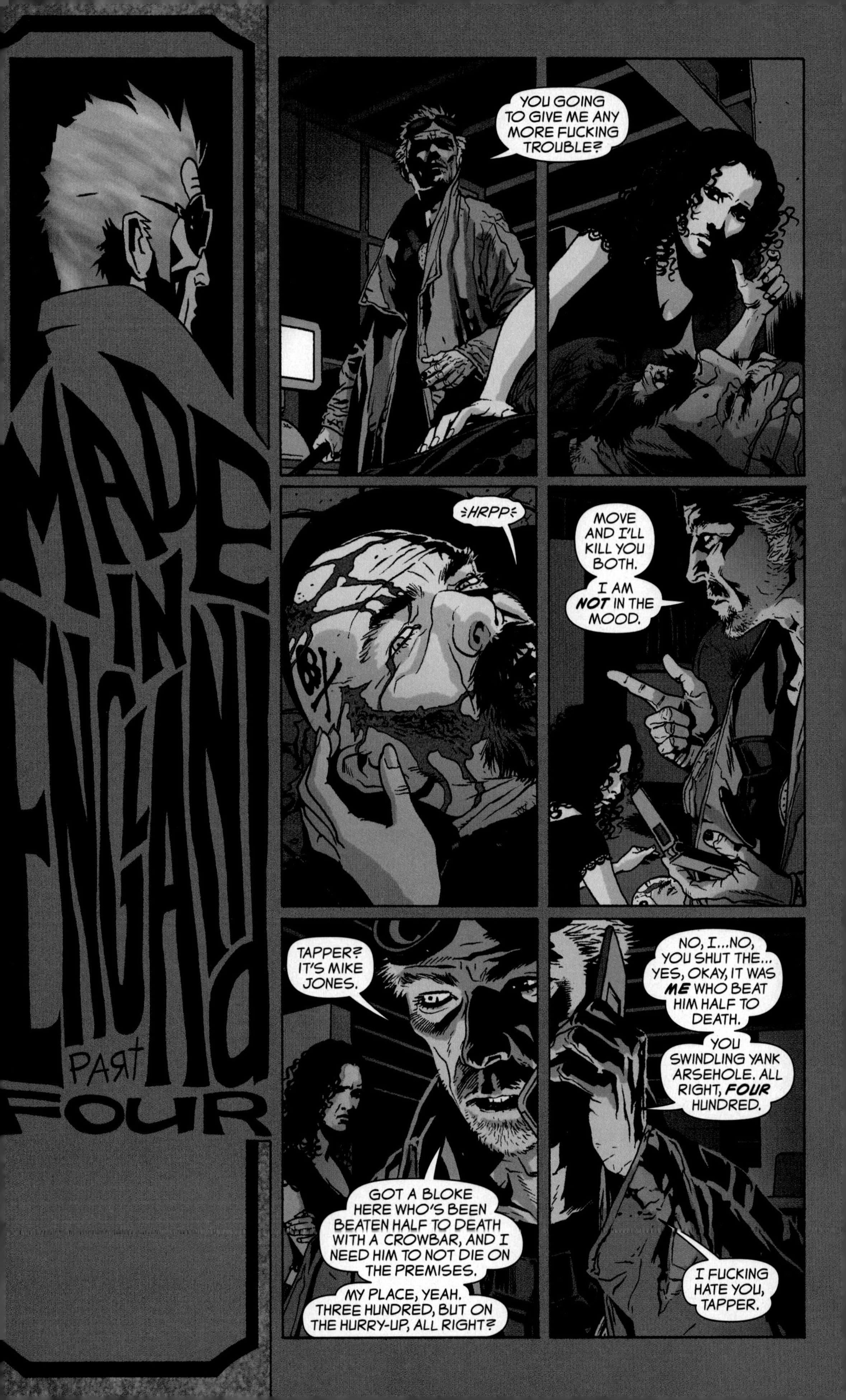
MADE IN ENGLAND
PART FOUR
YOU GOING TO GIVE ME ANY MORE FUCKING TROUBLE?
HRPP
MOVE AND I'LL KILL YOU BOTH.
I AM NOT IN THE MOOD.
TAPPER? IT'S MIKE JONES.
GOT A BLOKE HERE WHO'S BEEN BEATEN HALF TO DEATH WITH A CROWBAR, AND I NEED HIM TO NOT DIE ON THE PREMISES.
MY PLACE, YEAH. THREE HUNDRED, BUT ON THE HURRY-UP, ALL RIGHT?
NO, I...NO, YOU SHUT THE... YES, OKAY, IT WAS ME WHO BEAT HIM HALF TO DEATH.
YOU SWINDLING YANK ARSEHOLE. ALL RIGHT, FOUR HUNDRED.
I FUCKING HATE YOU, TAPPER.

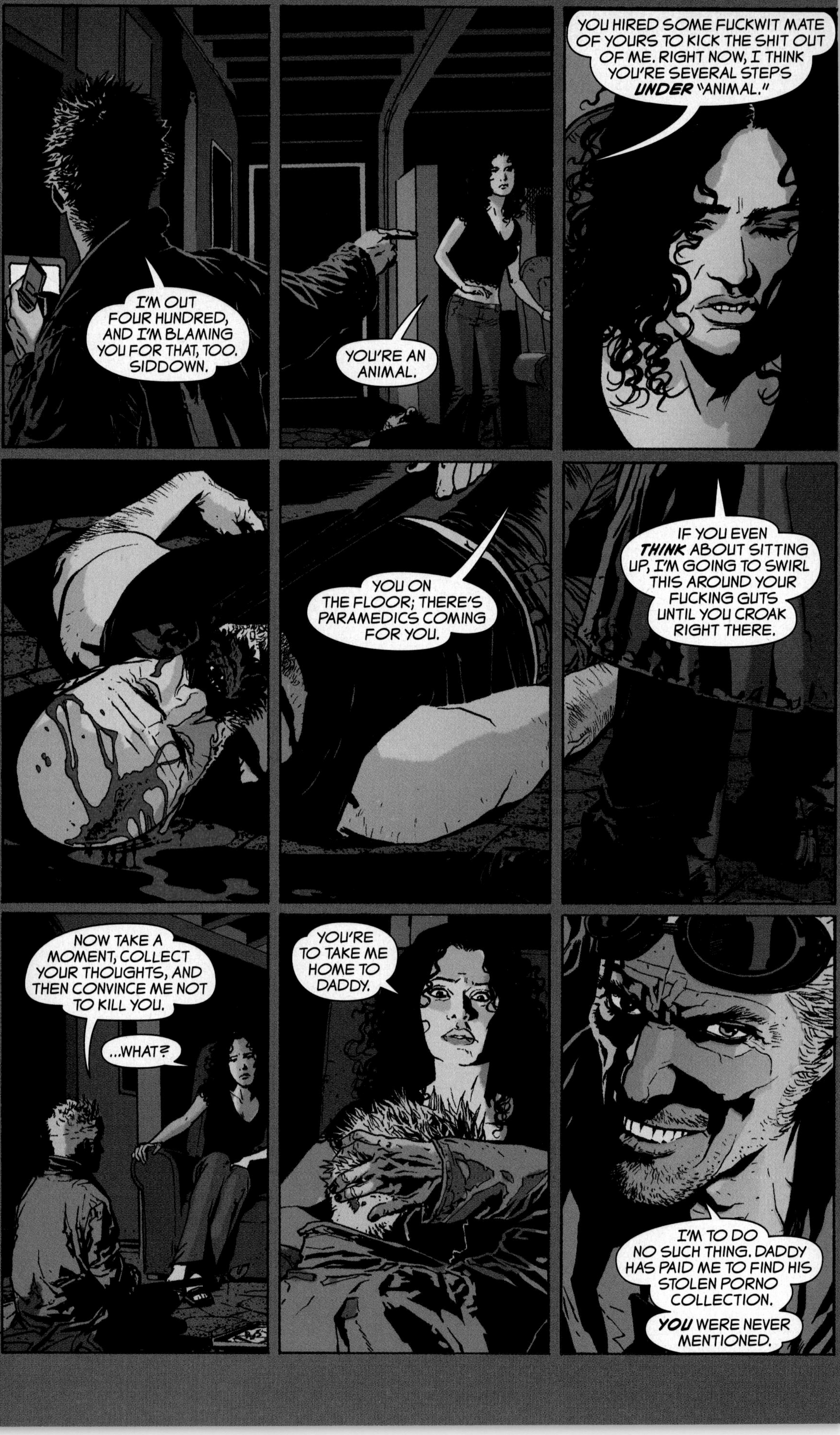
I'M OUT FOUR HUNDRED, AND I'M BLAMING YOU FOR THAT, TOO. SIDDOWN.
YOU'RE AN ANIMAL.
YOU HIRED SOME FUCKWIT MATE OF YOURS TO KICK THE SHIT OUT OF ME. RIGHT NOW, I THINK YOU'RE SEVERAL STEPS UNDER "ANIMAL."
YOU ON THE FLOOR; THERE'S PARAMEDICS COMING FOR YOU.
IF YOU EVEN THINK ABOUT SITTING UP, I'M GOING TO SWIRL THIS AROUND YOUR FUCKING GUTS UNTIL YOU CROAK RIGHT THERE.
NOW TAKE A MOMENT, COLLECT YOUR THOUGHTS, AND THEN CONVINCE ME NOT TO KILL YOU.
...WHAT?
YOU'RE TO TAKE ME HOME TO DADDY.
I'M TO DO NO SUCH THING. DADDY HAS PAID ME TO FIND HIS STOLEN PORNO COLLECTION.
YOU WERE NEVER MENTIONED.

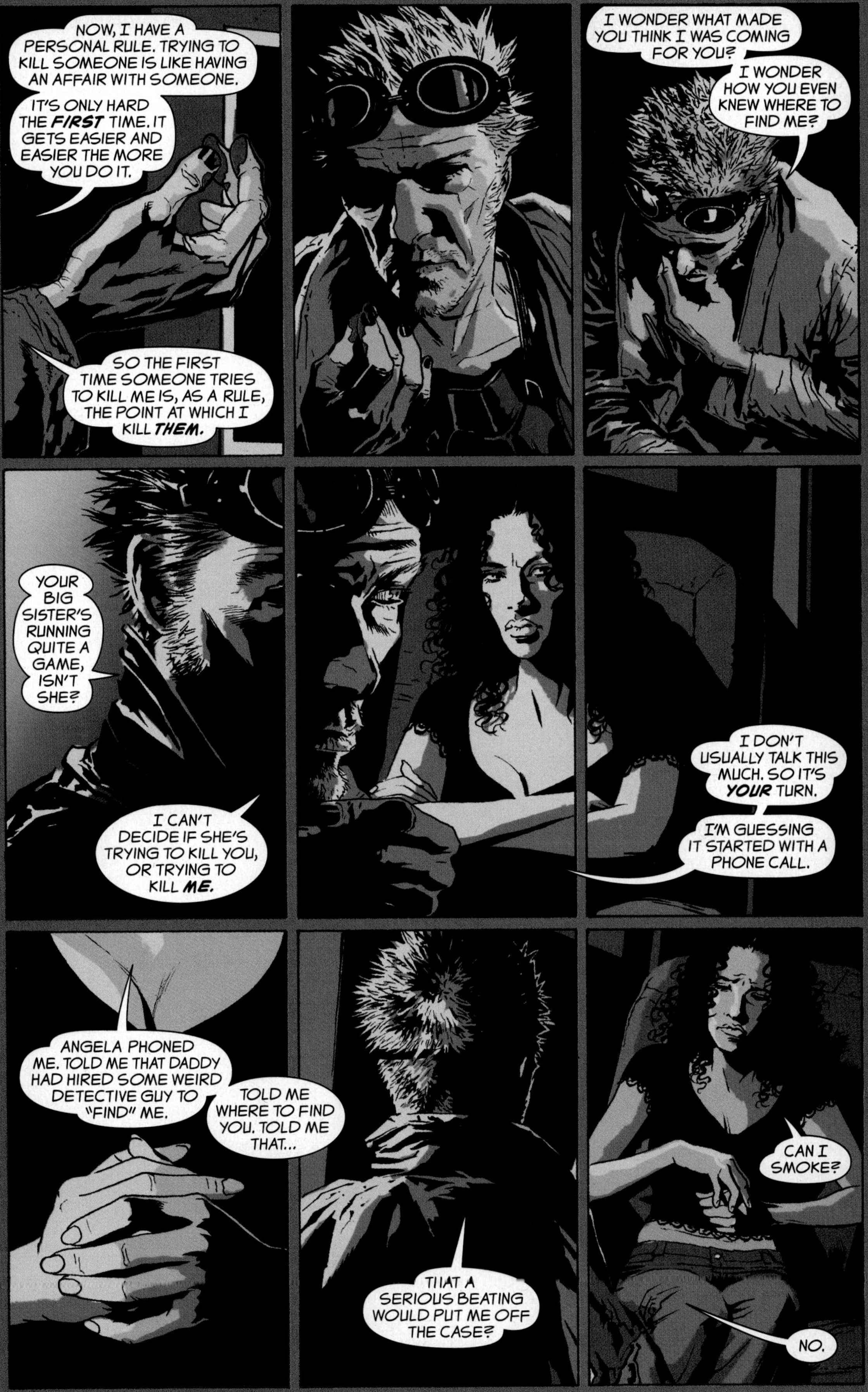
NOW, I HAVE A PERSONAL RULE. TRYING TO KILL SOMEONE IS LIKE HAVING AN AFFAIR WITH SOMEONE.
IT'S ONLY HARD THE *FIRST* TIME. IT GETS EASIER AND EASIER THE MORE YOU DO IT.
SO THE FIRST TIME SOMEONE TRIES TO KILL ME IS, AS A RULE, THE POINT AT WHICH I KILL *THEM.*
I WONDER WHAT MADE YOU THINK I WAS COMING FOR YOU?
I WONDER HOW YOU EVEN KNEW WHERE TO FIND ME?
YOUR BIG SISTER'S RUNNING QUITE A GAME, ISN'T SHE?
I CAN'T DECIDE IF SHE'S TRYING TO KILL YOU, OR TRYING TO KILL *ME.*
I DON'T USUALLY TALK THIS MUCH. SO IT'S *YOUR* TURN.
I'M GUESSING IT STARTED WITH A PHONE CALL.
ANGELA PHONED ME. TOLD ME THAT DADDY HAD HIRED SOME WEIRD DETECTIVE GUY TO "FIND" ME.
TOLD ME WHERE TO FIND YOU. TOLD ME THAT...
THAT A SERIOUS BEATING WOULD PUT ME OFF THE CASE?
CAN I SMOKE?
NO.

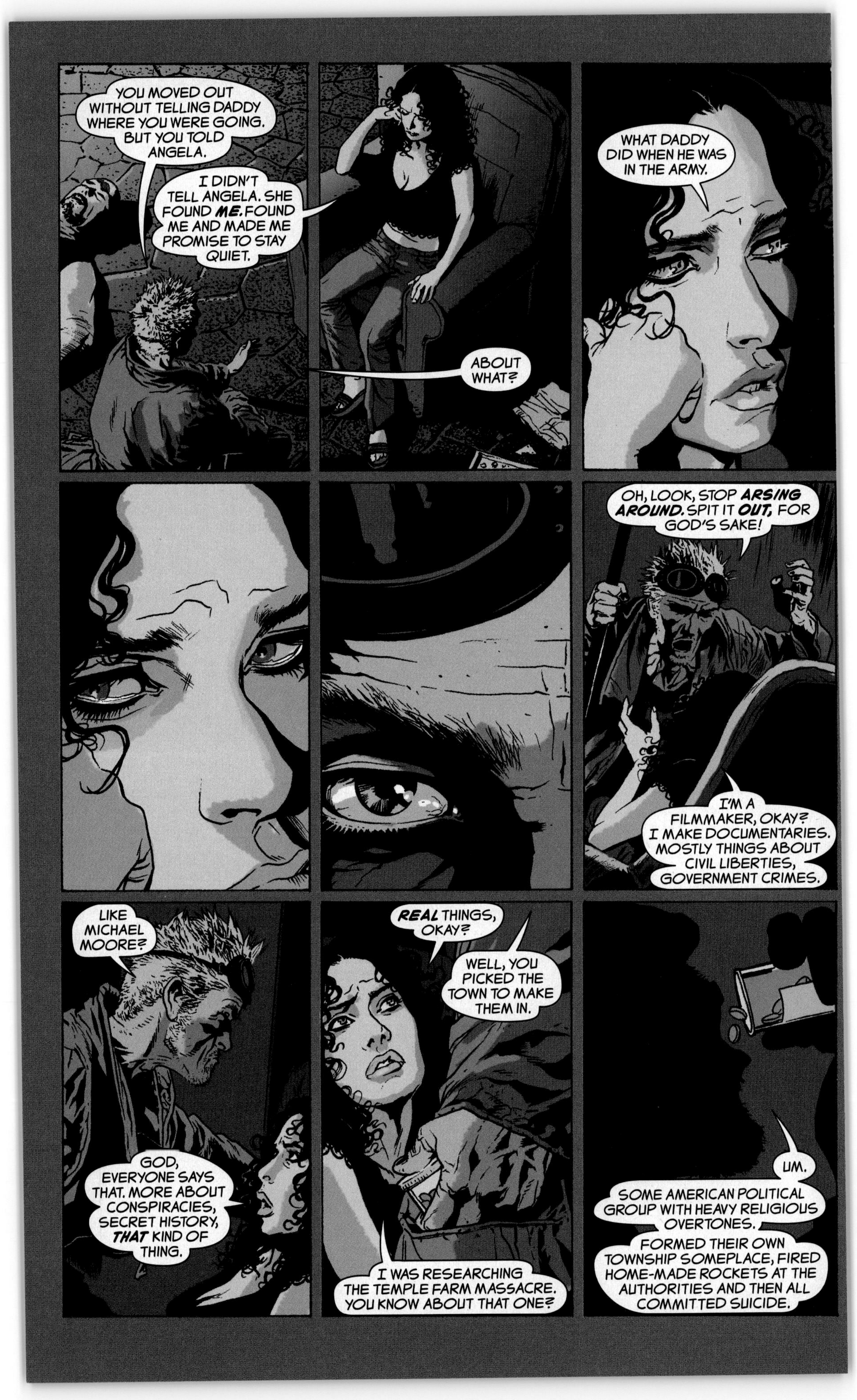

YOU MOVED OUT WITHOUT TELLING DADDY WHERE YOU WERE GOING. BUT YOU TOLD ANGELA.
I DIDN'T TELL ANGELA. SHE FOUND ME. FOUND ME AND MADE ME PROMISE TO STAY QUIET.
ABOUT WHAT?
WHAT DADDY DID WHEN HE WAS IN THE ARMY.
OH, LOOK, STOP ARSING AROUND. SPIT IT OUT, FOR GOD'S SAKE!
I'M A FILMMAKER, OKAY? I MAKE DOCUMENTARIES. MOSTLY THINGS ABOUT CIVIL LIBERTIES, GOVERNMENT CRIMES.
LIKE MICHAEL MOORE?
GOD, EVERYONE SAYS THAT. MORE ABOUT CONSPIRACIES, SECRET HISTORY, THAT KIND OF THING.
REAL THINGS, OKAY?
WELL, YOU PICKED THE TOWN TO MAKE THEM IN.
I WAS RESEARCHING THE TEMPLE FARM MASSACRE. YOU KNOW ABOUT THAT ONE?
UM.
SOME AMERICAN POLITICAL GROUP WITH HEAVY RELIGIOUS OVERTONES.
FORMED THEIR OWN TOWNSHIP SOMEPLACE, FIRED HOME-MADE ROCKETS AT THE AUTHORITIES AND THEN ALL COMMITTED SUICIDE.

THAT'S RIGHT.

IN THE COURSE OF MY RESEARCH, DADDY'S *NAME* CAME UP. AT LEAST TWO OF THE TEMPLE FARM ELDERS HAD ONCE BEEN UNDER DADDY'S COMMAND.

DADDY KEEPS RECORDS ON EVERYTHING. IT'S ALL AT HOME.

SO I WENT THROUGH THEM.

AND FUCK *YOU*, MISTER JONES.

TRYING TO PROVE HIS INVOLVE-MENT?

TRYING TO PROVE HE *WASN'T* INVOLVED. I DIDN'T WANT HIM NEAR IT.

AND...

TEMPLE FARM WAS ALL HIS FAULT. IT WAS ALL HIM.

THE GUY WHO RAN THE WHOLE THING? ALL HIS ADVISORS, ALL HIS FRIENDS--THEY WORKED FOR DADDY.

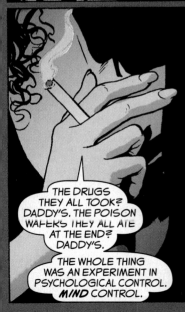
THE DRUGS THEY ALL TOOK? DADDY'S. THE POISON WAFERS THEY ALL ATE AT THE END? DADDY'S.

THE WHOLE THING WAS AN EXPERIMENT IN PSYCHOLOGICAL CONTROL. *MIND* CONTROL.

I...I JUST COULDN'T LOOK AT HIM AFTERWARDS. I GOT OUT.

BUT NOT BEFORE YOU TOLD YOUR SISTERS.

JUST ANGELA.

ANGELA HATED THE WORK I DID. I THOUGHT THAT IF I TOLD HER, AND PROMISED MY SILENCE, AND JUST GOT OUT...

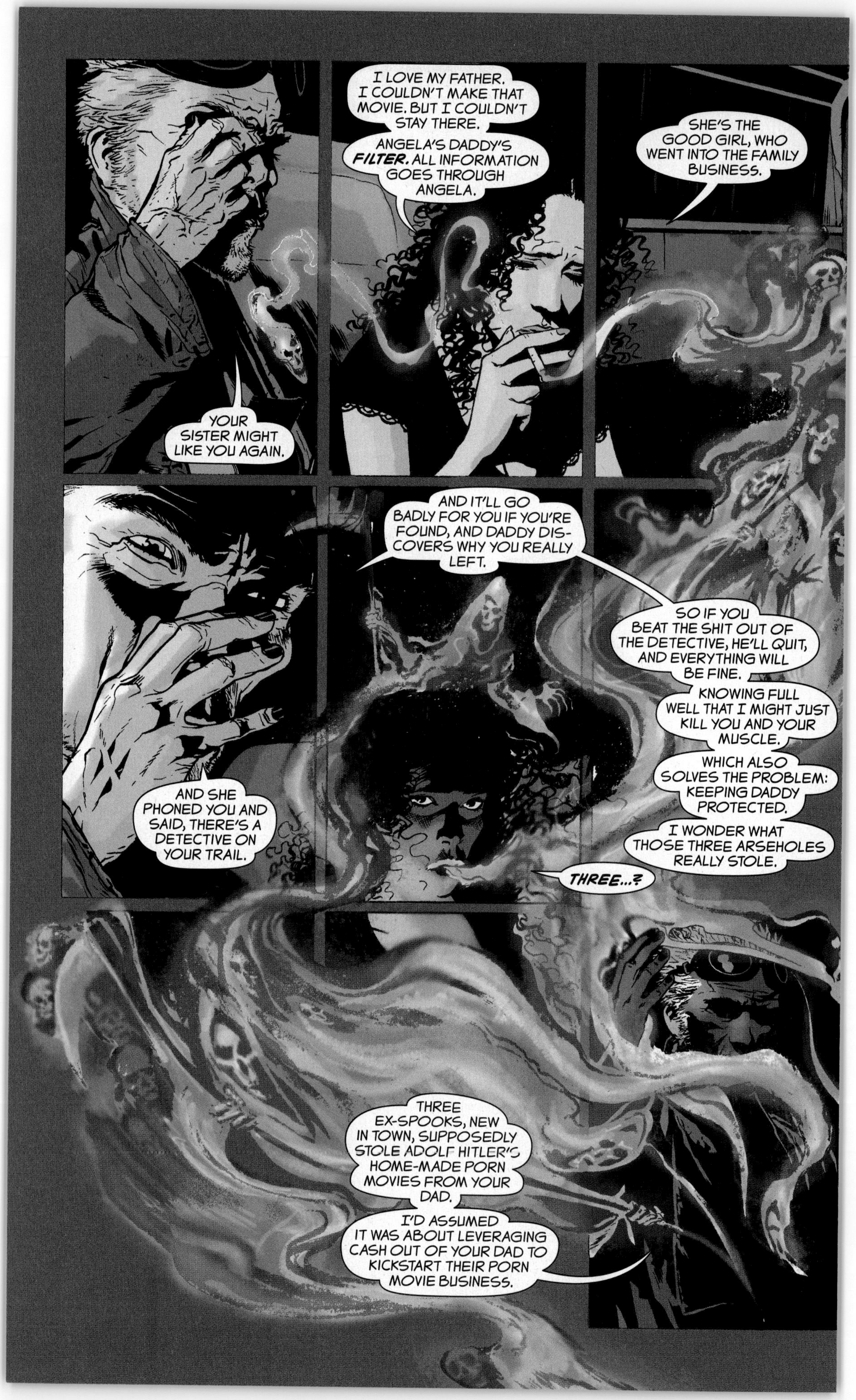

I LOVE MY FATHER. I COULDN'T MAKE THAT MOVIE. BUT I COULDN'T STAY THERE.
ANGELA'S DADDY'S **FILTER.** ALL INFORMATION GOES THROUGH ANGELA.
SHE'S THE GOOD GIRL, WHO WENT INTO THE FAMILY BUSINESS.
YOUR SISTER MIGHT LIKE YOU AGAIN.
AND SHE PHONED YOU AND SAID, THERE'S A DETECTIVE ON YOUR TRAIL.
AND IT'LL GO BADLY FOR YOU IF YOU'RE FOUND, AND DADDY DISCOVERS WHY YOU REALLY LEFT.
SO IF YOU BEAT THE SHIT OUT OF THE DETECTIVE, HE'LL QUIT, AND EVERYTHING WILL BE FINE.
KNOWING FULL WELL THAT I MIGHT JUST KILL YOU AND YOUR MUSCLE.
WHICH ALSO SOLVES THE PROBLEM: KEEPING DADDY PROTECTED.
I WONDER WHAT THOSE THREE ARSEHOLES REALLY STOLE.
THREE...?
THREE EX-SPOOKS, NEW IN TOWN, SUPPOSEDLY STOLE ADOLF HITLER'S HOME-MADE PORN MOVIES FROM YOUR DAD.
I'D ASSUMED IT WAS ABOUT LEVERAGING CASH OUT OF YOUR DAD TO KICKSTART THEIR PORN MOVIE BUSINESS.

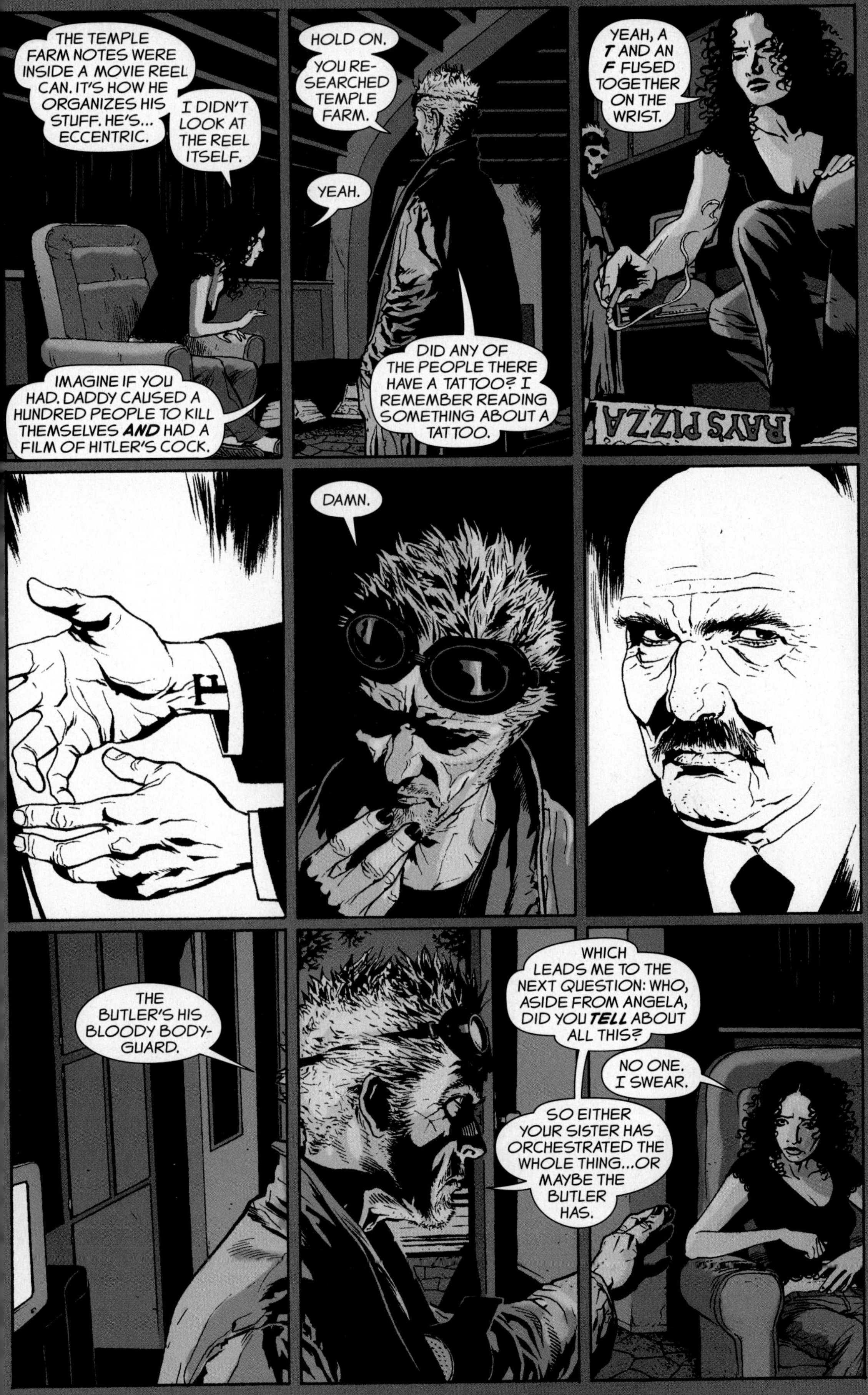
THE TEMPLE FARM NOTES WERE INSIDE A MOVIE REEL CAN. IT'S HOW HE ORGANIZES HIS STUFF. HE'S... ECCENTRIC.
I DIDN'T LOOK AT THE REEL ITSELF.
IMAGINE IF YOU HAD. DADDY CAUSED A HUNDRED PEOPLE TO KILL THEMSELVES AND HAD A FILM OF HITLER'S COCK.
HOLD ON.
YOU RE-SEARCHED TEMPLE FARM.
YEAH.
DID ANY OF THE PEOPLE THERE HAVE A TATTOO? I REMEMBER READING SOMETHING ABOUT A TATTOO.
YEAH, A T AND AN F FUSED TOGETHER ON THE WRIST.
RAY'S PIZZA
DAMN.
THE BUTLER'S HIS BLOODY BODY-GUARD.
WHICH LEADS ME TO THE NEXT QUESTION: WHO, ASIDE FROM ANGELA, DID YOU TELL ABOUT ALL THIS?
NO ONE. I SWEAR.
SO EITHER YOUR SISTER HAS ORCHESTRATED THE WHOLE THING...OR MAYBE THE BUTLER HAS.

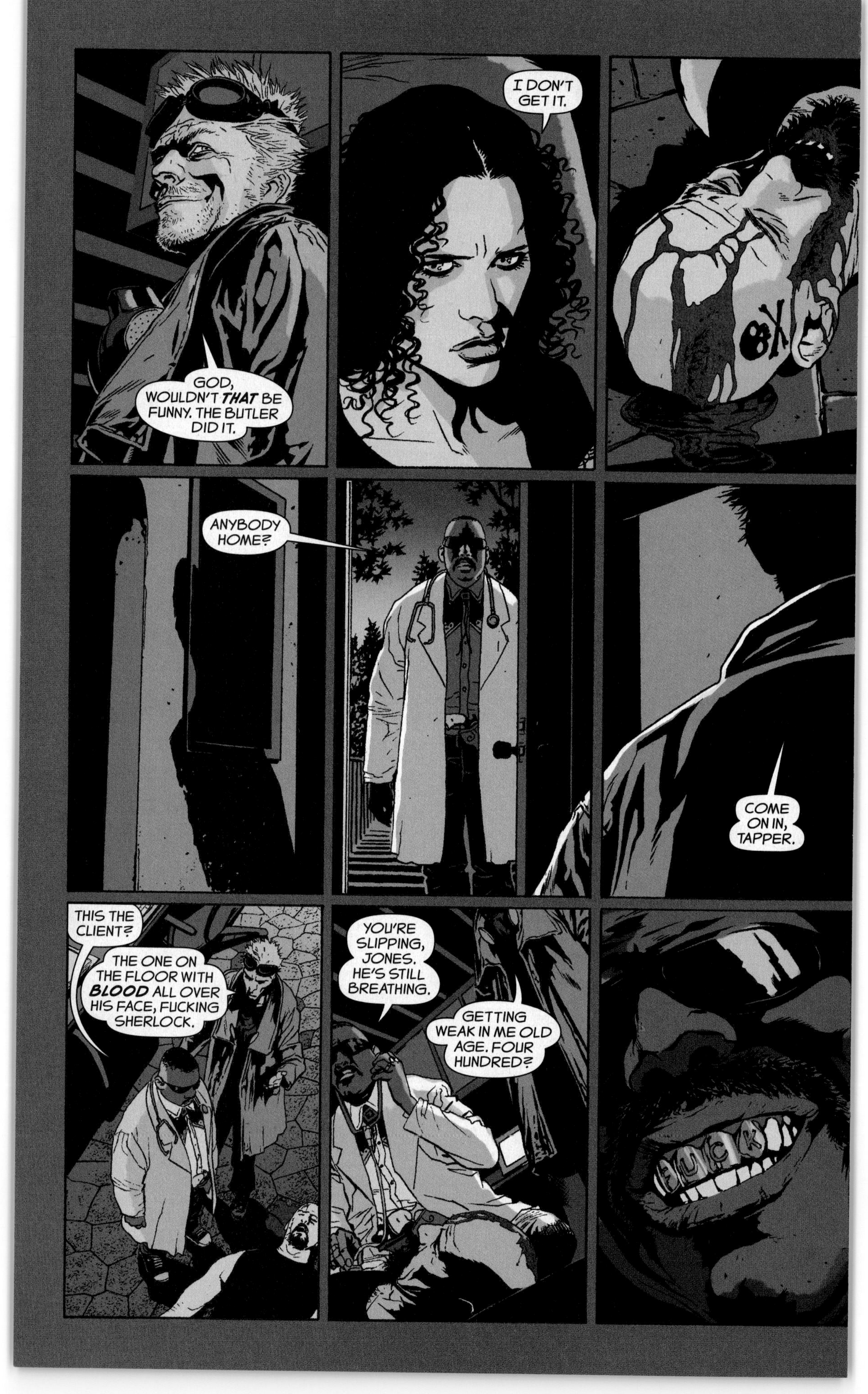

GOD, WOULDN'T *THAT* BE FUNNY. THE BUTLER DID IT.
I DON'T GET IT.
ANYBODY HOME?
COME ON IN, TAPPER.
THIS THE CLIENT?
THE ONE ON THE FLOOR WITH *BLOOD* ALL OVER HIS FACE, FUCKING SHERLOCK.
YOU'RE SLIPPING, JONES. HE'S STILL BREATHING.
GETTING WEAK IN ME OLD AGE. FOUR HUNDRED?

WHAT'S GOING ON?

IN YOUR RESEARCH, DID YOU EVER HEAR ABOUT A COMMUNITY OF EX-INTELLIGENCE OPERATIVES CONFINED TO THE LOS ANGELES AREA?

ONLY RUMORS.

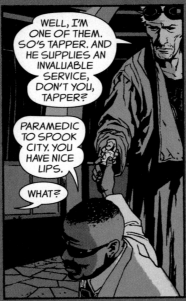

WELL, I'M ONE OF THEM. SO'S TAPPER. AND HE SUPPLIES AN INVALUABLE SERVICE, DON'T YOU, TAPPER?

PARAMEDIC TO SPOOK CITY. YOU HAVE NICE LIPS.

WHAT?

NICE LIPS. IT'S NOT DIFFICULT. ARE YOU A LITTLE BACKWARDS?

NO, I MEAN...SECRET AGENTS? A SECRET MEDICAL OPERATION?

BECAUSE, YOU KNOW, I'VE DONE IT TO BACKWARDS GIRLS TOO, AND THEY'VE LIKED IT.

TAPPER. JUST DEAL WITH THE GUY, WOULD YOU?

FRACTURED SKULL. DUNNO IF IT'S SURGICAL. I'LL LET YOU KNOW.

BOYS! I GOT A PACKAGE!

WHERE ARE YOU TAKING HIM?

SECRET HOSPITAL. I IMAGINE HE'LL BE OUT ON THE STREET IN A COUPLE OF DAYS.

HE WON'T REMEMBER MUCH. YOU MIGHT WANT TO START GETTING A STORY TOGETHER FOR HIM.

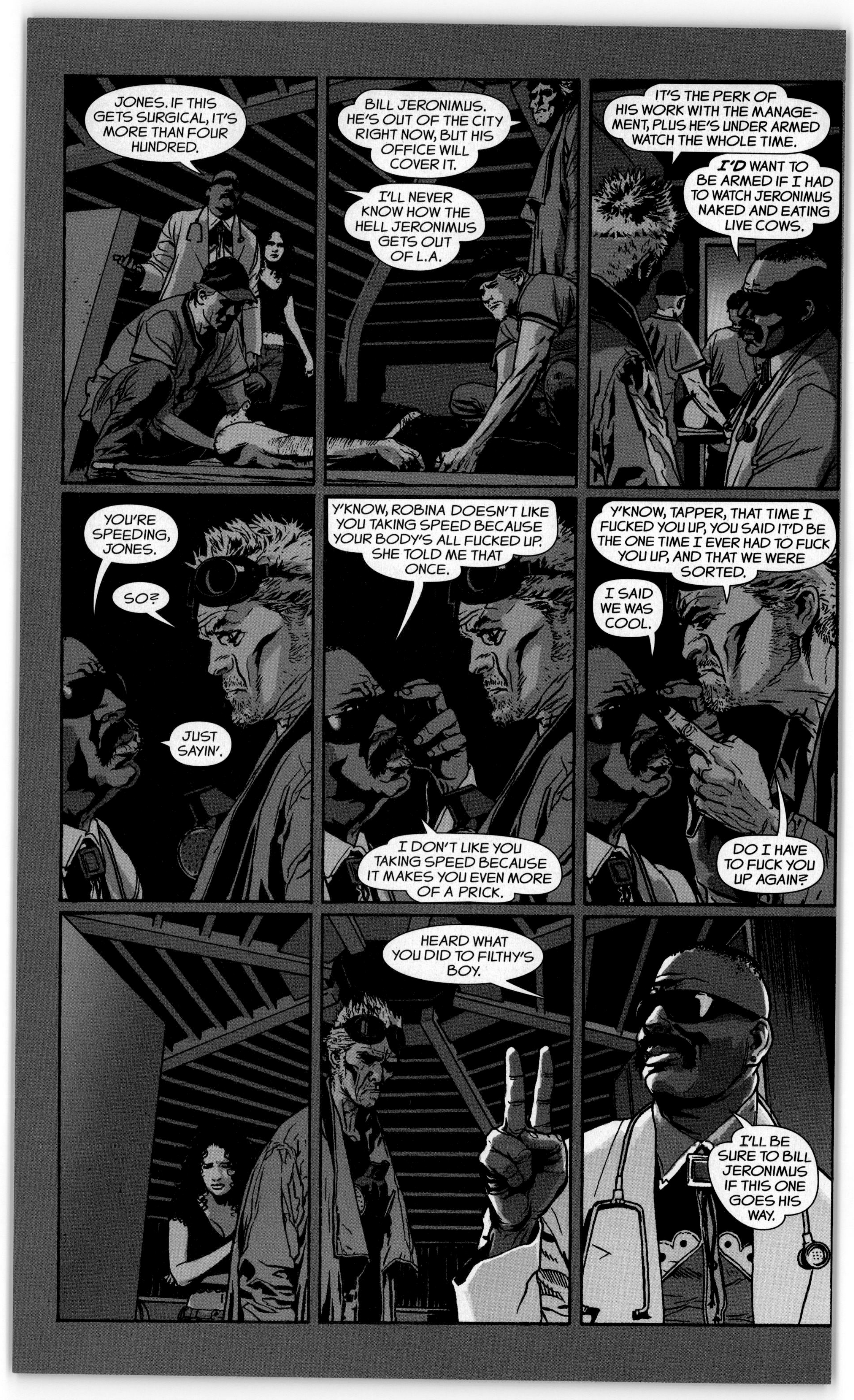
JONES. IF THIS GETS SURGICAL, IT'S MORE THAN FOUR HUNDRED.
BILL JERONIMUS. HE'S OUT OF THE CITY RIGHT NOW, BUT HIS OFFICE WILL COVER IT.
I'LL NEVER KNOW HOW THE HELL JERONIMUS GETS OUT OF L.A.
IT'S THE PERK OF HIS WORK WITH THE MANAGEMENT, PLUS HE'S UNDER ARMED WATCH THE WHOLE TIME.
I'D WANT TO BE ARMED IF I HAD TO WATCH JERONIMUS NAKED AND EATING LIVE COWS.
YOU'RE SPEEDING, JONES.
SO?
JUST SAYIN'.
Y'KNOW, ROBINA DOESN'T LIKE YOU TAKING SPEED BECAUSE YOUR BODY'S ALL FUCKED UP. SHE TOLD ME THAT ONCE.
I DON'T LIKE YOU TAKING SPEED BECAUSE IT MAKES YOU EVEN MORE OF A PRICK.
Y'KNOW, TAPPER, THAT TIME I FUCKED YOU UP, YOU SAID IT'D BE THE ONE TIME I EVER HAD TO FUCK YOU UP, AND THAT WE WERE SORTED.
I SAID WE WAS COOL.
DO I HAVE TO FUCK YOU UP AGAIN?
HEARD WHAT YOU DID TO FILTHY'S BOY.
I'LL BE SURE TO BILL JERONIMUS IF THIS ONE GOES HIS WAY.

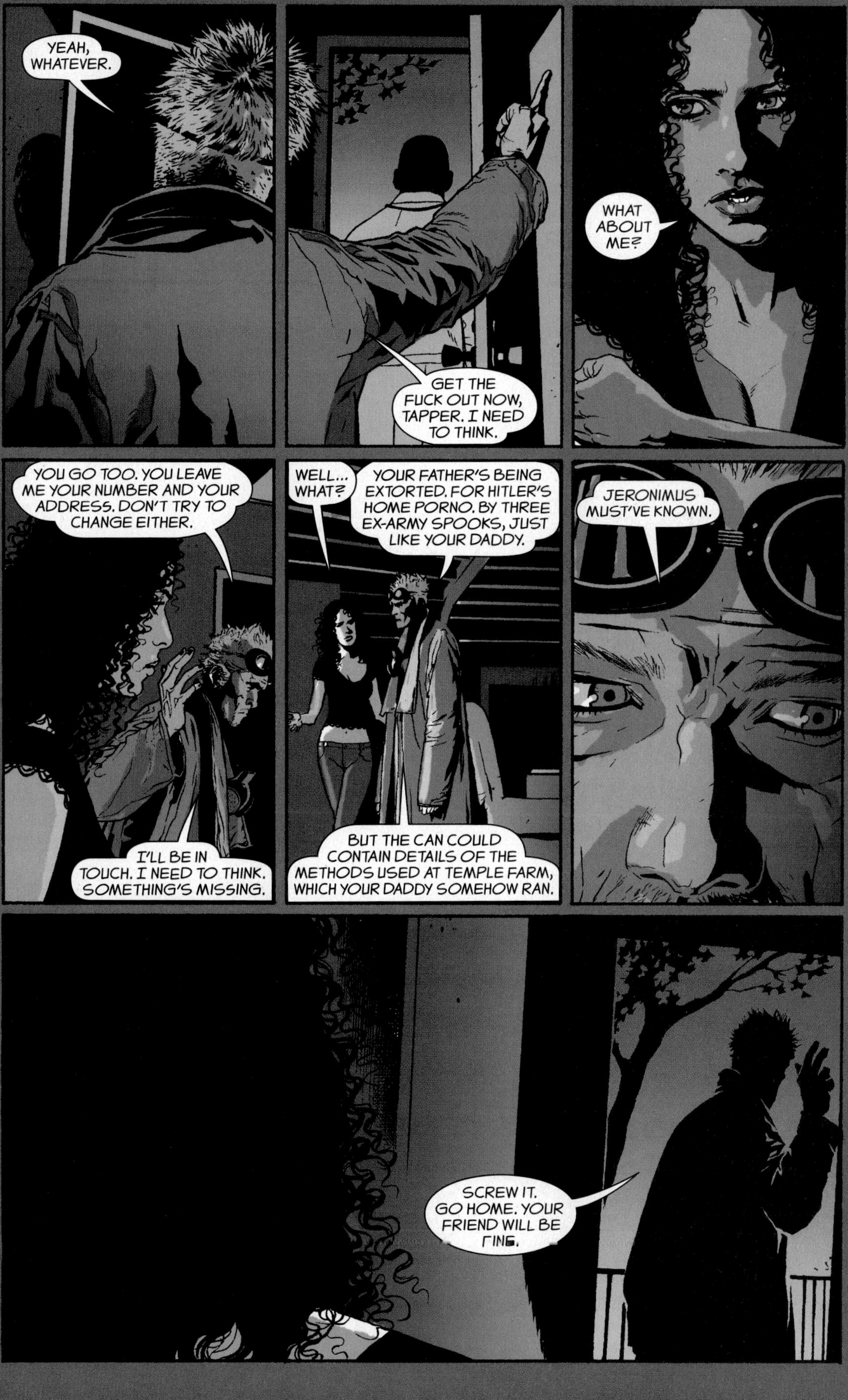
YEAH, WHATEVER.
GET THE FUCK OUT NOW, TAPPER. I NEED TO THINK.
WHAT ABOUT ME?
YOU GO TOO. YOU LEAVE ME YOUR NUMBER AND YOUR ADDRESS. DON'T TRY TO CHANGE EITHER.
I'LL BE IN TOUCH. I NEED TO THINK. SOMETHING'S MISSING.
WELL... WHAT?
YOUR FATHER'S BEING EXTORTED. FOR HITLER'S HOME PORNO. BY THREE EX-ARMY SPOOKS, JUST LIKE YOUR DADDY.
BUT THE CAN COULD CONTAIN DETAILS OF THE METHODS USED AT TEMPLE FARM, WHICH YOUR DADDY SOMEHOW RAN.
JERONIMUS MUST'VE KNOWN.
SCREW IT. GO HOME. YOUR FRIEND WILL BE FINE.

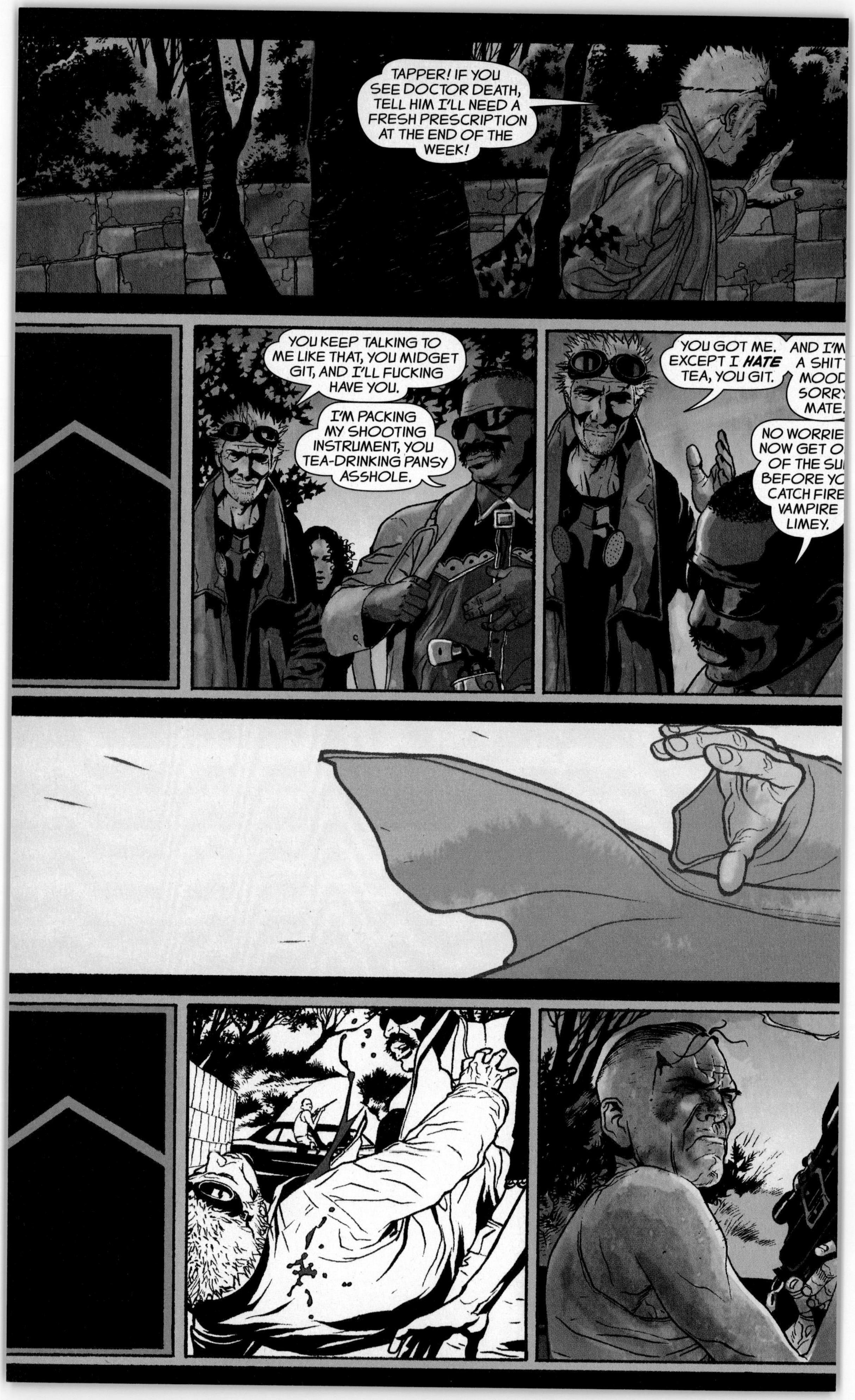

TAPPER! IF YOU SEE DOCTOR DEATH, TELL HIM I'LL NEED A FRESH PRESCRIPTION AT THE END OF THE WEEK!
YOU KEEP TALKING TO ME LIKE THAT, YOU MIDGET GIT, AND I'LL FUCKING HAVE YOU.
I'M PACKING MY SHOOTING INSTRUMENT, YOU TEA-DRINKING PANSY ASSHOLE.
YOU GOT ME. EXCEPT I HATE TEA, YOU GIT.
AND I'M A SHIT MOOD SORRY MATE.
NO WORRIE NOW GET O OF THE SU BEFORE YO CATCH FIRE VAMPIRE LIMEY.

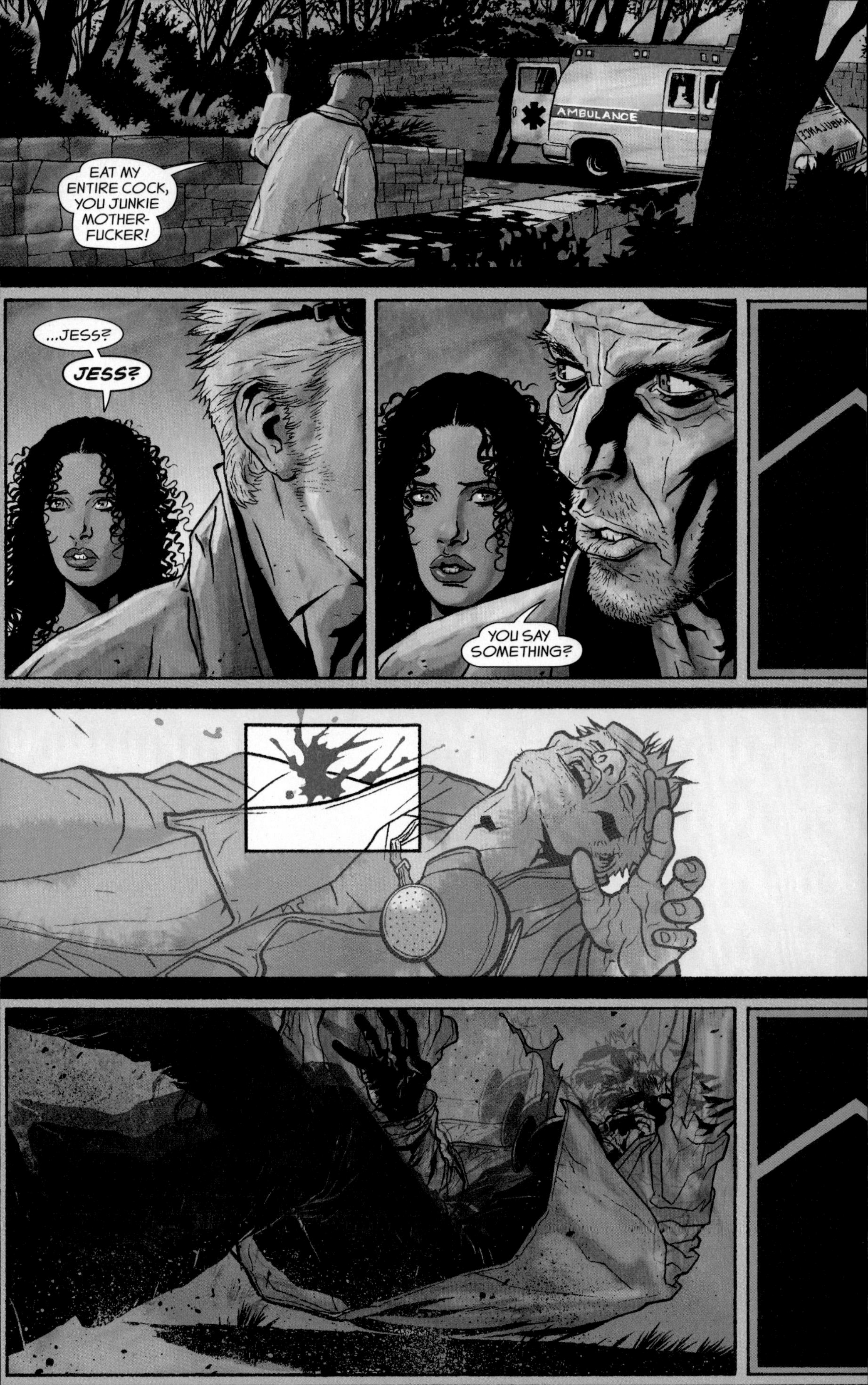
EAT MY ENTIRE COCK, YOU JUNKIE MOTHER-FUCKER!
...JESS?
JESS?
YOU SAY SOMETHING?
AMBULANCE

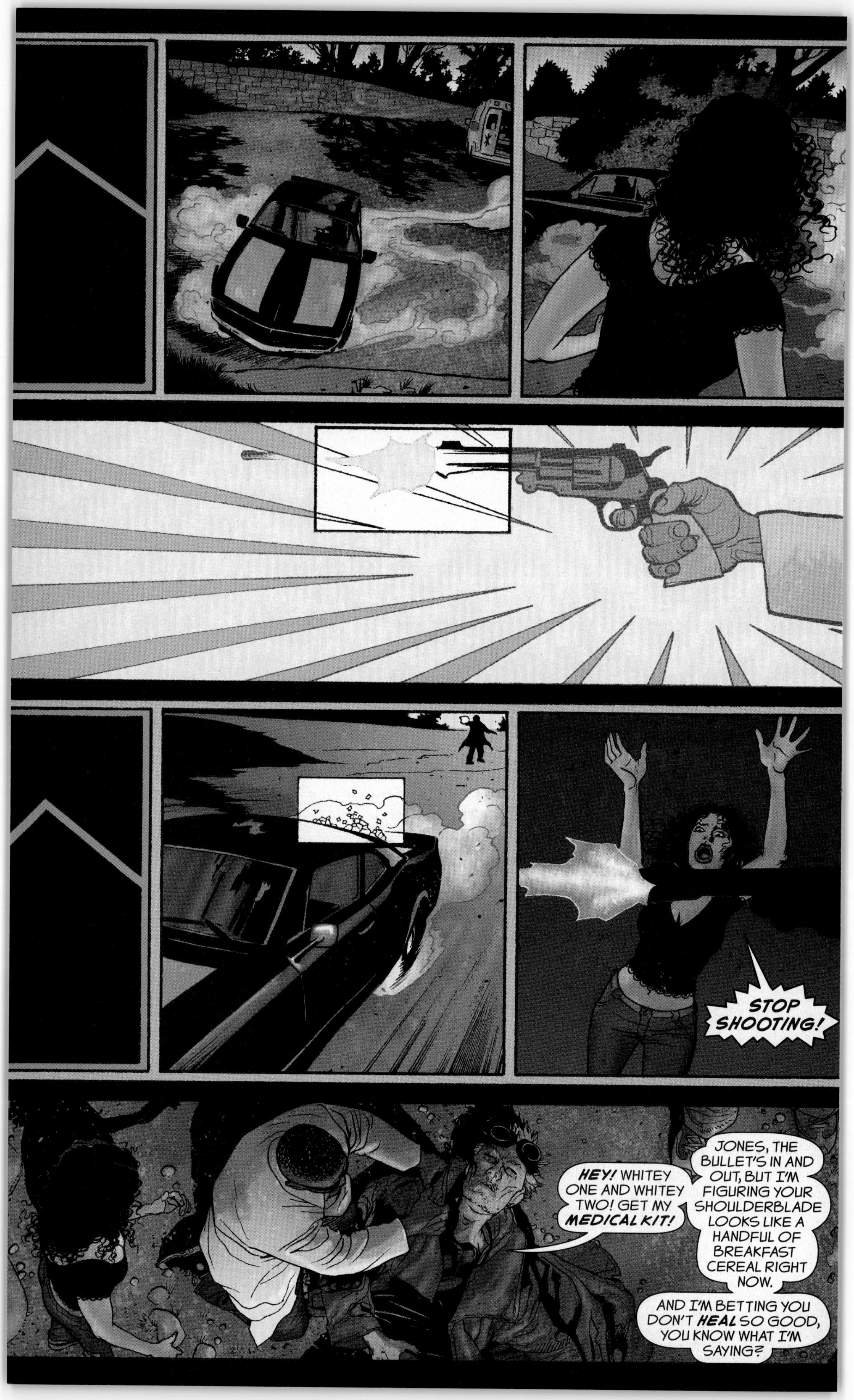
STOP SHOOTING!
HEY! WHITEY ONE AND WHITEY TWO! GET MY MEDICAL KIT!
JONES, THE BULLET'S IN AND OUT, BUT I'M FIGURING YOUR SHOULDERBLADE LOOKS LIKE A HANDFUL OF BREAKFAST CEREAL RIGHT NOW.
AND I'M BETTING YOU DON'T HEAL SO GOOD, YOU KNOW WHAT I'M SAYING?

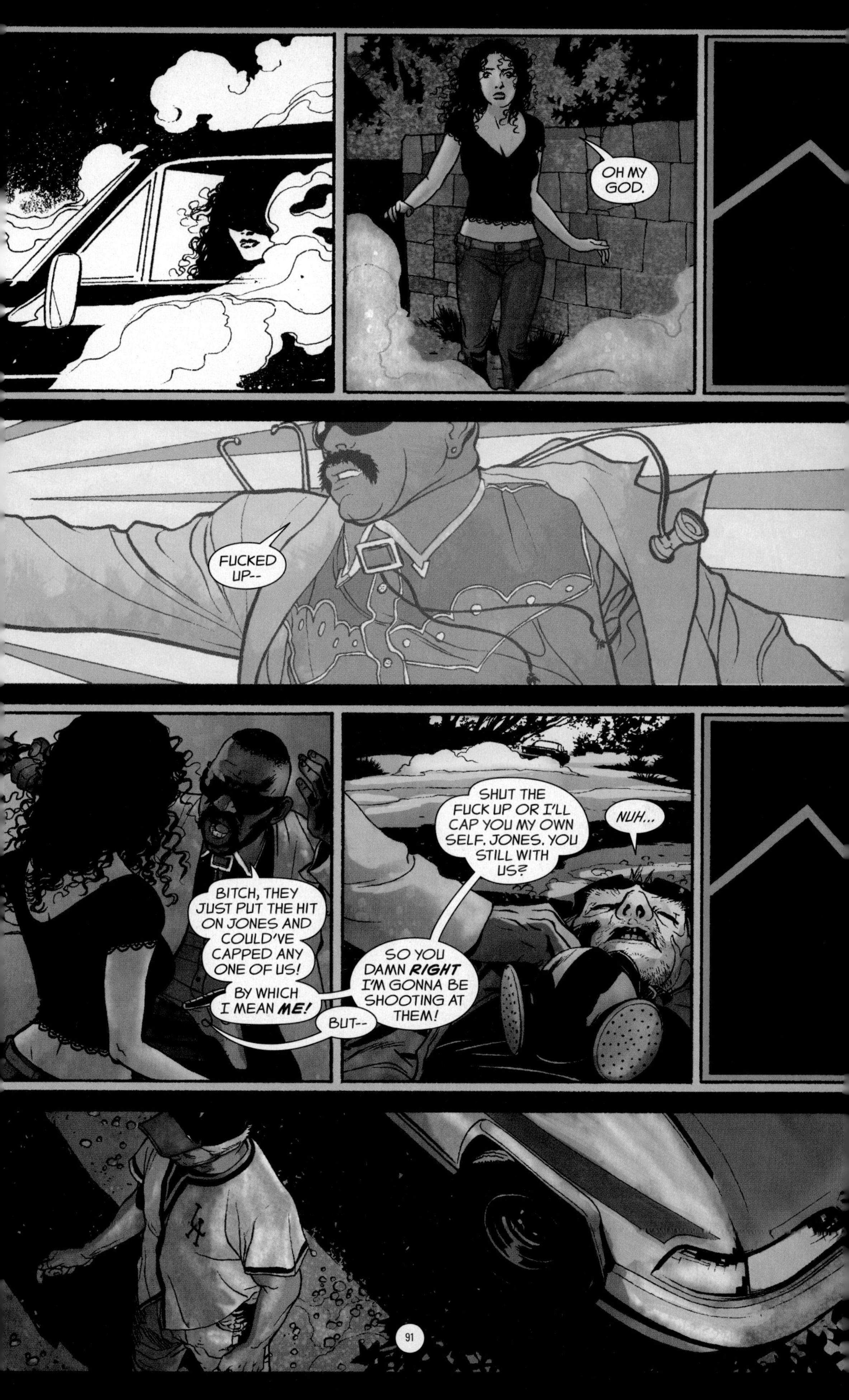
OH MY GOD.
FUCKED UP--
BITCH, THEY JUST PUT THE HIT ON JONES AND COULD'VE CAPPED ANY ONE OF US!
BY WHICH I MEAN **ME!**
BUT--
SO YOU DAMN **RIGHT** I'M GONNA BE SHOOTING AT THEM!
SHUT THE FUCK UP OR I'LL CAP YOU MY OWN SELF. JONES. YOU STILL WITH US?
NUH...

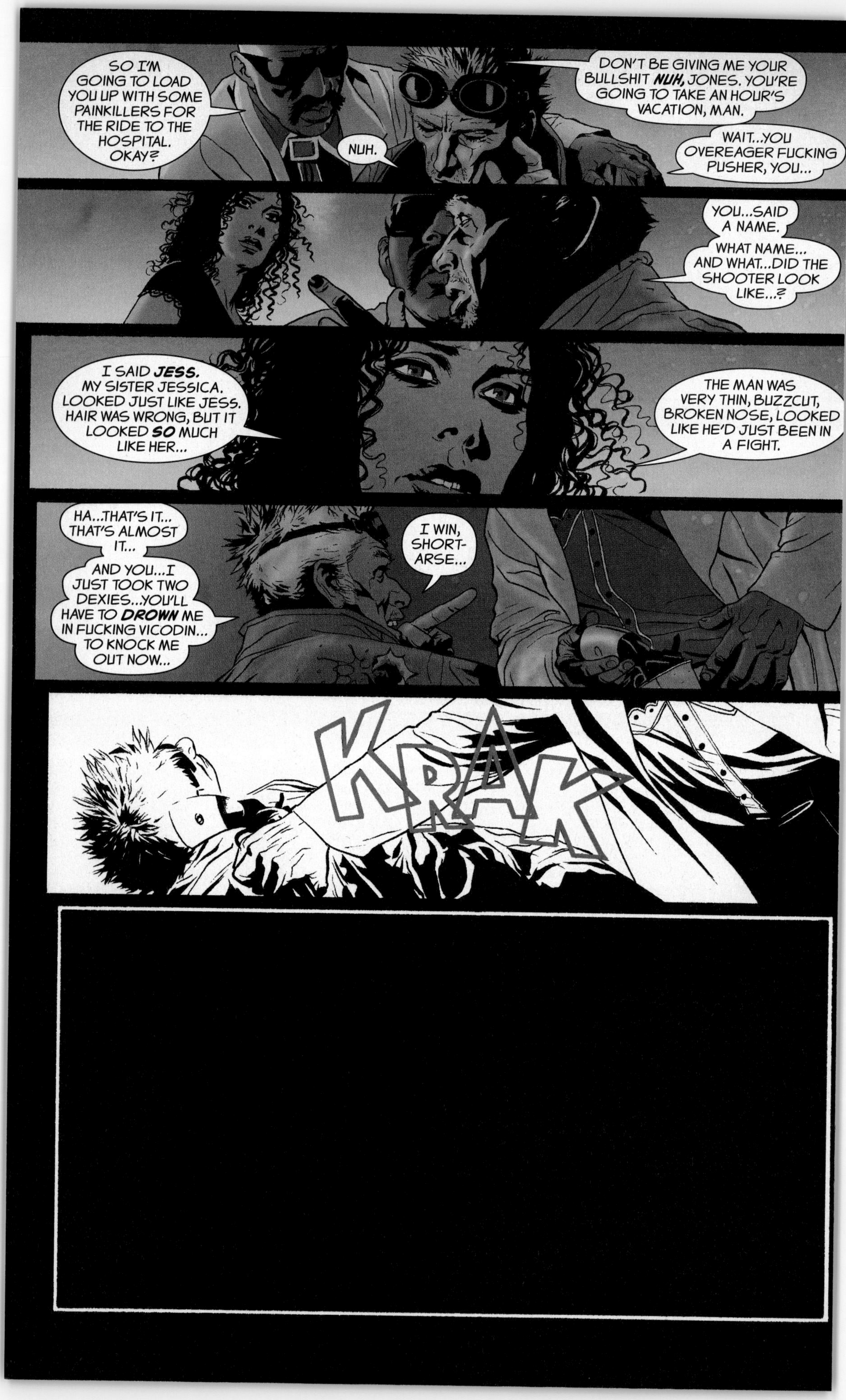
SO I'M GOING TO LOAD YOU UP WITH SOME PAINKILLERS FOR THE RIDE TO THE HOSPITAL. OKAY?
NUH.
DON'T BE GIVING ME YOUR BULLSHIT **NUH,** JONES. YOU'RE GOING TO TAKE AN HOUR'S VACATION, MAN.
WAIT...YOU OVEREAGER FUCKING PUSHER, YOU...
YOU...SAID A NAME.
WHAT NAME... AND WHAT...DID THE SHOOTER LOOK LIKE...?
I SAID **JESS.** MY SISTER JESSICA. LOOKED JUST LIKE JESS. HAIR WAS WRONG, BUT IT LOOKED **SO** MUCH LIKE HER...
THE MAN WAS VERY THIN, BUZZCUT, BROKEN NOSE, LOOKED LIKE HE'D JUST BEEN IN A FIGHT.
HA...THAT'S IT... THAT'S ALMOST IT...
AND YOU...I JUST TOOK TWO DEXIES...YOU'LL HAVE TO **DROWN** ME IN FUCKING VICODIN... TO KNOCK ME OUT NOW...
I WIN, SHORT-ARSE...
KRAK

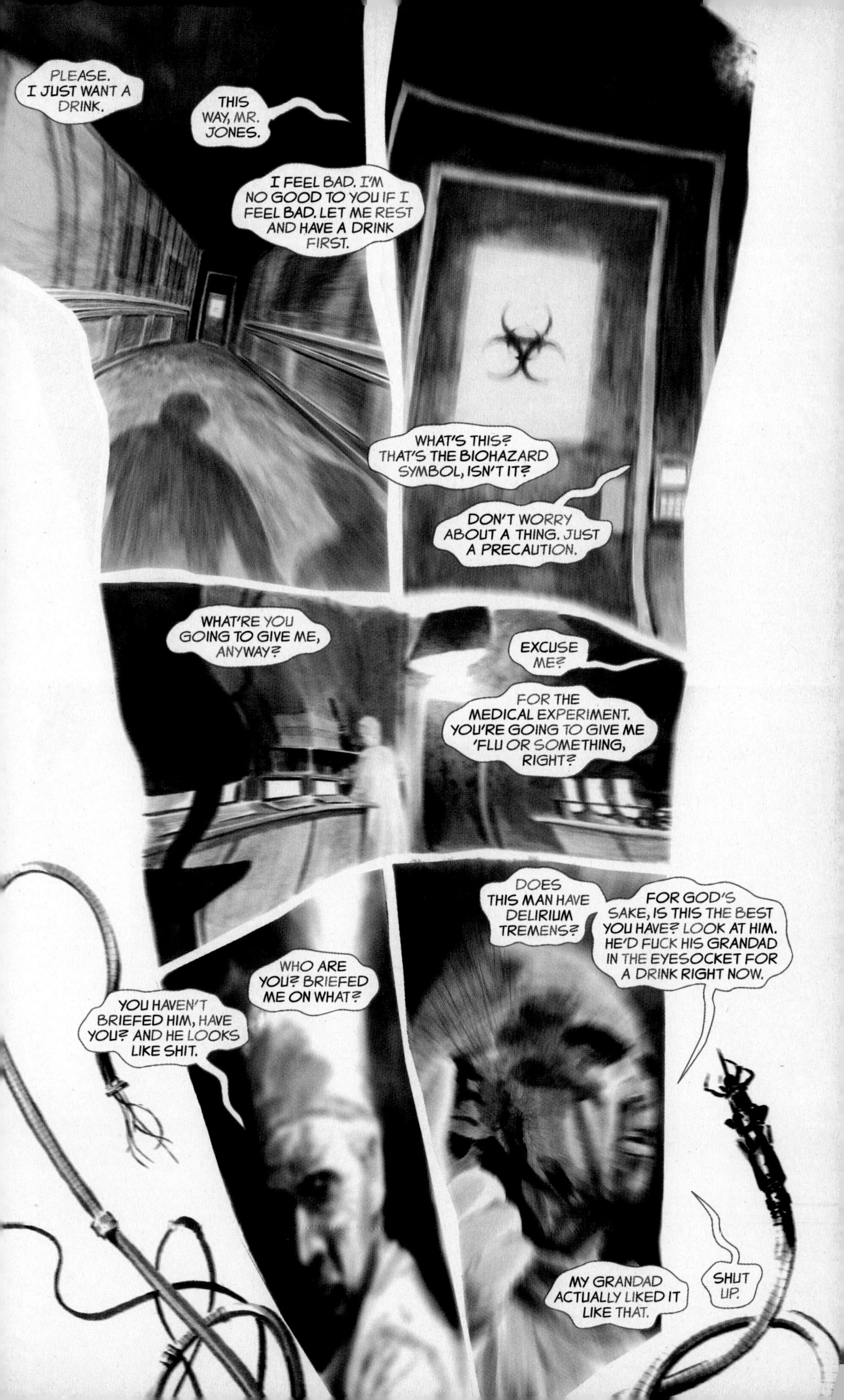
PLEASE. I JUST WANT A DRINK.
THIS WAY, MR. JONES.
I FEEL BAD. I'M NO GOOD TO YOU IF I FEEL BAD. LET ME REST AND HAVE A DRINK FIRST.
WHAT'S THIS? THAT'S THE BIOHAZARD SYMBOL, ISN'T IT?
DON'T WORRY ABOUT A THING. JUST A PRECAUTION.
WHAT'RE YOU GOING TO GIVE ME, ANYWAY?
EXCUSE ME?
FOR THE MEDICAL EXPERIMENT. YOU'RE GOING TO GIVE ME 'FLU OR SOMETHING, RIGHT?
DOES THIS MAN HAVE DELIRIUM TREMENS?
FOR GOD'S SAKE, IS THIS THE BEST YOU HAVE? LOOK AT HIM. HE'D FUCK HIS GRANDAD IN THE EYESOCKET FOR A DRINK RIGHT NOW.
YOU HAVEN'T BRIEFED HIM, HAVE YOU? AND HE LOOKS LIKE SHIT.
WHO ARE YOU? BRIEFED ME ON WHAT?
MY GRANDAD ACTUALLY LIKED IT LIKE THAT.
SHUT UP.

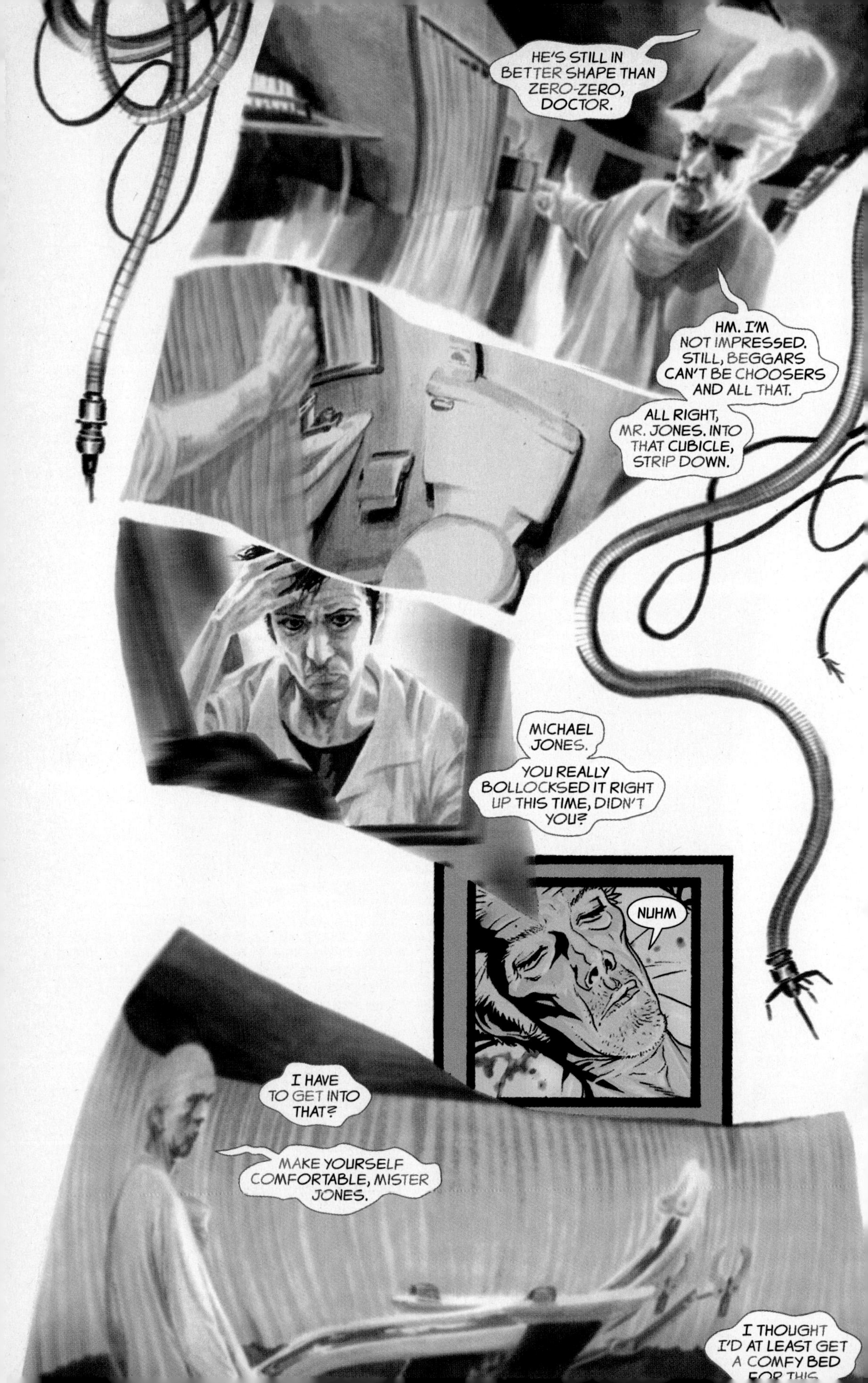
HE'S STILL IN BETTER SHAPE THAN ZERO-ZERO, DOCTOR.
HM. I'M NOT IMPRESSED. STILL, BEGGARS CAN'T BE CHOOSERS AND ALL THAT.
ALL RIGHT, MR. JONES. INTO THAT CUBICLE, STRIP DOWN.
MICHAEL JONES.
YOU REALLY BOLLOCKSED IT RIGHT UP THIS TIME, DIDN'T YOU?
NUHM
I HAVE TO GET INTO THAT?
MAKE YOURSELF COMFORTABLE, MISTER JONES.
I THOUGHT I'D AT LEAST GET A COMFY BED

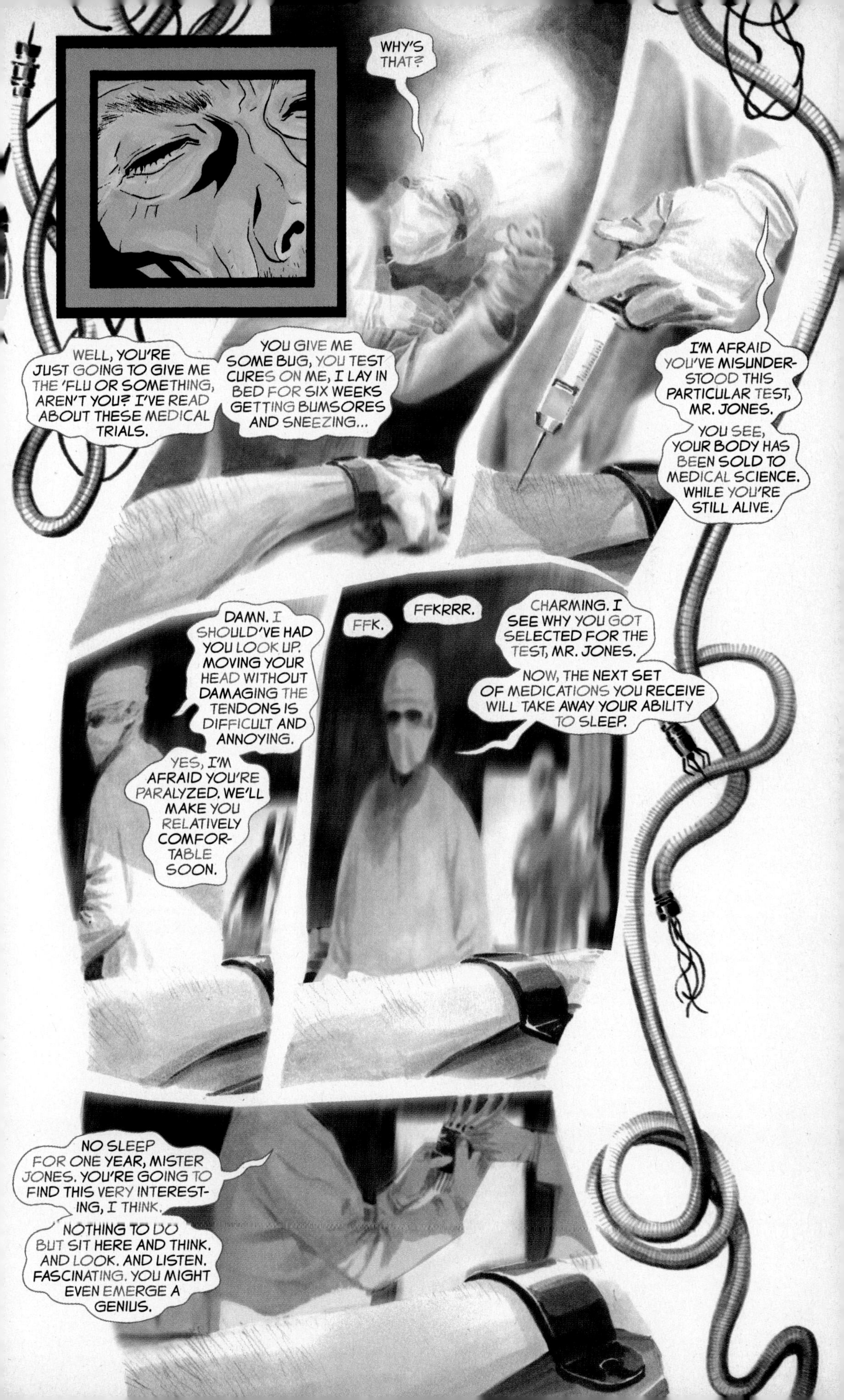
WHY'S THAT?
WELL, YOU'RE JUST GOING TO GIVE ME THE 'FLU OR SOMETHING, AREN'T YOU? I'VE READ ABOUT THESE MEDICAL TRIALS.
YOU GIVE ME SOME BUG, YOU TEST CURES ON ME, I LAY IN BED FOR SIX WEEKS GETTING BUMSORES AND SNEEZING...
I'M AFRAID YOU'VE MISUNDERSTOOD THIS PARTICULAR TEST, MR. JONES.
YOU SEE, YOUR BODY HAS BEEN SOLD TO MEDICAL SCIENCE. WHILE YOU'RE STILL ALIVE.
DAMN. I SHOULD'VE HAD YOU LOOK UP. MOVING YOUR HEAD WITHOUT DAMAGING THE TENDONS IS DIFFICULT AND ANNOYING.
YES, I'M AFRAID YOU'RE PARALYZED. WE'LL MAKE YOU RELATIVELY COMFORTABLE SOON.
FFK.
FFKRRR.
CHARMING. I SEE WHY YOU GOT SELECTED FOR THE TEST, MR. JONES.
NOW, THE NEXT SET OF MEDICATIONS YOU RECEIVE WILL TAKE AWAY YOUR ABILITY TO SLEEP.
NO SLEEP FOR ONE YEAR, MISTER JONES. YOU'RE GOING TO FIND THIS VERY INTERESTING, I THINK.
NOTHING TO DO BUT SIT HERE AND THINK. AND LOOK. AND LISTEN. FASCINATING. YOU MIGHT EVEN EMERGE A GENIUS.

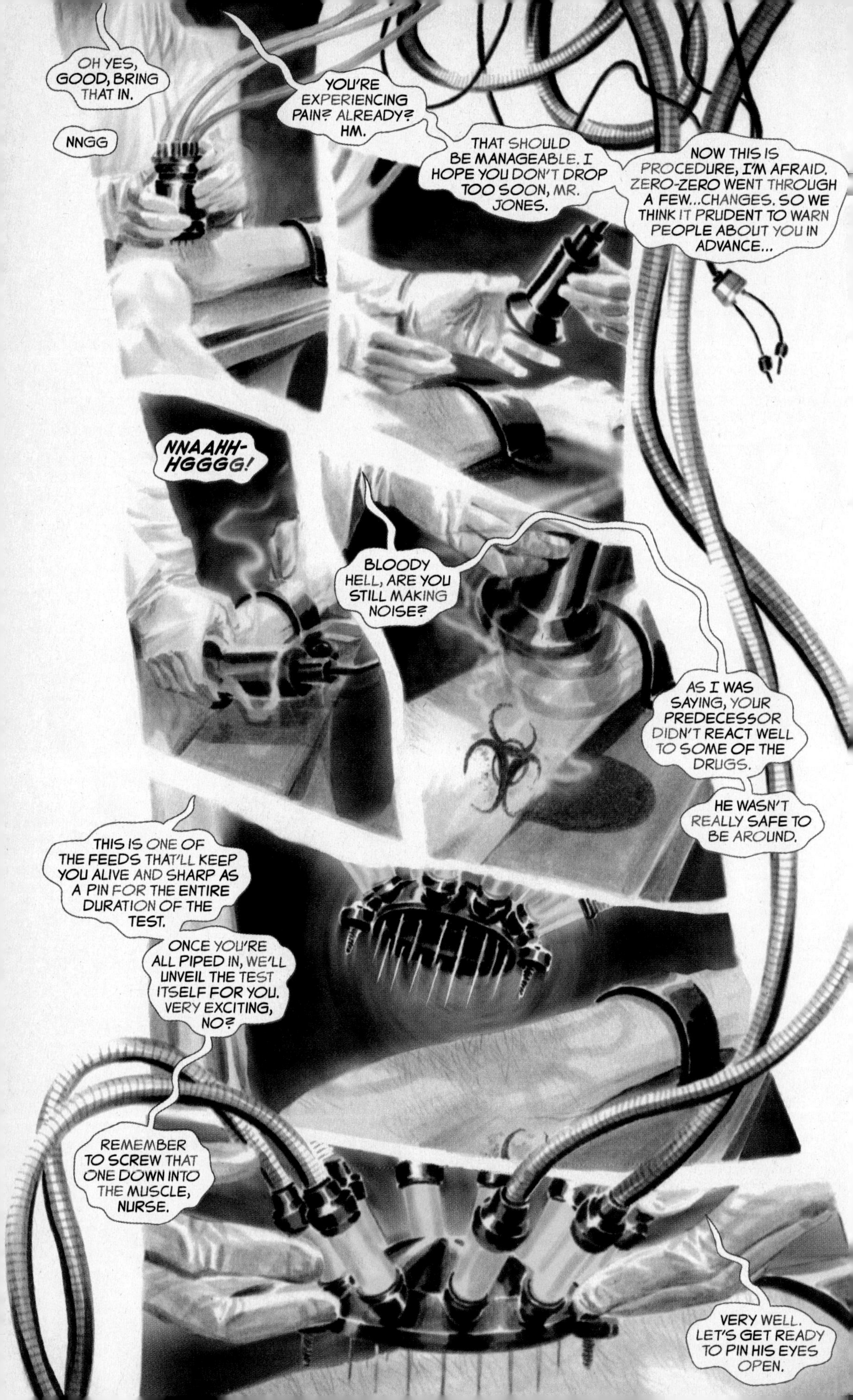
OH YES, GOOD, BRING THAT IN.
NNGG
YOU'RE EXPERIENCING PAIN? ALREADY? HM.
THAT SHOULD BE MANAGEABLE. I HOPE YOU DON'T DROP TOO SOON, MR. JONES.
NOW THIS IS PROCEDURE, I'M AFRAID. ZERO-ZERO WENT THROUGH A FEW...CHANGES. SO WE THINK IT PRUDENT TO WARN PEOPLE ABOUT YOU IN ADVANCE...
NNAAHH-HGGGG!
BLOODY HELL, ARE YOU STILL MAKING NOISE?
AS I WAS SAYING, YOUR PREDECESSOR DIDN'T REACT WELL TO SOME OF THE DRUGS.
HE WASN'T REALLY SAFE TO BE AROUND.
THIS IS ONE OF THE FEEDS THAT'LL KEEP YOU ALIVE AND SHARP AS A PIN FOR THE ENTIRE DURATION OF THE TEST.
ONCE YOU'RE ALL PIPED IN, WE'LL UNVEIL THE TEST ITSELF FOR YOU. VERY EXCITING, NO?
REMEMBER TO SCREW THAT ONE DOWN INTO THE MUSCLE, NURSE.
VERY WELL. LET'S GET READY TO PIN HIS EYES OPEN.

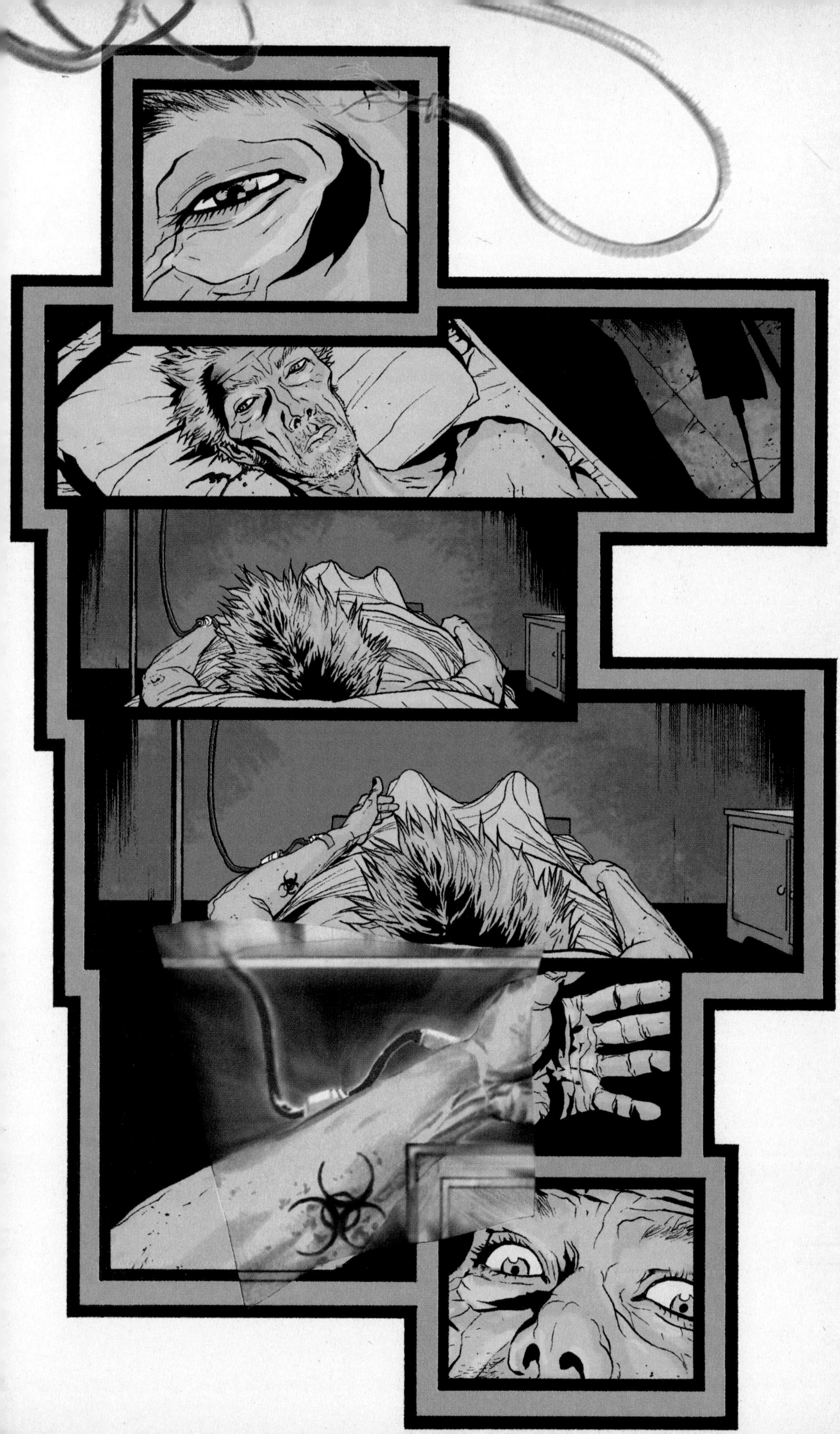

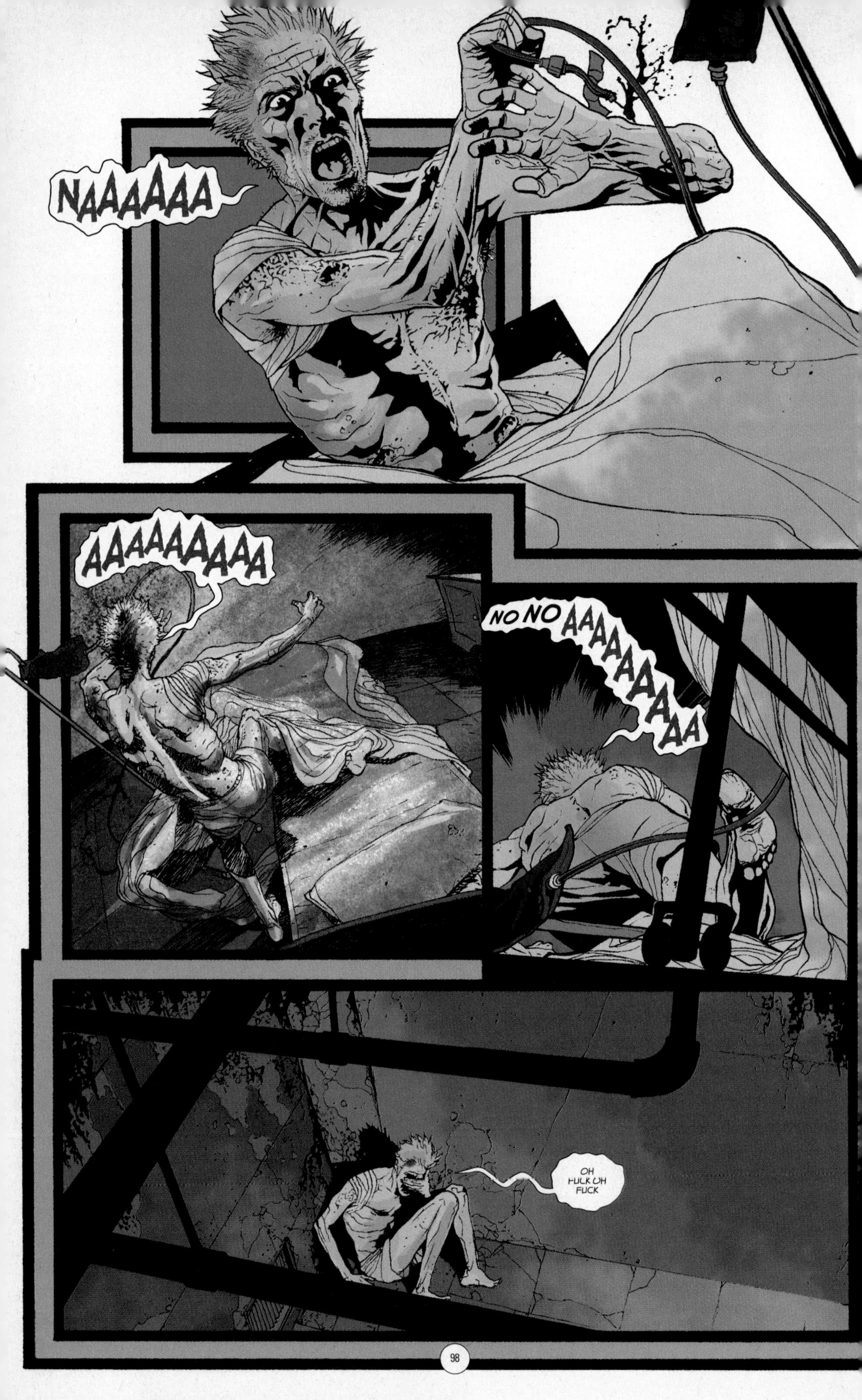
NAAAAAA
AAAAAAAAA
NO NO AAAAAAAAAAA
OH FUCK OH FUCK

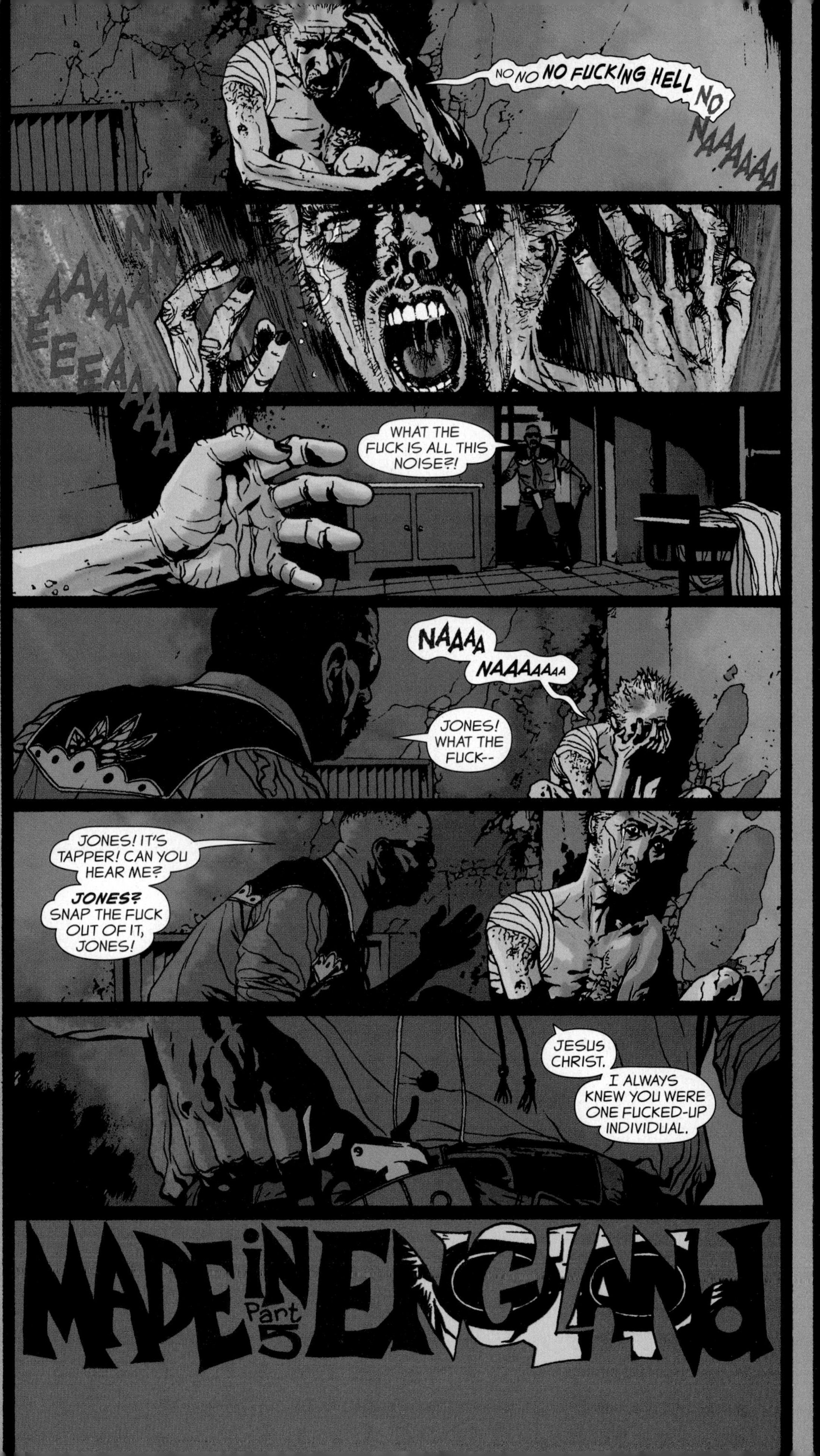
NO NO NO FUCKING HELL NO
NAAAAAA
AAAAAAN
EEEAAAAA
WHAT THE FUCK IS ALL THIS NOISE?!
NAAAA NAAAaaaa
JONES! WHAT THE FUCK--
JONES! IT'S TAPPER! CAN YOU HEAR ME?
JONES? SNAP THE FUCK OUT OF IT, JONES!
JESUS CHRIST.
I ALWAYS KNEW YOU WERE ONE FUCKED-UP INDIVIDUAL.
MADE IN ENGLAND Part 5

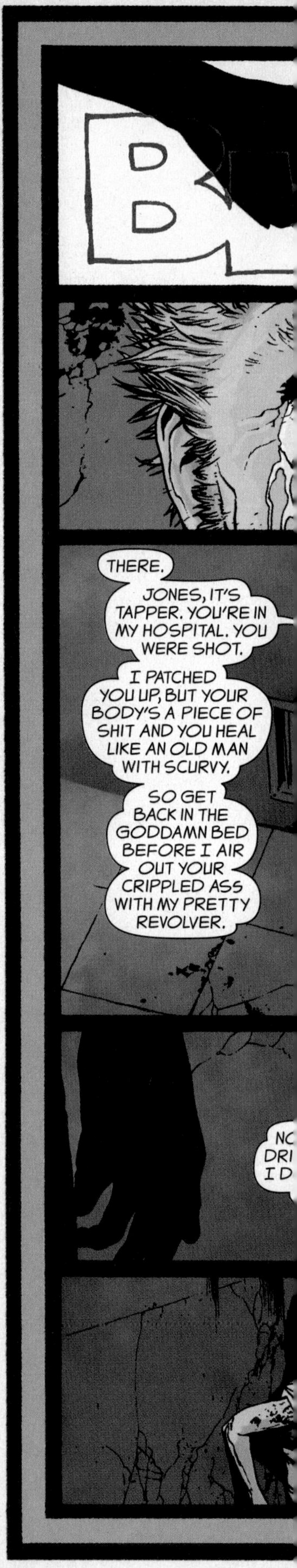
THERE.
JONES, IT'S TAPPER. YOU'RE IN MY HOSPITAL. YOU WERE SHOT.
I PATCHED YOU UP, BUT YOUR BODY'S A PIECE OF SHIT AND YOU HEAL LIKE AN OLD MAN WITH SCURVY.
SO GET BACK IN THE GODDAMN BED BEFORE I AIR OUT YOUR CRIPPLED ASS WITH MY PRETTY REVOLVER.

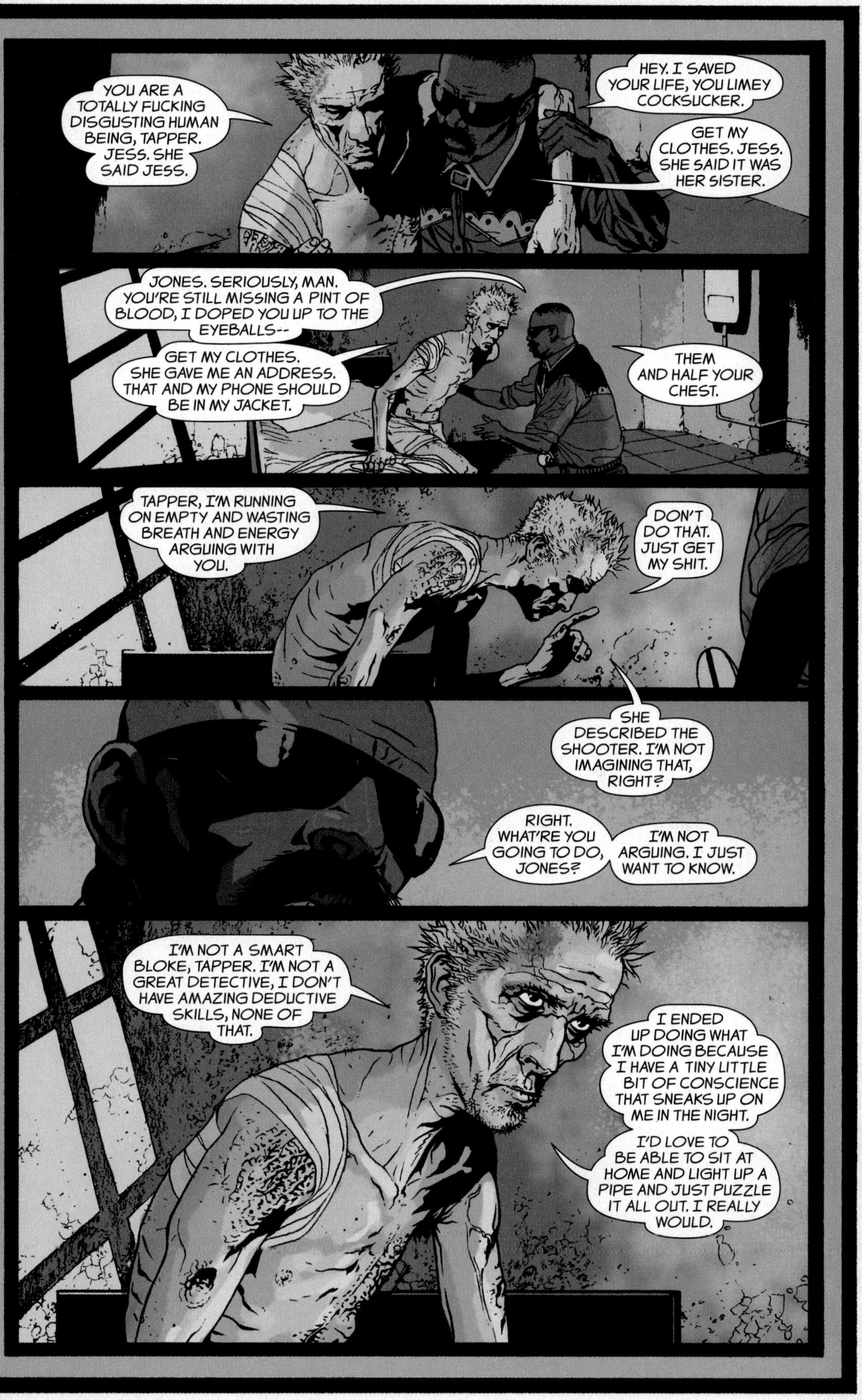

YOU ARE A TOTALLY FUCKING DISGUSTING HUMAN BEING, TAPPER. JESS. SHE SAID JESS.
HEY. I SAVED YOUR LIFE, YOU LIMEY COCKSUCKER.
GET MY CLOTHES. JESS. SHE SAID IT WAS HER SISTER.
JONES. SERIOUSLY, MAN. YOU'RE STILL MISSING A PINT OF BLOOD, I DOPED YOU UP TO THE EYEBALLS--
GET MY CLOTHES. SHE GAVE ME AN ADDRESS. THAT AND MY PHONE SHOULD BE IN MY JACKET.
THEM AND HALF YOUR CHEST.
TAPPER, I'M RUNNING ON EMPTY AND WASTING BREATH AND ENERGY ARGUING WITH YOU.
DON'T DO THAT. JUST GET MY SHIT.
SHE DESCRIBED THE SHOOTER. I'M NOT IMAGINING THAT, RIGHT?
RIGHT. WHAT'RE YOU GOING TO DO, JONES?
I'M NOT ARGUING. I JUST WANT TO KNOW.
I'M NOT A SMART BLOKE, TAPPER. I'M NOT A GREAT DETECTIVE, I DON'T HAVE AMAZING DEDUCTIVE SKILLS, NONE OF THAT.
I ENDED UP DOING WHAT I'M DOING BECAUSE I HAVE A TINY LITTLE BIT OF CONSCIENCE THAT SNEAKS UP ON ME IN THE NIGHT.
I'D LOVE TO BE ABLE TO SIT AT HOME AND LIGHT UP A PIPE AND JUST PUZZLE IT ALL OUT. I REALLY WOULD.

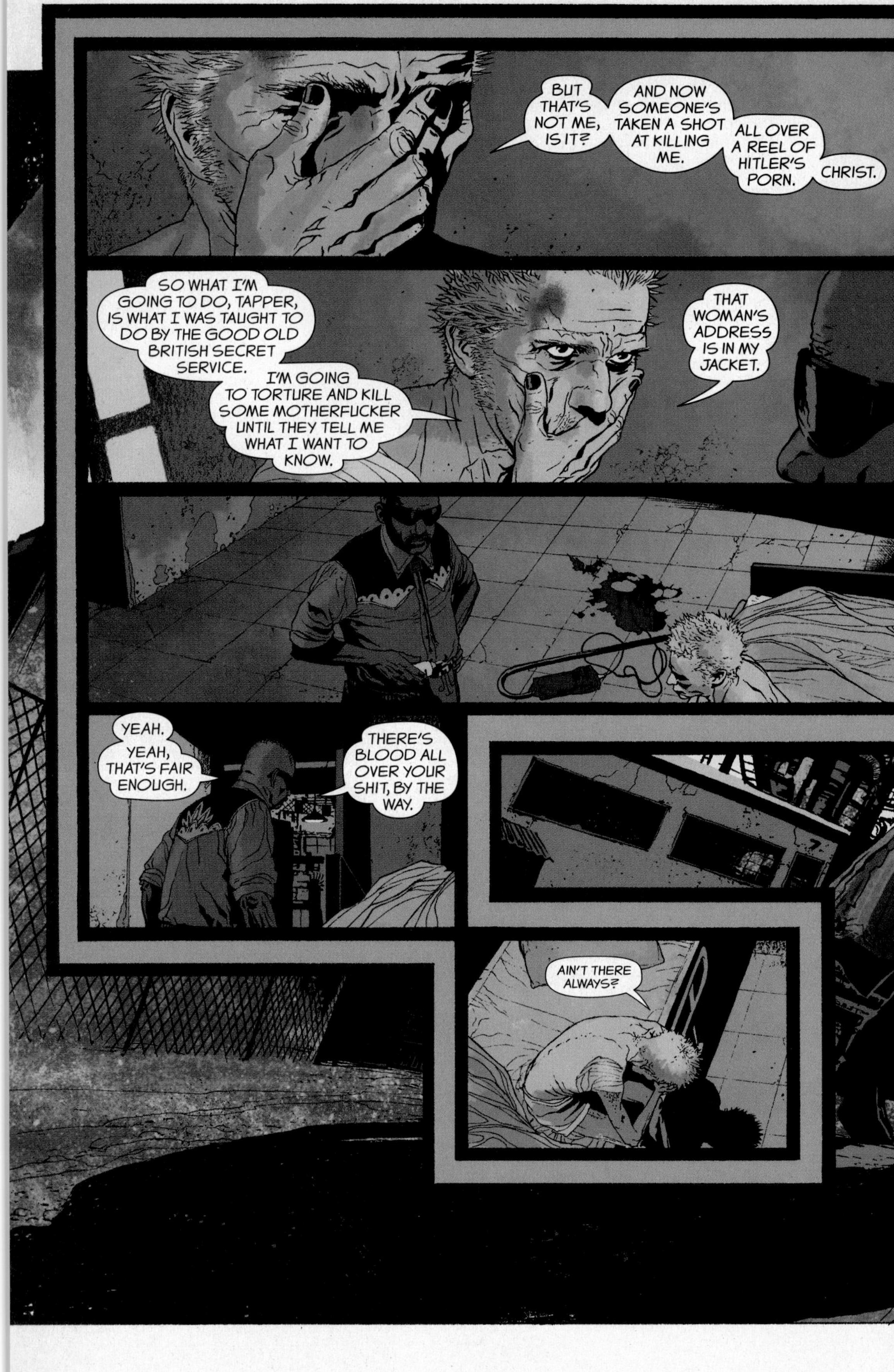
BUT THAT'S NOT ME, IS IT?
AND NOW SOMEONE'S TAKEN A SHOT AT KILLING ME.
ALL OVER A REEL OF HITLER'S PORN.
CHRIST.
SO WHAT I'M GOING TO DO, TAPPER, IS WHAT I WAS TAUGHT TO DO BY THE GOOD OLD BRITISH SECRET SERVICE.
I'M GOING TO TORTURE AND KILL SOME MOTHERFUCKER UNTIL THEY TELL ME WHAT I WANT TO KNOW.
THAT WOMAN'S ADDRESS IS IN MY JACKET.
YEAH. YEAH, THAT'S FAIR ENOUGH.
THERE'S BLOOD ALL OVER YOUR SHIT, BY THE WAY.
AIN'T THERE ALWAYS?

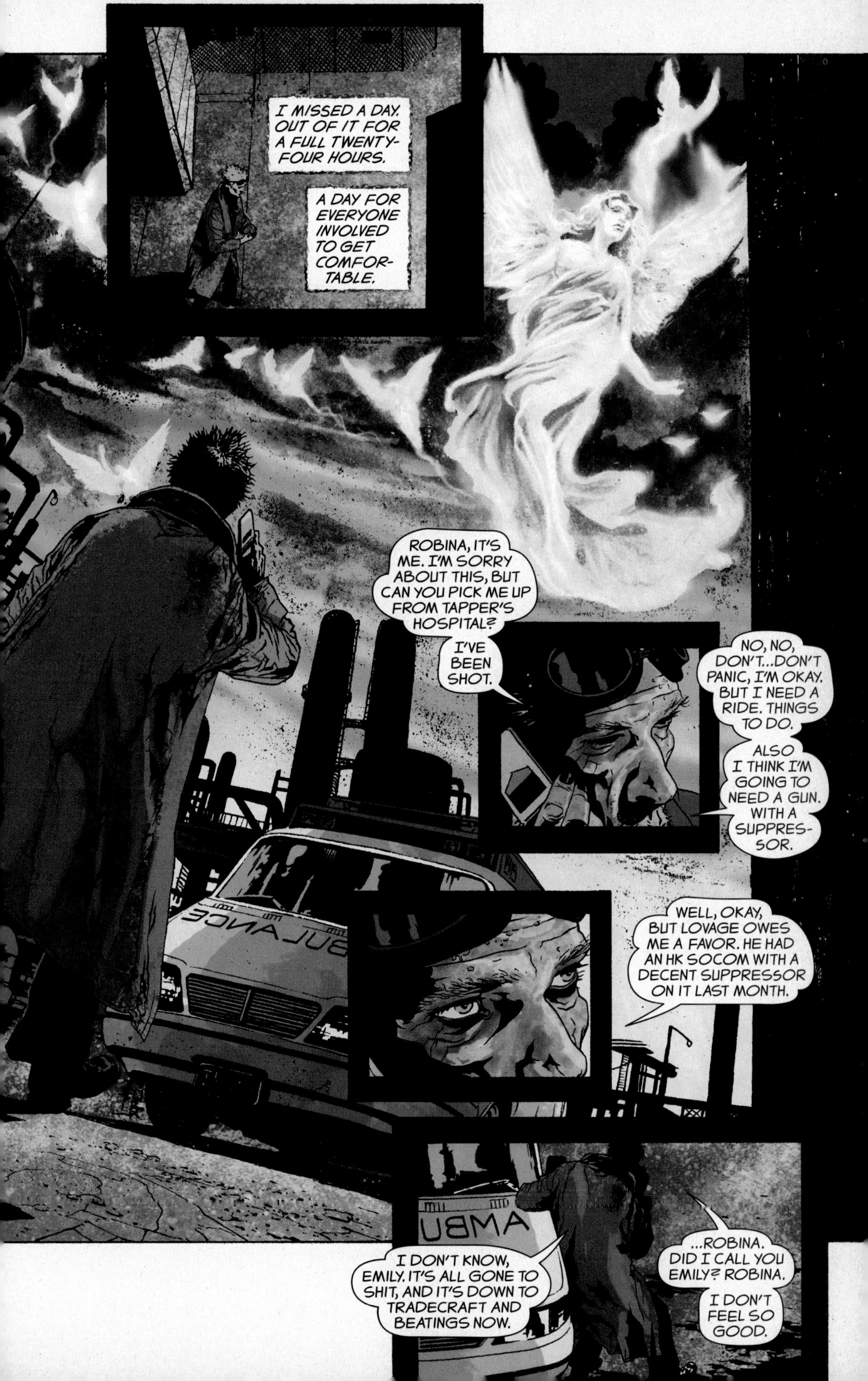
I MISSED A DAY. OUT OF IT FOR A FULL TWENTY-FOUR HOURS.
A DAY FOR EVERYONE INVOLVED TO GET COMFOR-TABLE.
ROBINA, IT'S ME. I'M SORRY ABOUT THIS, BUT CAN YOU PICK ME UP FROM TAPPER'S HOSPITAL?
I'VE BEEN SHOT.
NO, NO, DON'T...DON'T PANIC, I'M OKAY. BUT I NEED A RIDE. THINGS TO DO.
ALSO I THINK I'M GOING TO NEED A GUN. WITH A SUPPRES-SOR.
WELL, OKAY, BUT LOVAGE OWES ME A FAVOR. HE HAD AN HK SOCOM WITH A DECENT SUPPRESSOR ON IT LAST MONTH.
I DON'T KNOW, EMILY. IT'S ALL GONE TO SHIT, AND IT'S DOWN TO TRADECRAFT AND BEATINGS NOW.
...ROBINA. DID I CALL YOU EMILY? ROBINA.
I DON'T FEEL SO GOOD.

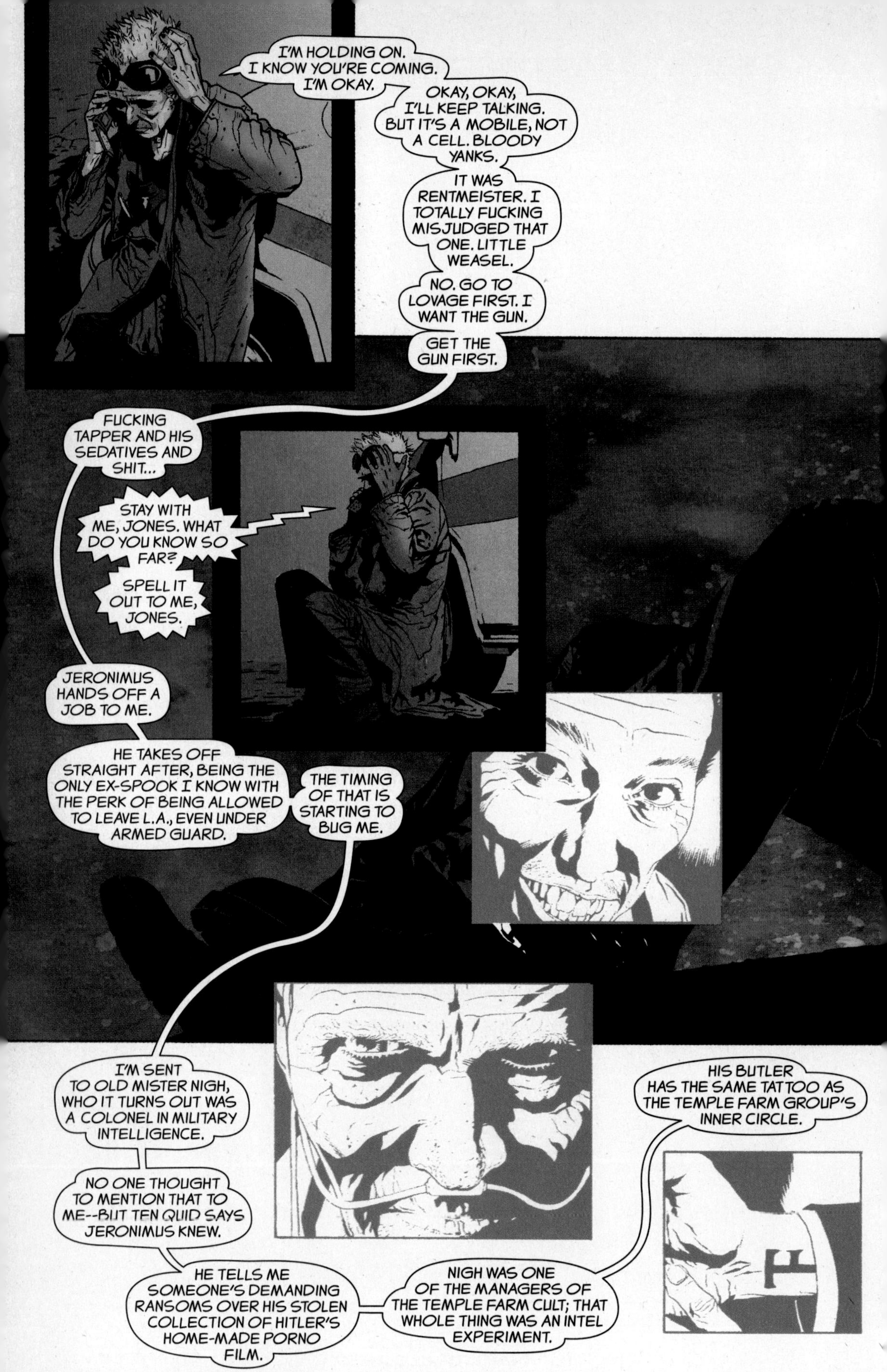

I'M HOLDING ON. I KNOW YOU'RE COMING. I'M OKAY.
OKAY, OKAY, I'LL KEEP TALKING. BUT IT'S A MOBILE, NOT A CELL. BLOODY YANKS.
IT WAS RENTMEISTER. I TOTALLY FUCKING MISJUDGED THAT ONE. LITTLE WEASEL.
NO. GO TO LOVAGE FIRST. I WANT THE GUN.
GET THE GUN FIRST.
FUCKING TAPPER AND HIS SEDATIVES AND SHIT...
STAY WITH ME, JONES. WHAT DO YOU KNOW SO FAR?
SPELL IT OUT TO ME, JONES.
JERONIMUS HANDS OFF A JOB TO ME.
HE TAKES OFF STRAIGHT AFTER, BEING THE ONLY EX-SPOOK I KNOW WITH THE PERK OF BEING ALLOWED TO LEAVE L.A., EVEN UNDER ARMED GUARD.
THE TIMING OF THAT IS STARTING TO BUG ME.
I'M SENT TO OLD MISTER NIGH, WHO IT TURNS OUT WAS A COLONEL IN MILITARY INTELLIGENCE.
NO ONE THOUGHT TO MENTION THAT TO ME--BUT TEN QUID SAYS JERONIMUS KNEW.
HE TELLS ME SOMEONE'S DEMANDING RANSOMS OVER HIS STOLEN COLLECTION OF HITLER'S HOME-MADE PORNO FILM.
NIGH WAS ONE OF THE MANAGERS OF THE TEMPLE FARM CULT; THAT WHOLE THING WAS AN INTEL EXPERIMENT.
HIS BUTLER HAS THE SAME TATTOO AS THE TEMPLE FARM GROUP'S INNER CIRCLE.

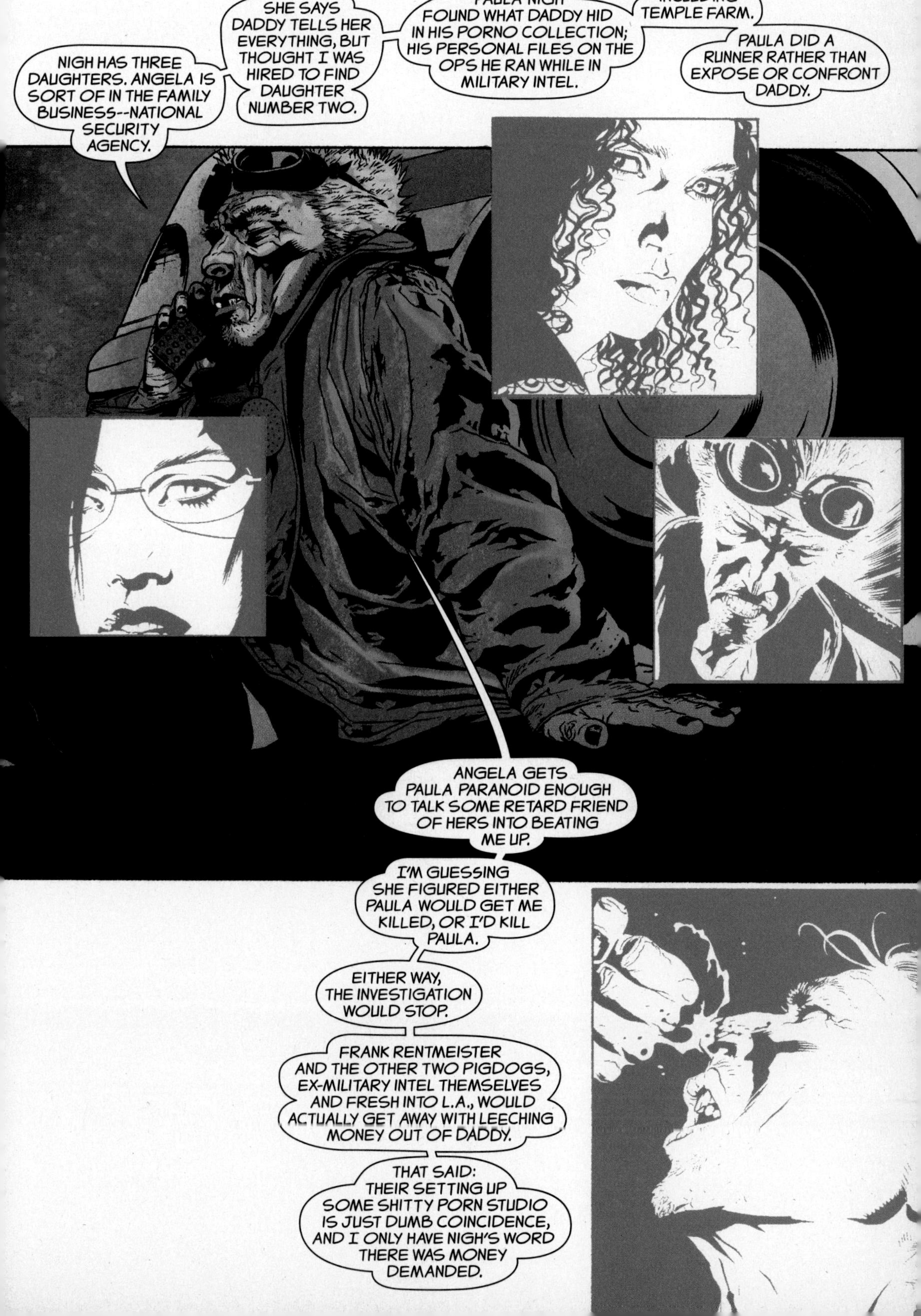
NIGH HAS THREE DAUGHTERS. ANGELA IS SORT OF IN THE FAMILY BUSINESS--NATIONAL SECURITY AGENCY.
SHE SAYS DADDY TELLS HER EVERYTHING, BUT THOUGHT I WAS HIRED TO FIND DAUGHTER NUMBER TWO.
PAULA NIGH FOUND WHAT DADDY HID IN HIS PORNO COLLECTION; HIS PERSONAL FILES ON THE OPS HE RAN WHILE IN MILITARY INTEL.
INCLUDING TEMPLE FARM.
PAULA DID A RUNNER RATHER THAN EXPOSE OR CONFRONT DADDY.
ANGELA GETS PAULA PARANOID ENOUGH TO TALK SOME RETARD FRIEND OF HERS INTO BEATING ME UP.
I'M GUESSING SHE FIGURED EITHER PAULA WOULD GET ME KILLED, OR I'D KILL PAULA.
EITHER WAY, THE INVESTIGATION WOULD STOP.
FRANK RENTMEISTER AND THE OTHER TWO PIGDOGS, EX-MILITARY INTEL THEMSELVES AND FRESH INTO L.A., WOULD ACTUALLY GET AWAY WITH LEECHING MONEY OUT OF DADDY.
THAT SAID: THEIR SETTING UP SOME SHITTY PORN STUDIO IS JUST DUMB COINCIDENCE, AND I ONLY HAVE NIGH'S WORD THERE WAS MONEY DEMANDED.

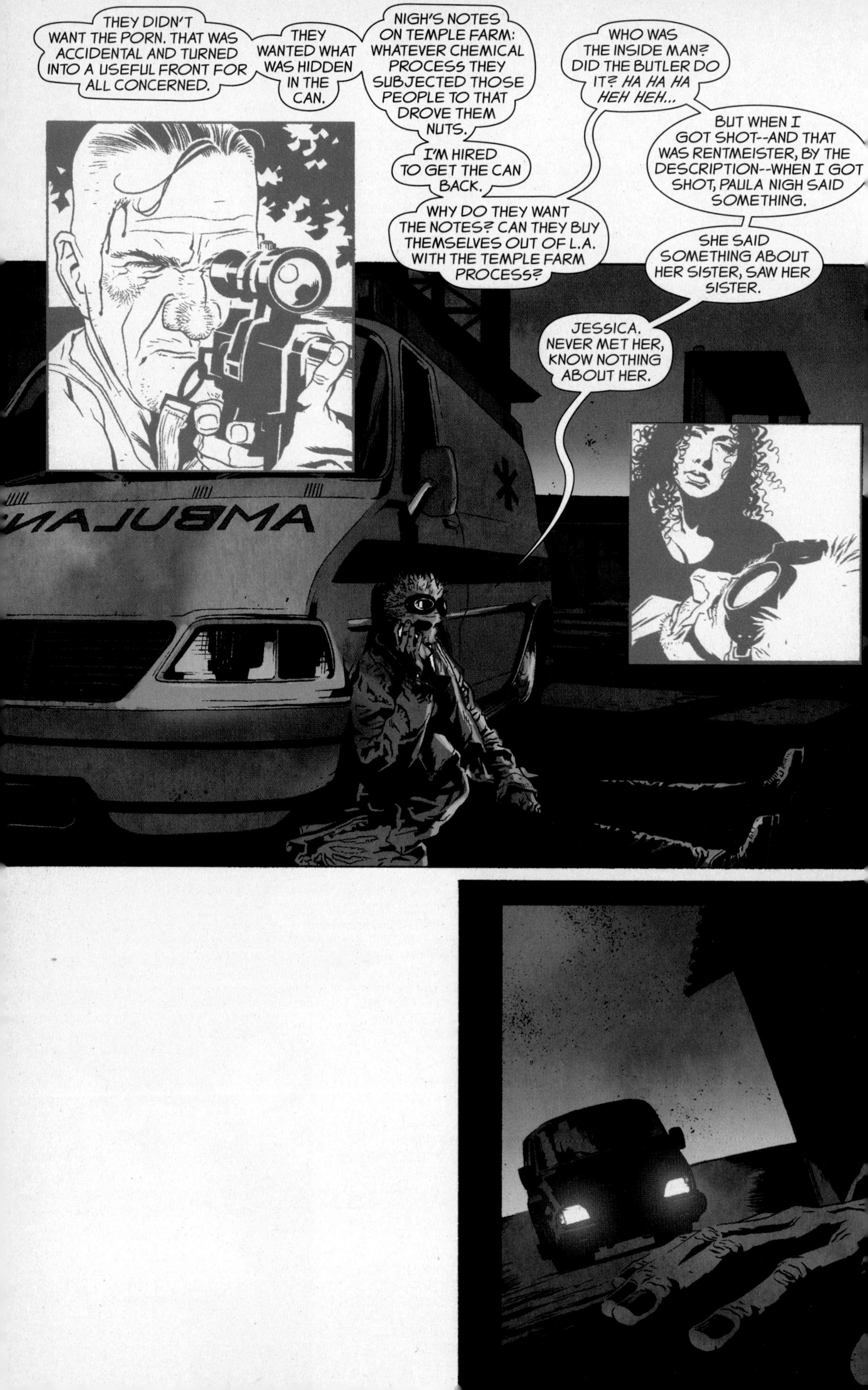
THEY DIDN'T WANT THE PORN. THAT WAS ACCIDENTAL AND TURNED INTO A USEFUL FRONT FOR ALL CONCERNED.
THEY WANTED WHAT WAS HIDDEN IN THE CAN.
NIGH'S NOTES ON TEMPLE FARM: WHATEVER CHEMICAL PROCESS THEY SUBJECTED THOSE PEOPLE TO THAT DROVE THEM NUTS.
I'M HIRED TO GET THE CAN BACK.
WHY DO THEY WANT THE NOTES? CAN THEY BUY THEMSELVES OUT OF L.A. WITH THE TEMPLE FARM PROCESS?
WHO WAS THE INSIDE MAN? DID THE BUTLER DO IT? *HA HA HA HEH HEH...*
BUT WHEN I GOT SHOT--AND THAT WAS RENTMEISTER, BY THE DESCRIPTION--WHEN I GOT SHOT, PAULA NIGH SAID SOMETHING.
SHE SAID SOMETHING ABOUT HER SISTER, SAW HER SISTER.
JESSICA. NEVER MET HER, KNOW NOTHING ABOUT HER.
AMBULAN

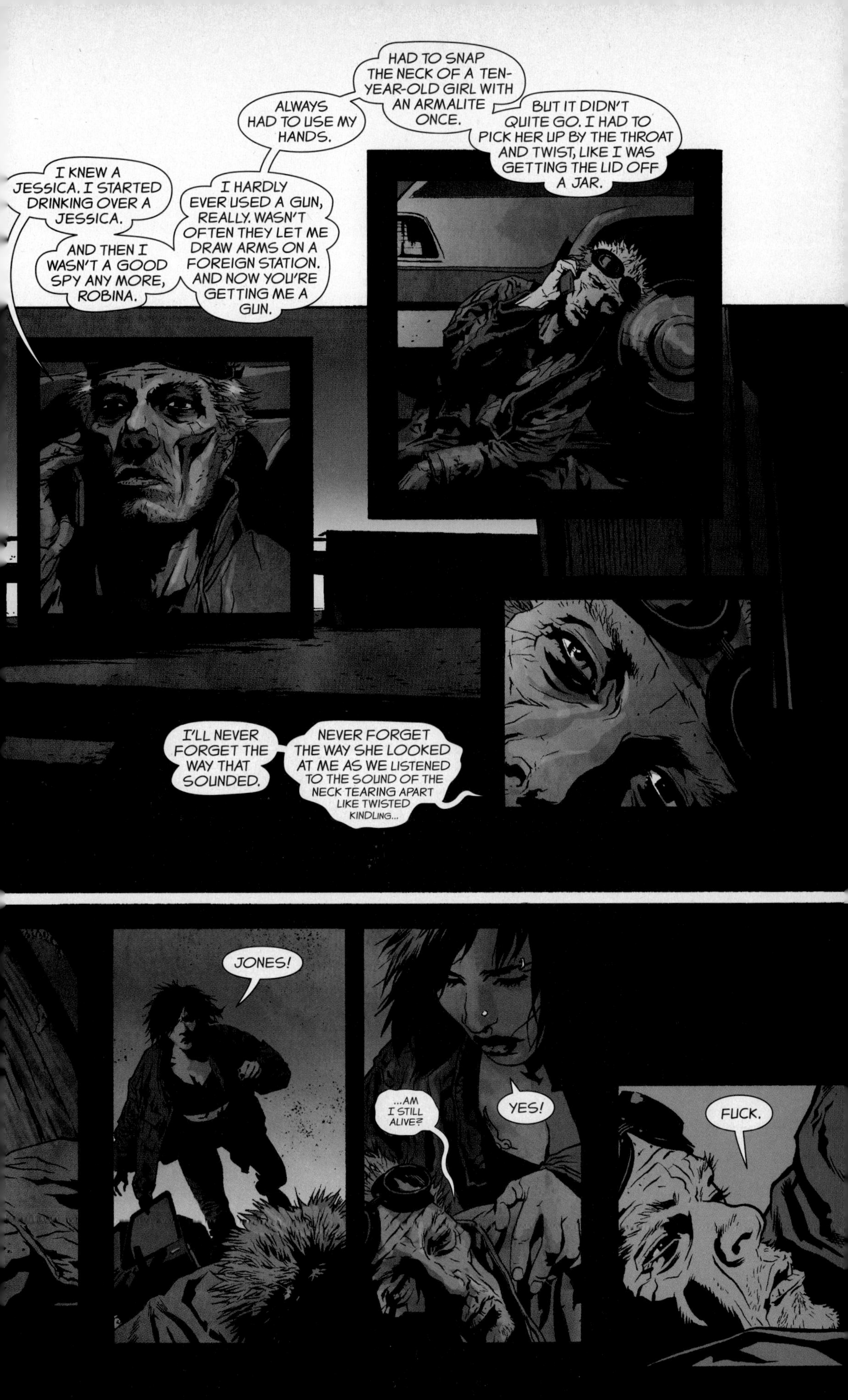
I KNEW A JESSICA. I STARTED DRINKING OVER A JESSICA.
AND THEN I WASN'T A GOOD SPY ANY MORE, ROBINA.
I HARDLY EVER USED A GUN, REALLY. WASN'T OFTEN THEY LET ME DRAW ARMS ON A FOREIGN STATION. AND NOW YOU'RE GETTING ME A GUN.
ALWAYS HAD TO USE MY HANDS.
HAD TO SNAP THE NECK OF A TEN-YEAR-OLD GIRL WITH AN ARMALITE ONCE.
BUT IT DIDN'T QUITE GO. I HAD TO PICK HER UP BY THE THROAT AND TWIST, LIKE I WAS GETTING THE LID OFF A JAR.
I'LL NEVER FORGET THE WAY THAT SOUNDED.
NEVER FORGET THE WAY SHE LOOKED AT ME AS WE LISTENED TO THE SOUND OF THE NECK TEARING APART LIKE TWISTED KINDLING...
JONES!
...AM I STILL ALIVE?
YES!
FUCK.

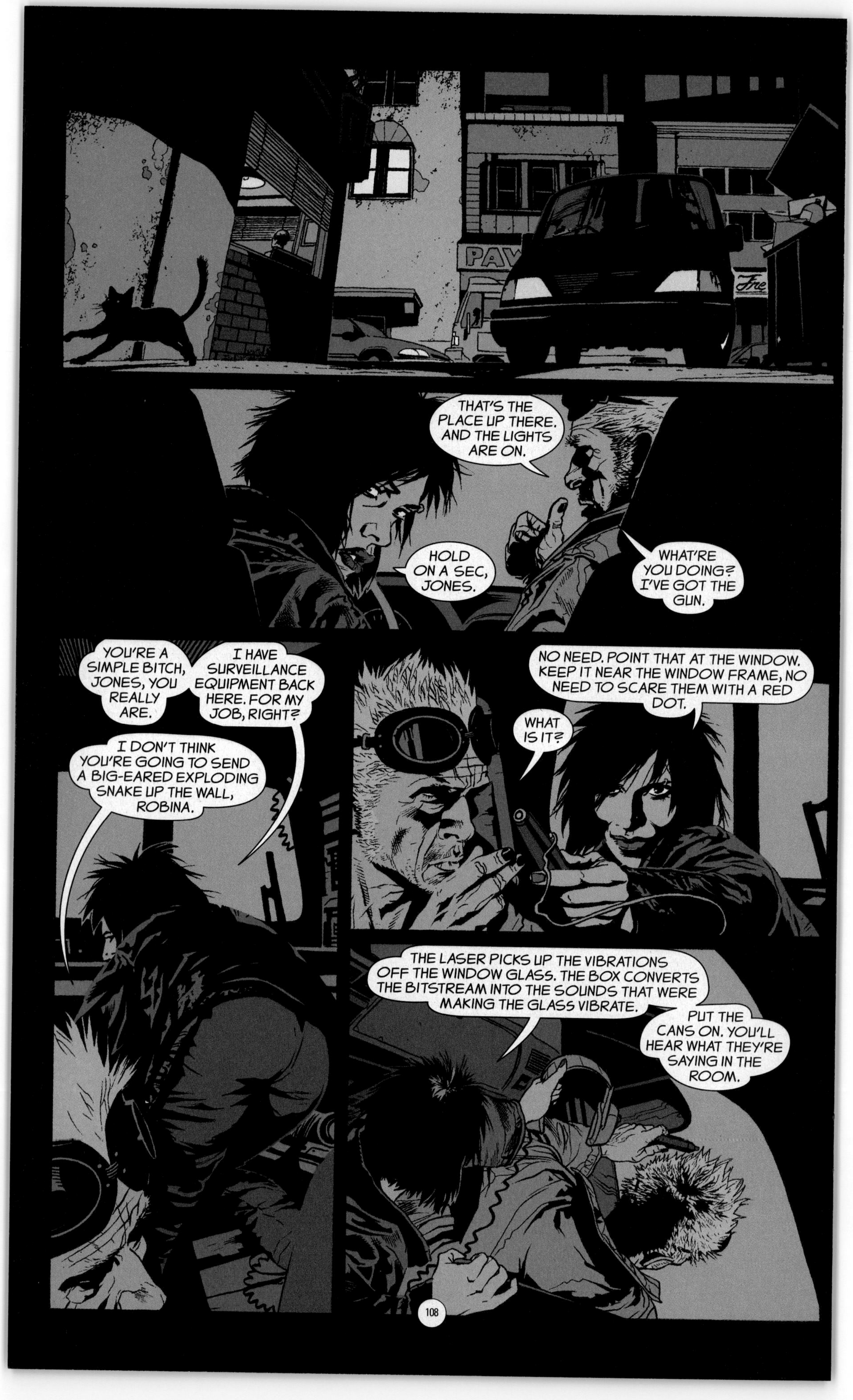

THAT'S THE PLACE UP THERE. AND THE LIGHTS ARE ON.
HOLD ON A SEC, JONES.
WHAT'RE YOU DOING? I'VE GOT THE GUN.
YOU'RE A SIMPLE BITCH, JONES, YOU REALLY ARE.
I HAVE SURVEILLANCE EQUIPMENT BACK HERE. FOR MY JOB, RIGHT?
I DON'T THINK YOU'RE GOING TO SEND A BIG-EARED EXPLODING SNAKE UP THE WALL, ROBINA.
NO NEED. POINT THAT AT THE WINDOW. KEEP IT NEAR THE WINDOW FRAME, NO NEED TO SCARE THEM WITH A RED DOT.
WHAT IS IT?
THE LASER PICKS UP THE VIBRATIONS OFF THE WINDOW GLASS. THE BOX CONVERTS THE BITSTREAM INTO THE SOUNDS THAT WERE MAKING THE GLASS VIBRATE.
PUT THE CANS ON. YOU'LL HEAR WHAT THEY'RE SAYING IN THE ROOM.

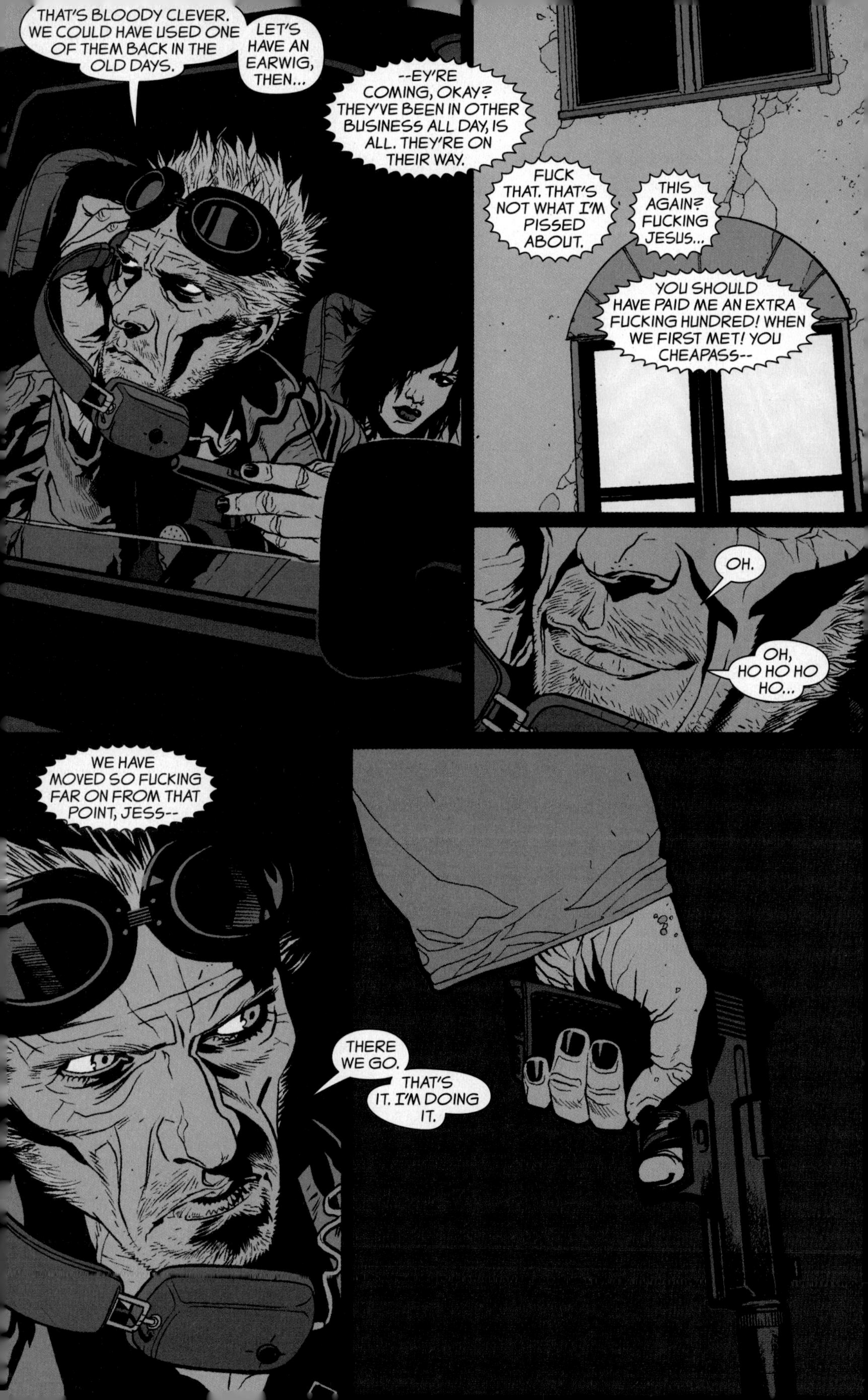
THAT'S BLOODY CLEVER. WE COULD HAVE USED ONE OF THEM BACK IN THE OLD DAYS.
LET'S HAVE AN EARWIG, THEN...
--EY'RE COMING, OKAY? THEY'VE BEEN IN OTHER BUSINESS ALL DAY, IS ALL. THEY'RE ON THEIR WAY.
FUCK THAT. THAT'S NOT WHAT I'M PISSED ABOUT.
THIS AGAIN? FUCKING JESUS...
YOU SHOULD HAVE PAID ME AN EXTRA FUCKING HUNDRED! WHEN WE FIRST MET! YOU CHEAPASS--
OH.
OH, HO HO HO HO...
WE HAVE MOVED SO FUCKING FAR ON FROM THAT POINT, JESS--
THERE WE GO.
THAT'S IT. I'M DOING IT.

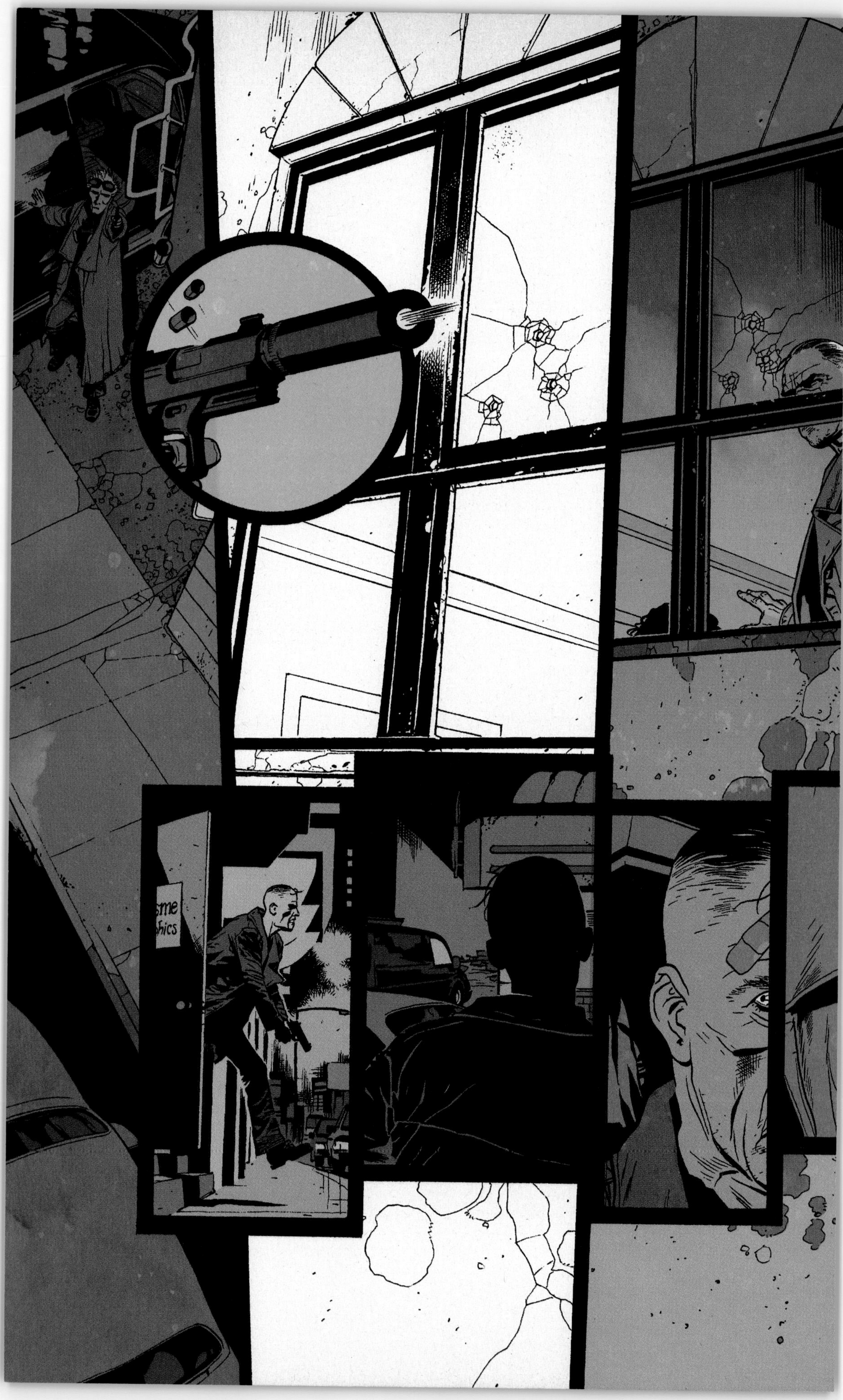
sme
phics

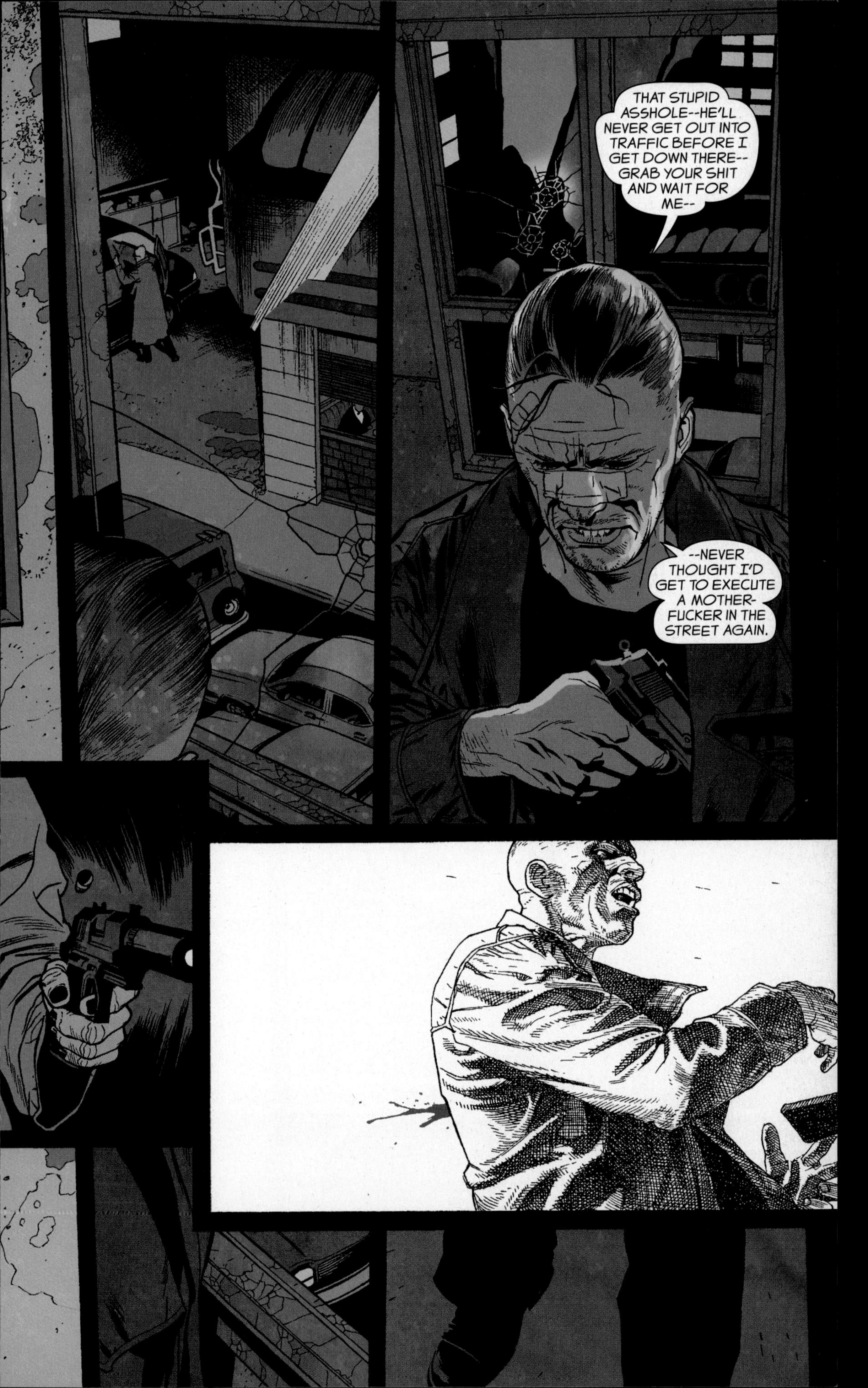
THAT STUPID ASSHOLE--HE'LL NEVER GET OUT INTO TRAFFIC BEFORE I GET DOWN THERE--GRAB YOUR SHIT AND WAIT FOR ME--
--NEVER THOUGHT I'D GET TO EXECUTE A MOTHER-FUCKER IN THE STREET AGAIN.

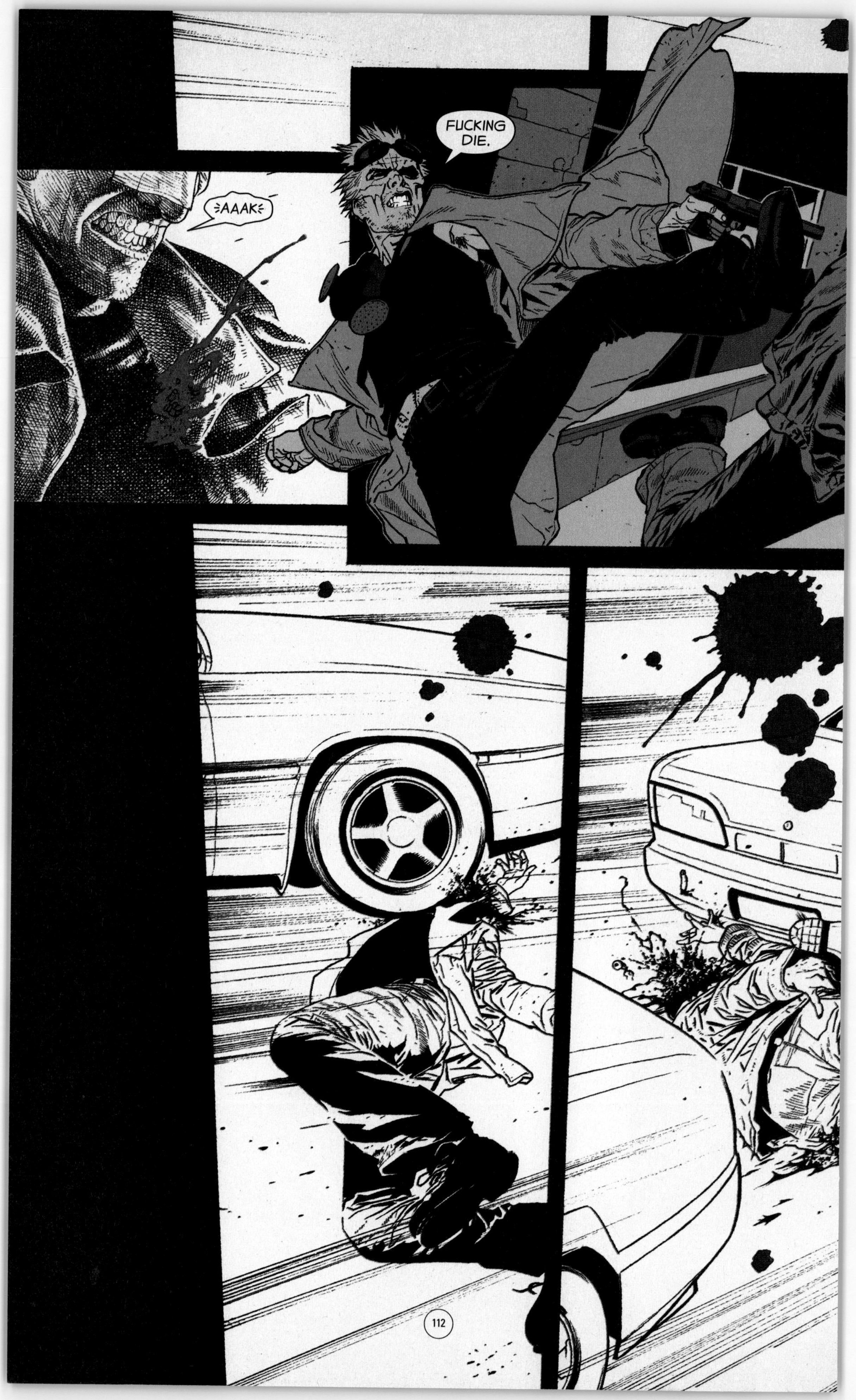
AAAK
FUCKING DIE.

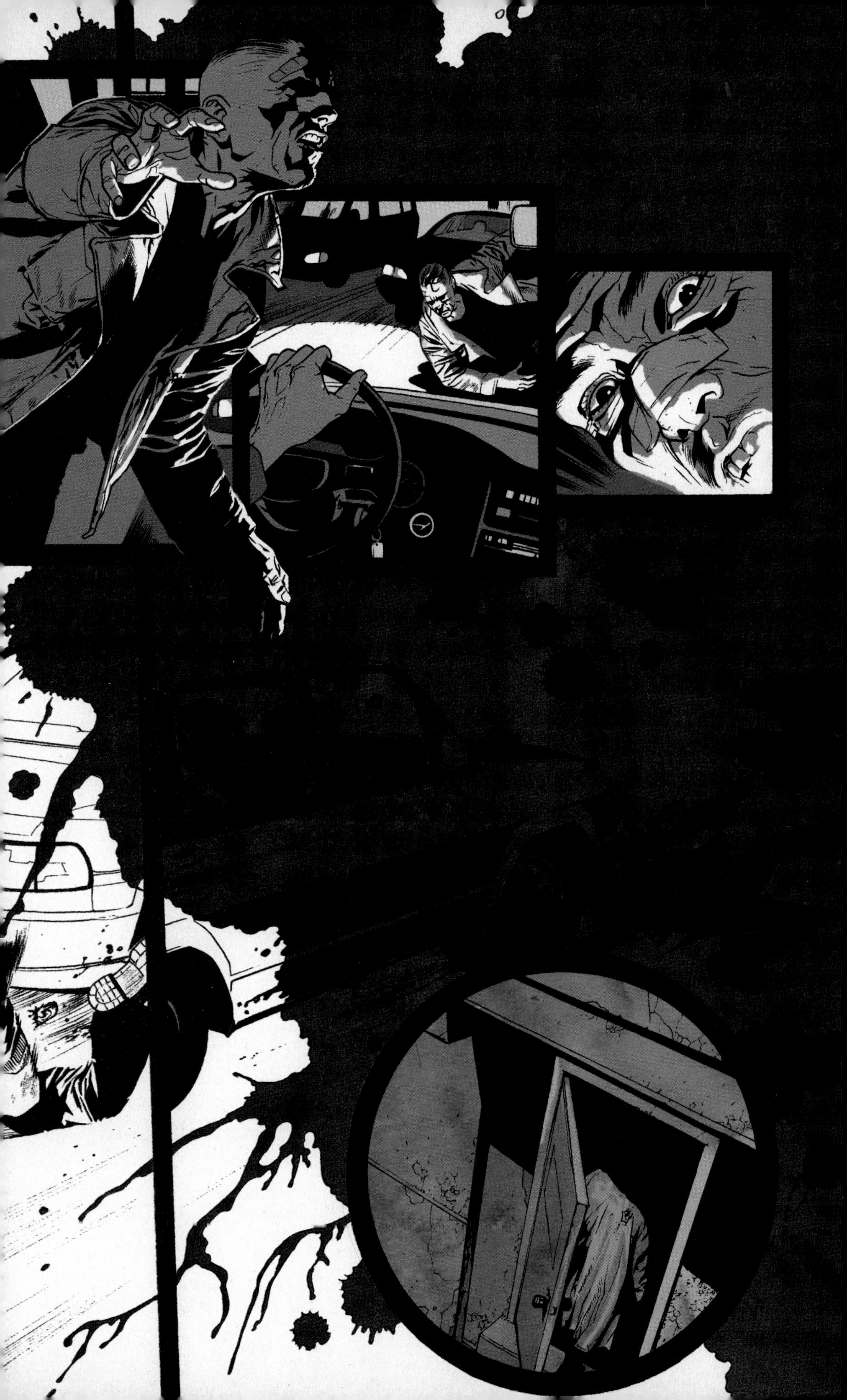

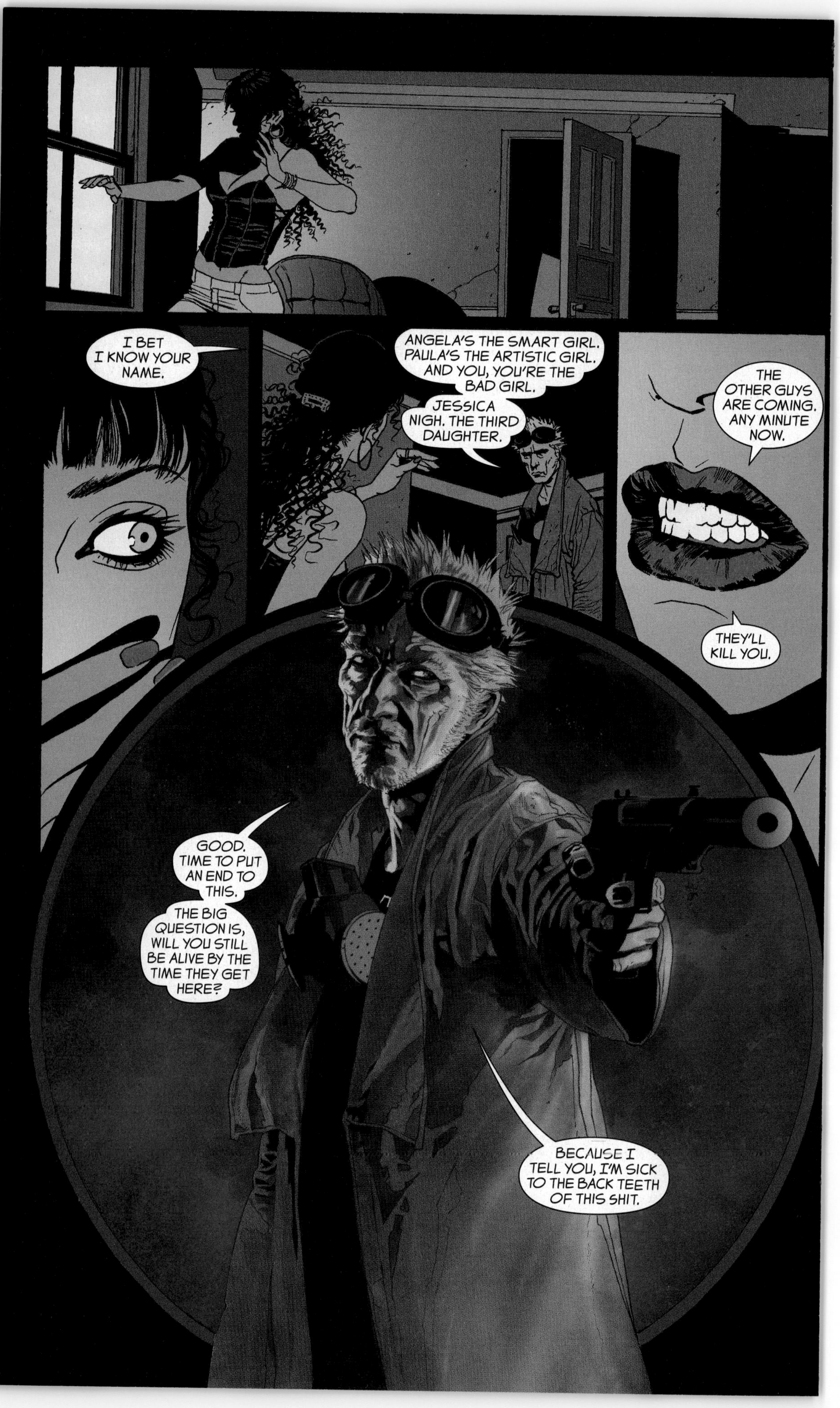
I BET I KNOW YOUR NAME.
ANGELA'S THE SMART GIRL. PAULA'S THE ARTISTIC GIRL. AND YOU, YOU'RE THE BAD GIRL.
JESSICA NIGH. THE THIRD DAUGHTER.
THE OTHER GUYS ARE COMING. ANY MINUTE NOW.
THEY'LL KILL YOU.
GOOD. TIME TO PUT AN END TO THIS.
THE BIG QUESTION IS, WILL YOU STILL BE ALIVE BY THE TIME THEY GET HERE?
BECAUSE I TELL YOU, I'M SICK TO THE BACK TEETH OF THIS SHIT.

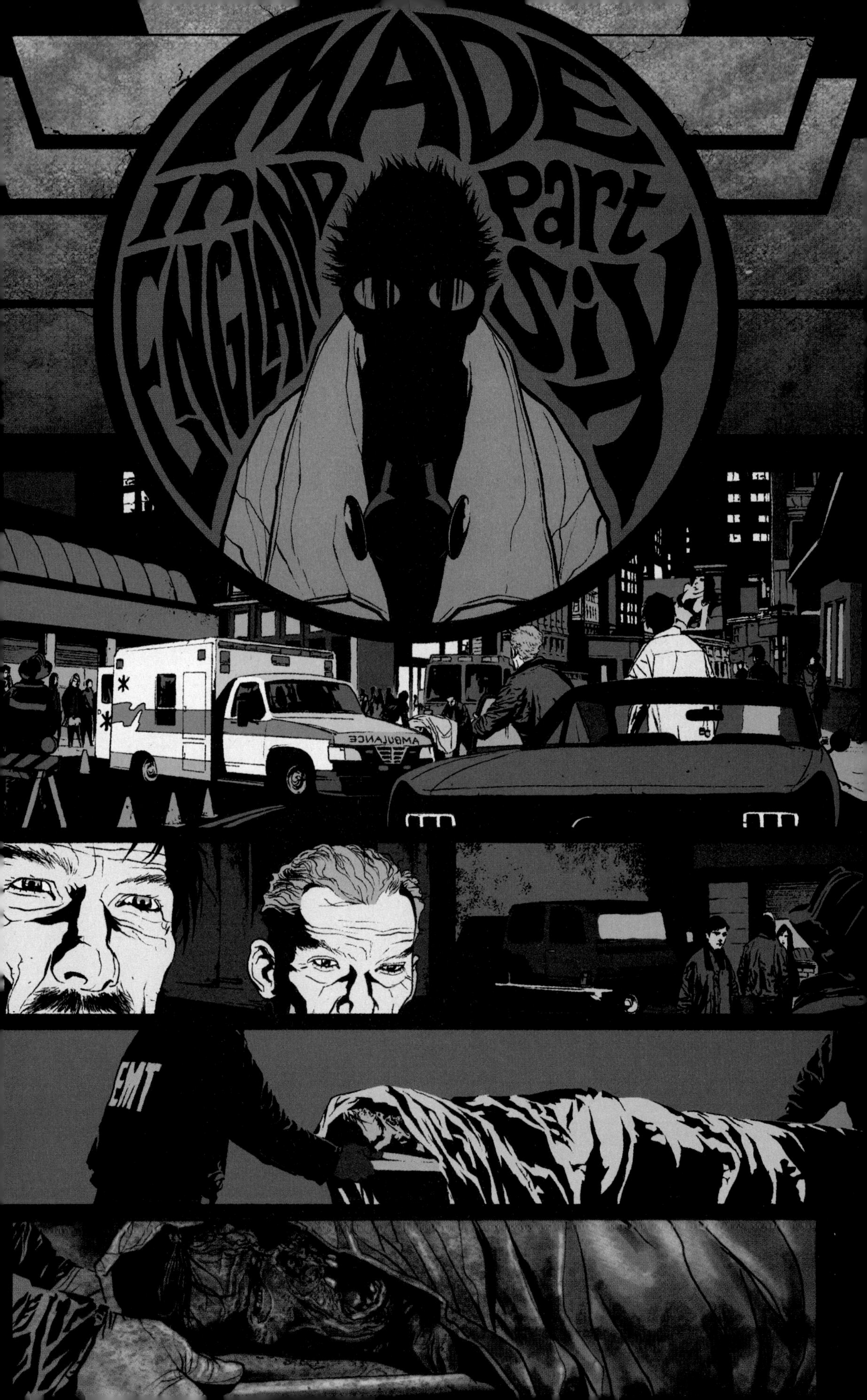
MADE IN ENGLAND
part SIX
AMBULANCE
EMT

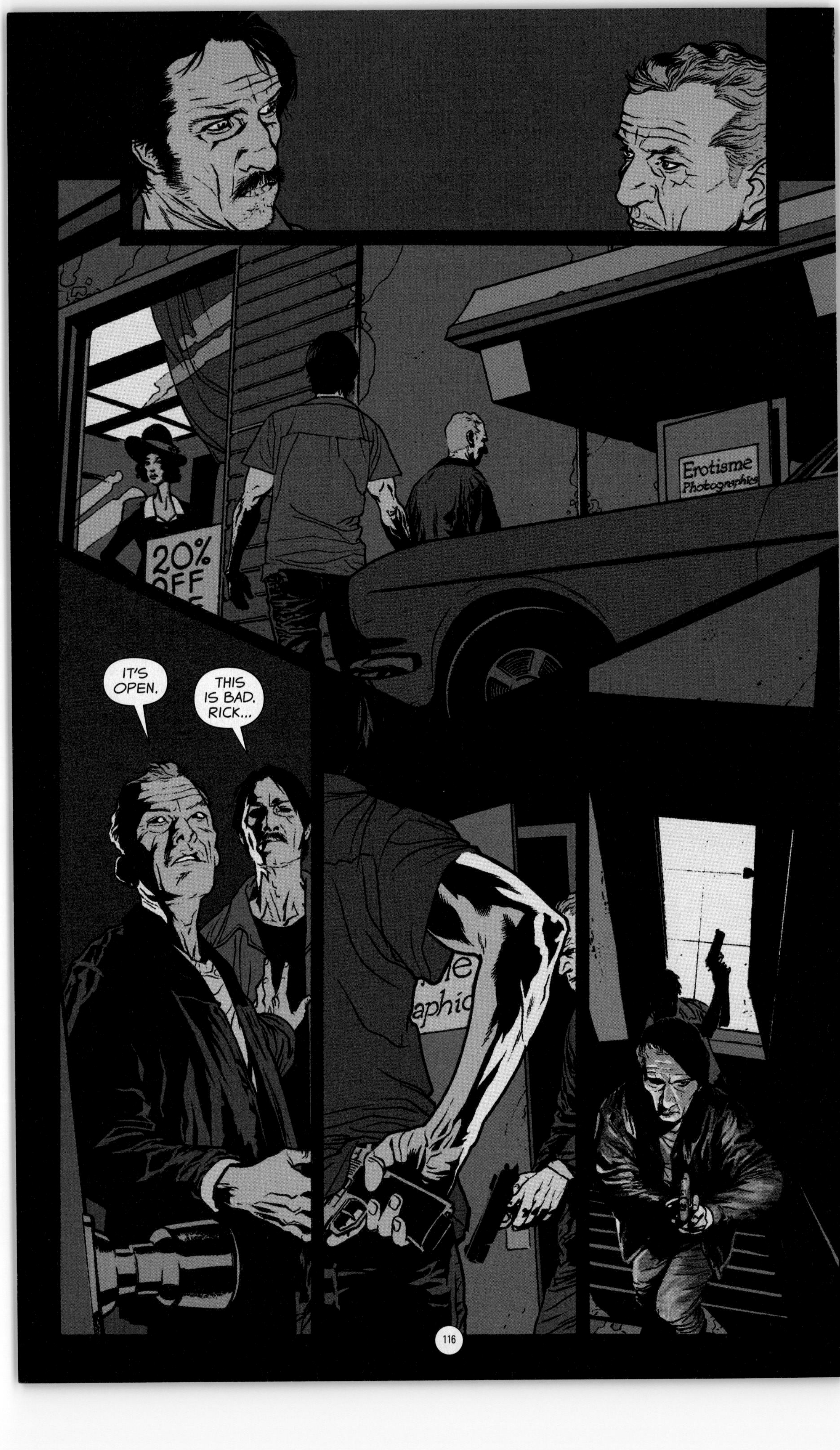
Erotisme
Photographies
20%
IT'S OPEN.
THIS IS BAD, RICK...

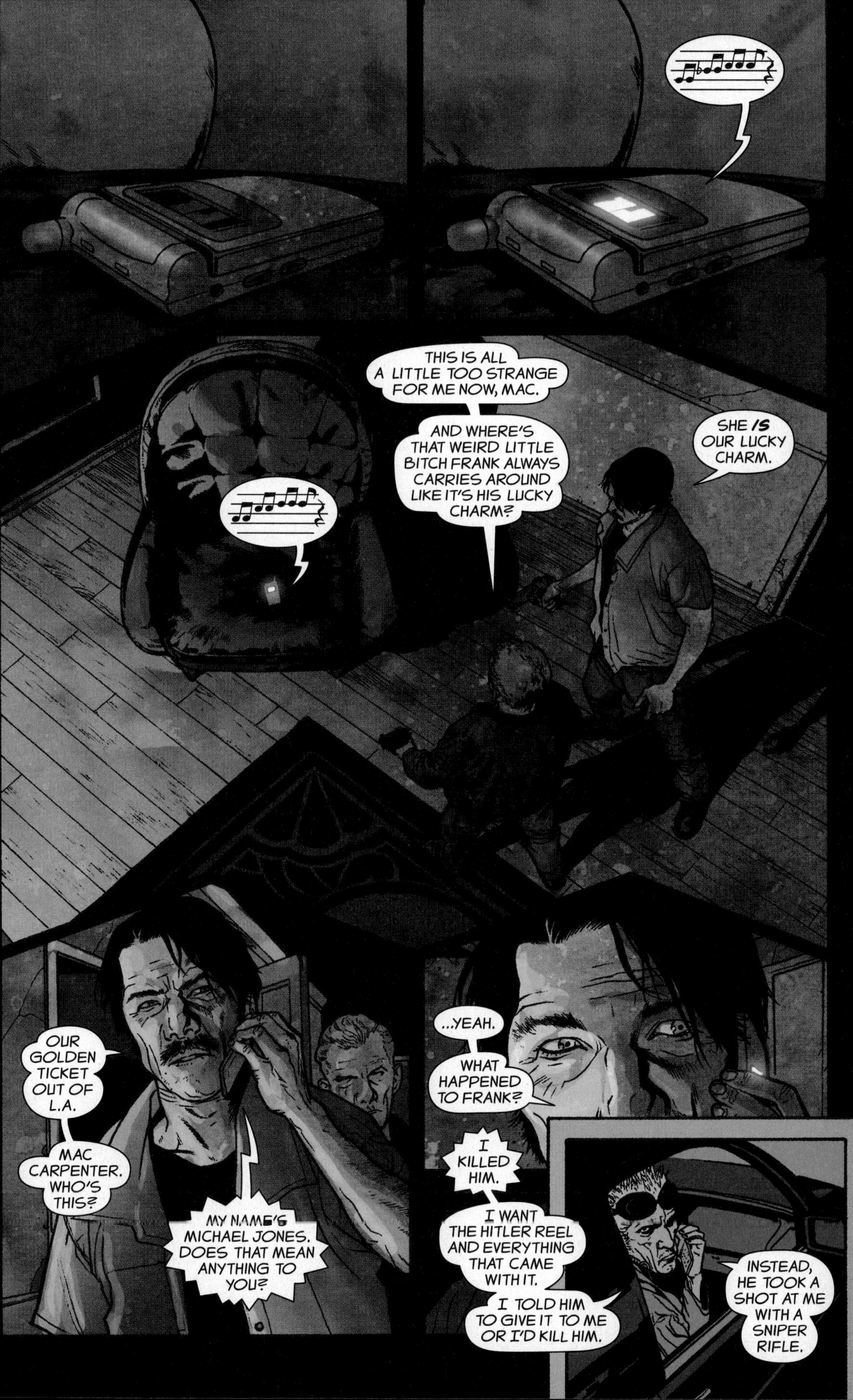
THIS IS ALL A LITTLE TOO STRANGE FOR ME NOW, MAC.
AND WHERE'S THAT WEIRD LITTLE BITCH FRANK ALWAYS CARRIES AROUND LIKE IT'S HIS LUCKY CHARM?
SHE IS OUR LUCKY CHARM.
OUR GOLDEN TICKET OUT OF L.A.
MAC CARPENTER. WHO'S THIS?
MY NAME'S MICHAEL JONES. DOES THAT MEAN ANYTHING TO YOU?
...YEAH.
WHAT HAPPENED TO FRANK?
I KILLED HIM.
I WANT THE HITLER REEL AND EVERYTHING THAT CAME WITH IT.
I TOLD HIM TO GIVE IT TO ME OR I'D KILL HIM.
INSTEAD, HE TOOK A SHOT AT ME WITH A SNIPER RIFLE.

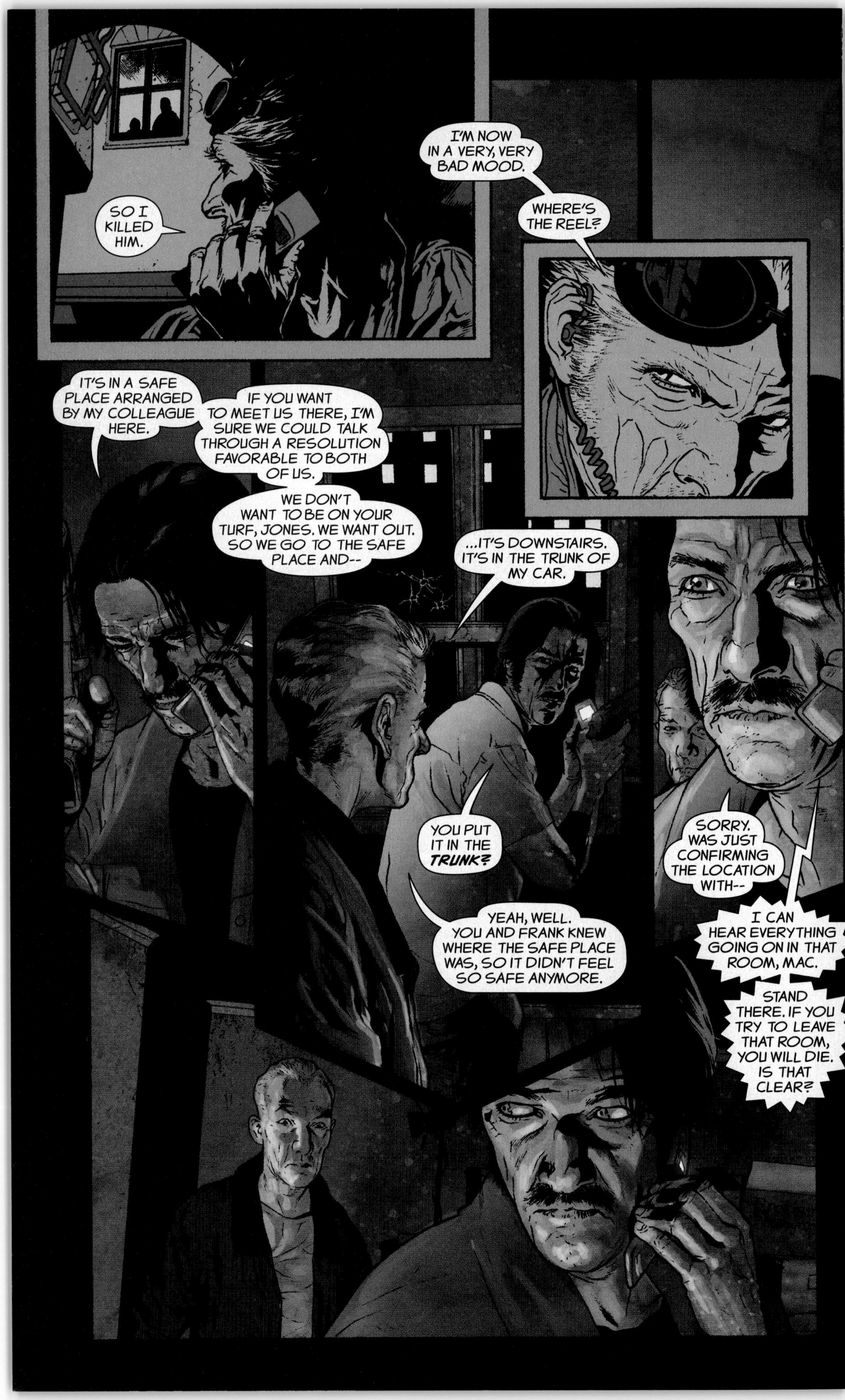
SO I KILLED HIM.
I'M NOW IN A VERY, VERY BAD MOOD.
WHERE'S THE REEL?
IT'S IN A SAFE PLACE ARRANGED BY MY COLLEAGUE HERE.
IF YOU WANT TO MEET US THERE, I'M SURE WE COULD TALK THROUGH A RESOLUTION FAVORABLE TO BOTH OF US.
WE DON'T WANT TO BE ON YOUR TURF, JONES. WE WANT OUT. SO WE GO TO THE SAFE PLACE AND--
...IT'S DOWNSTAIRS. IT'S IN THE TRUNK OF MY CAR.
YOU PUT IT IN THE TRUNK?
YEAH, WELL. YOU AND FRANK KNEW WHERE THE SAFE PLACE WAS, SO IT DIDN'T FEEL SO SAFE ANYMORE.
SORRY. WAS JUST CONFIRMING THE LOCATION WITH--
I CAN HEAR EVERYTHING GOING ON IN THAT ROOM, MAC.
STAND THERE. IF YOU TRY TO LEAVE THAT ROOM, YOU WILL DIE. IS THAT CLEAR?

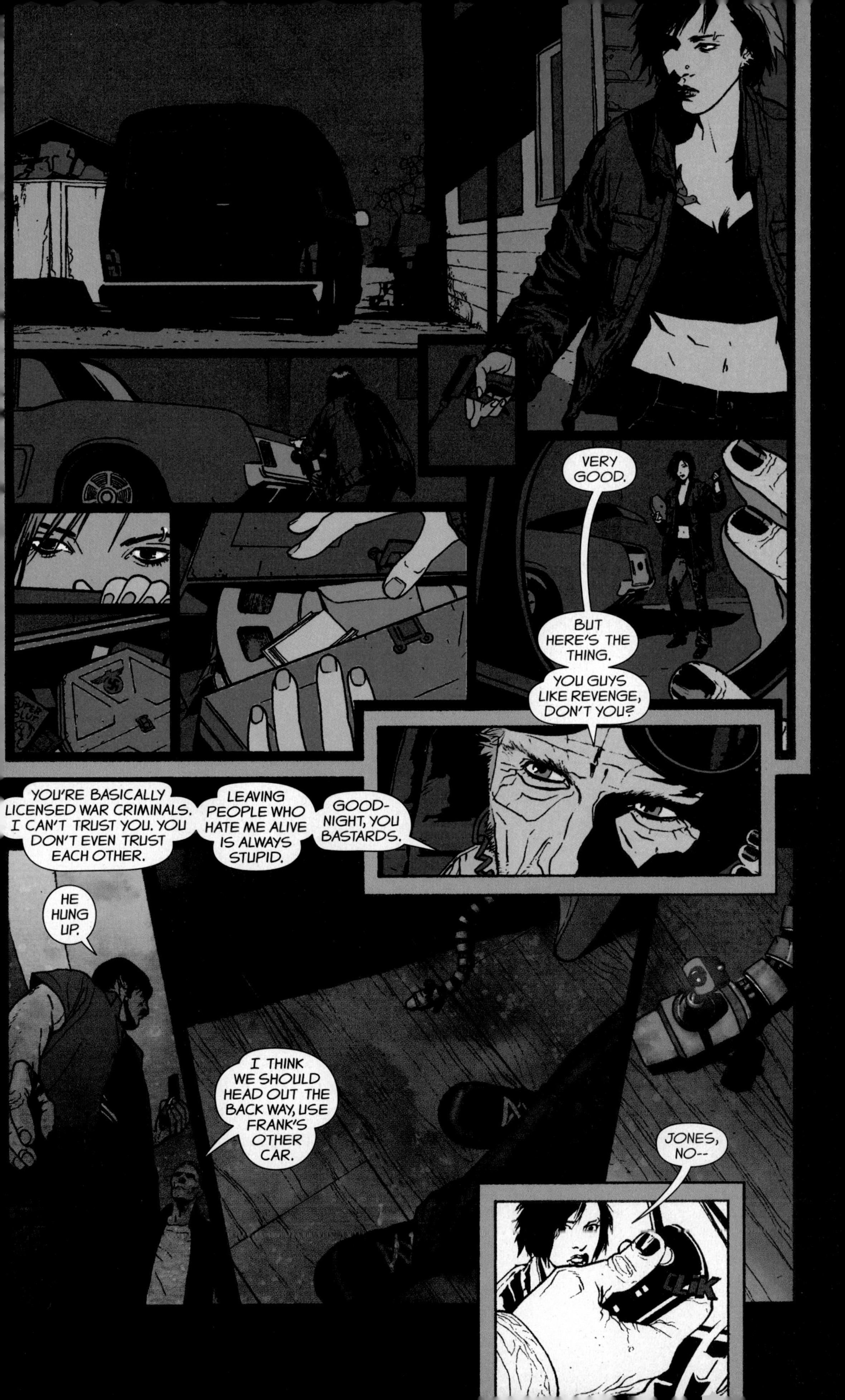
VERY GOOD.
BUT HERE'S THE THING.
YOU GUYS LIKE REVENGE, DON'T YOU?
YOU'RE BASICALLY LICENSED WAR CRIMINALS. I CAN'T TRUST YOU. YOU DON'T EVEN TRUST EACH OTHER.
LEAVING PEOPLE WHO HATE ME ALIVE IS ALWAYS STUPID.
GOOD-NIGHT, YOU BASTARDS.
HE HUNG UP.
I THINK WE SHOULD HEAD OUT THE BACK WAY, USE FRANK'S OTHER CAR.
JONES, NO--
CLIK

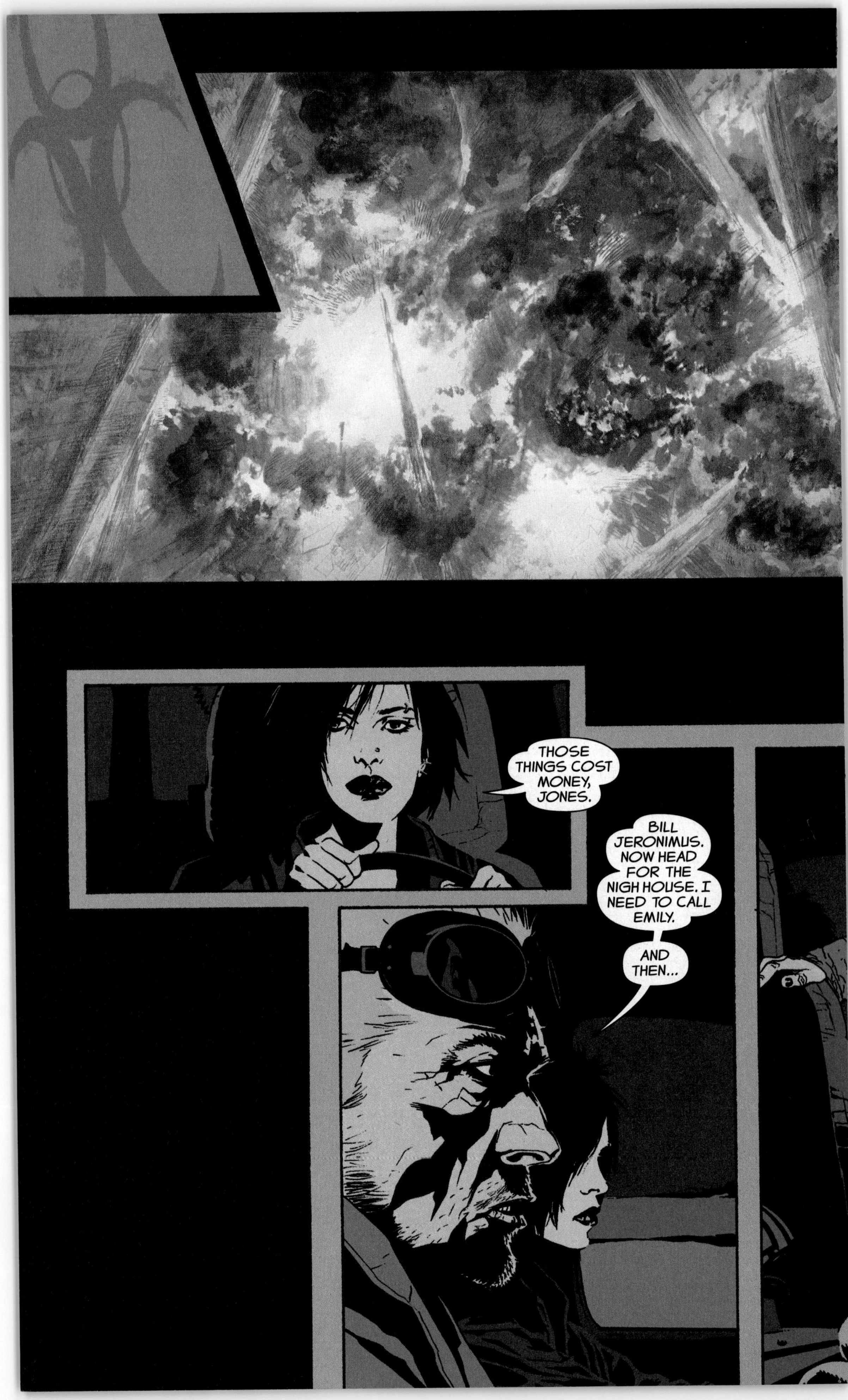
THOSE THINGS COST MONEY, JONES.
BILL JERONIMUS. NOW HEAD FOR THE NIGH HOUSE. I NEED TO CALL EMILY.
AND THEN...

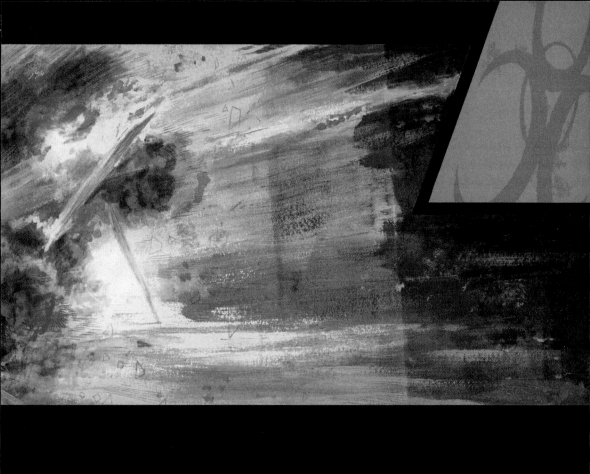

...I NEED TO HAVE A LITTLE CHINWAG WITH THE COLONEL'S YOUNGEST DAUGHTER.

FKR.

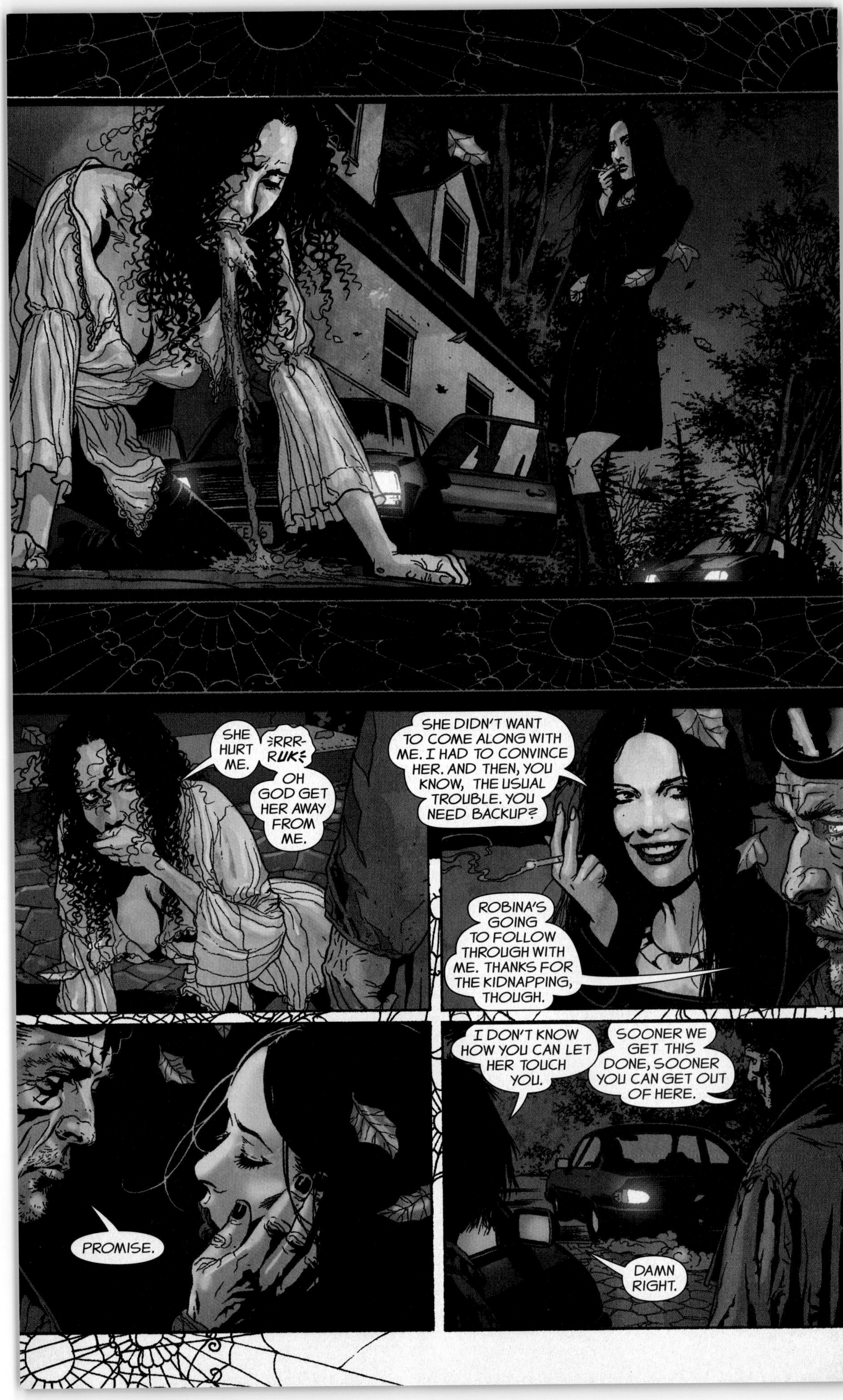
SHE HURT ME.
RRR-RUK
OH GOD GET HER AWAY FROM ME.
SHE DIDN'T WANT TO COME ALONG WITH ME. I HAD TO CONVINCE HER. AND THEN, YOU KNOW, THE USUAL TROUBLE. YOU NEED BACKUP?
ROBINA'S GOING TO FOLLOW THROUGH WITH ME. THANKS FOR THE KIDNAPPING, THOUGH.
PROMISE.
I DON'T KNOW HOW YOU CAN LET HER TOUCH YOU.
SOONER WE GET THIS DONE, SOONER YOU CAN GET OUT OF HERE.
DAMN RIGHT.

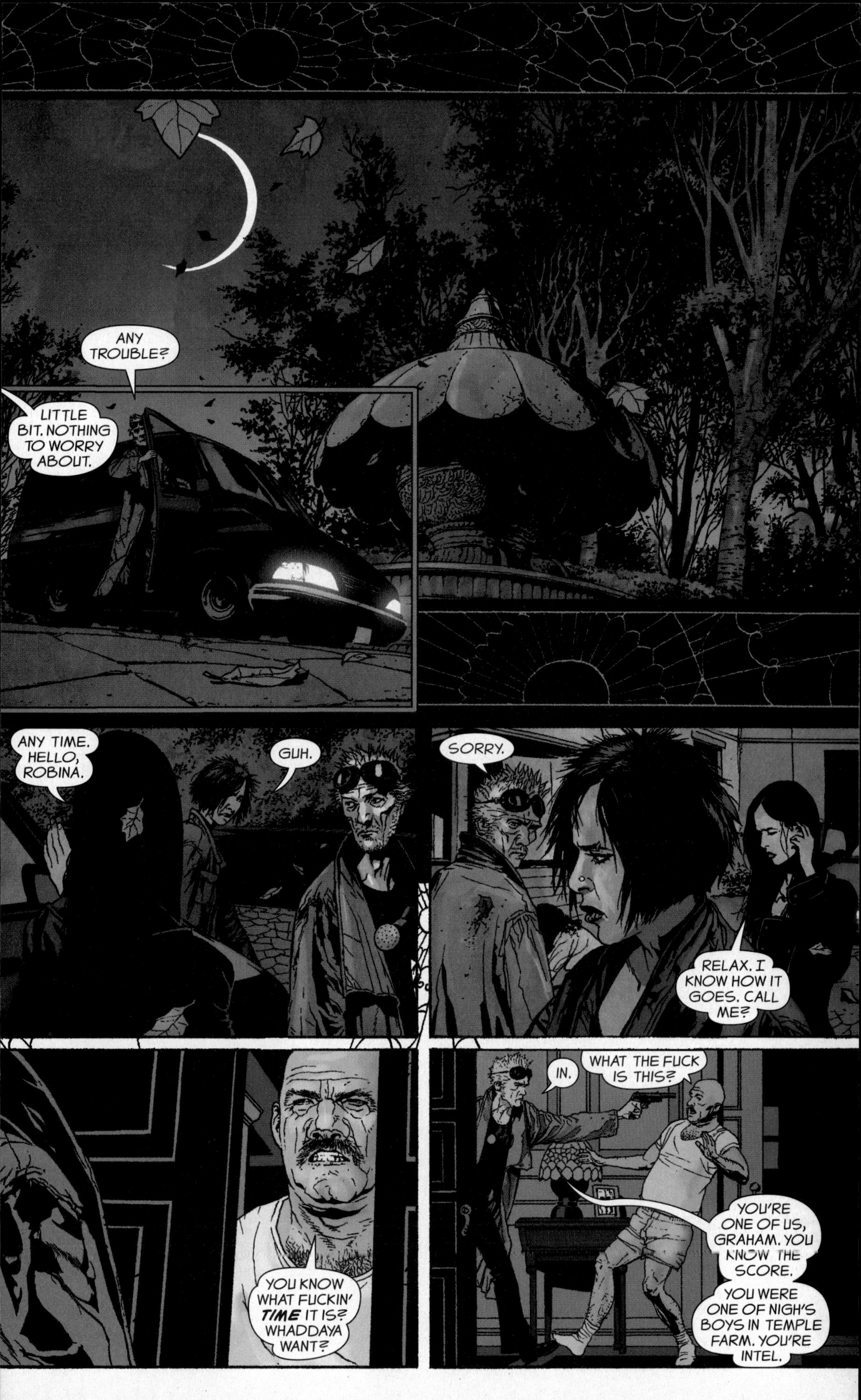
ANY TROUBLE?
LITTLE BIT. NOTHING TO WORRY ABOUT.
ANY TIME. HELLO, ROBINA.
GUH.
SORRY.
RELAX. I KNOW HOW IT GOES. CALL ME?
YOU KNOW WHAT FUCKIN' TIME IT IS? WHADDAYA WANT?
IN.
WHAT THE FUCK IS THIS?
YOU'RE ONE OF US, GRAHAM. YOU KNOW THE SCORE.
YOU WERE ONE OF NIGH'S BOYS IN TEMPLE FARM. YOU'RE INTEL.

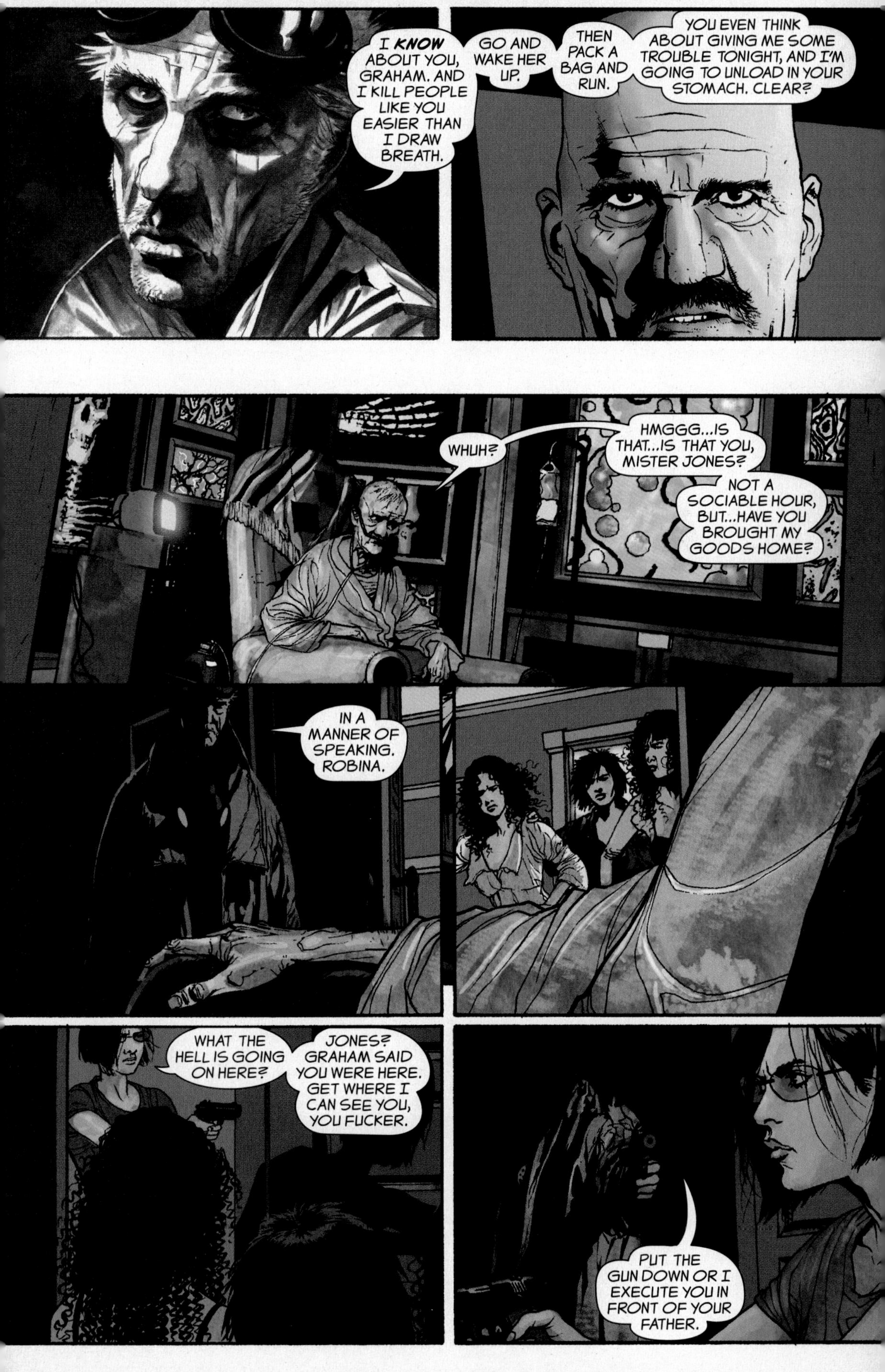
I KNOW ABOUT YOU, GRAHAM. AND I KILL PEOPLE LIKE YOU EASIER THAN I DRAW BREATH.
GO AND WAKE HER UP.
THEN PACK A BAG AND RUN.
YOU EVEN THINK ABOUT GIVING ME SOME TROUBLE TONIGHT, AND I'M GOING TO UNLOAD IN YOUR STOMACH. CLEAR?
WHUH?
HMGGG...IS THAT...IS THAT YOU, MISTER JONES?
NOT A SOCIABLE HOUR, BUT...HAVE YOU BROUGHT MY GOODS HOME?
IN A MANNER OF SPEAKING. ROBINA.
WHAT THE HELL IS GOING ON HERE?
JONES? GRAHAM SAID YOU WERE HERE. GET WHERE I CAN SEE YOU, YOU FUCKER.
PUT THE GUN DOWN OR I EXECUTE YOU IN FRONT OF YOUR FATHER.

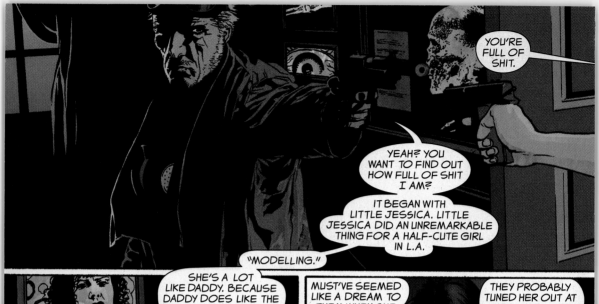

YOU'RE FULL OF SHIT.

YEAH? YOU WANT TO FIND OUT HOW FULL OF SHIT I AM?

IT BEGAN WITH LITTLE JESSICA. LITTLE JESSICA DID AN UNREMARKABLE THING FOR A HALF-CUTE GIRL IN L.A.

"MODELLING."

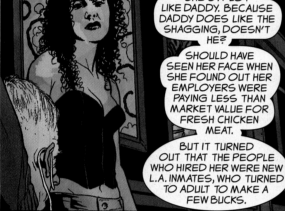

SHE'S A LOT LIKE DADDY. BECAUSE DADDY DOES LIKE THE SHAGGING, DOESN'T HE?

SHOULD HAVE SEEN HER FACE WHEN SHE FOUND OUT HER EMPLOYERS WERE PAYING LESS THAN MARKET VALUE FOR FRESH CHICKEN MEAT.

BUT IT TURNED OUT THAT THE PEOPLE WHO HIRED HER WERE NEW L.A. INMATES, WHO TURNED TO ADULT TO MAKE A FEW BUCKS.

MUST'VE SEEMED LIKE A DREAM TO THEM WHEN SHE STARTED TALKING ABOUT HER LIFE.

THEY PROBABLY TUNED HER OUT AT FIRST. AND THEN SHE DROPPED THE MAGIC WORDS.

THEY WERE REALLY BLACKMAILING YOU, THOUGH, WEREN'T THEY?

YES.

MY DAUGHTERS, EH? MY STUPID, LAZY DAUGHTERS.

NONE OF THEM COULD BRING THEM-SELVES TO LOOK IN THE FILM CAN MARKED "STALIN MASTURBATING."

AH, PAULA. YOU LEFT RATHER THAN HURT ME.

BUT YOU'RE STUPID AS MUD, YOU REALLY ARE.

AND ANGELA...

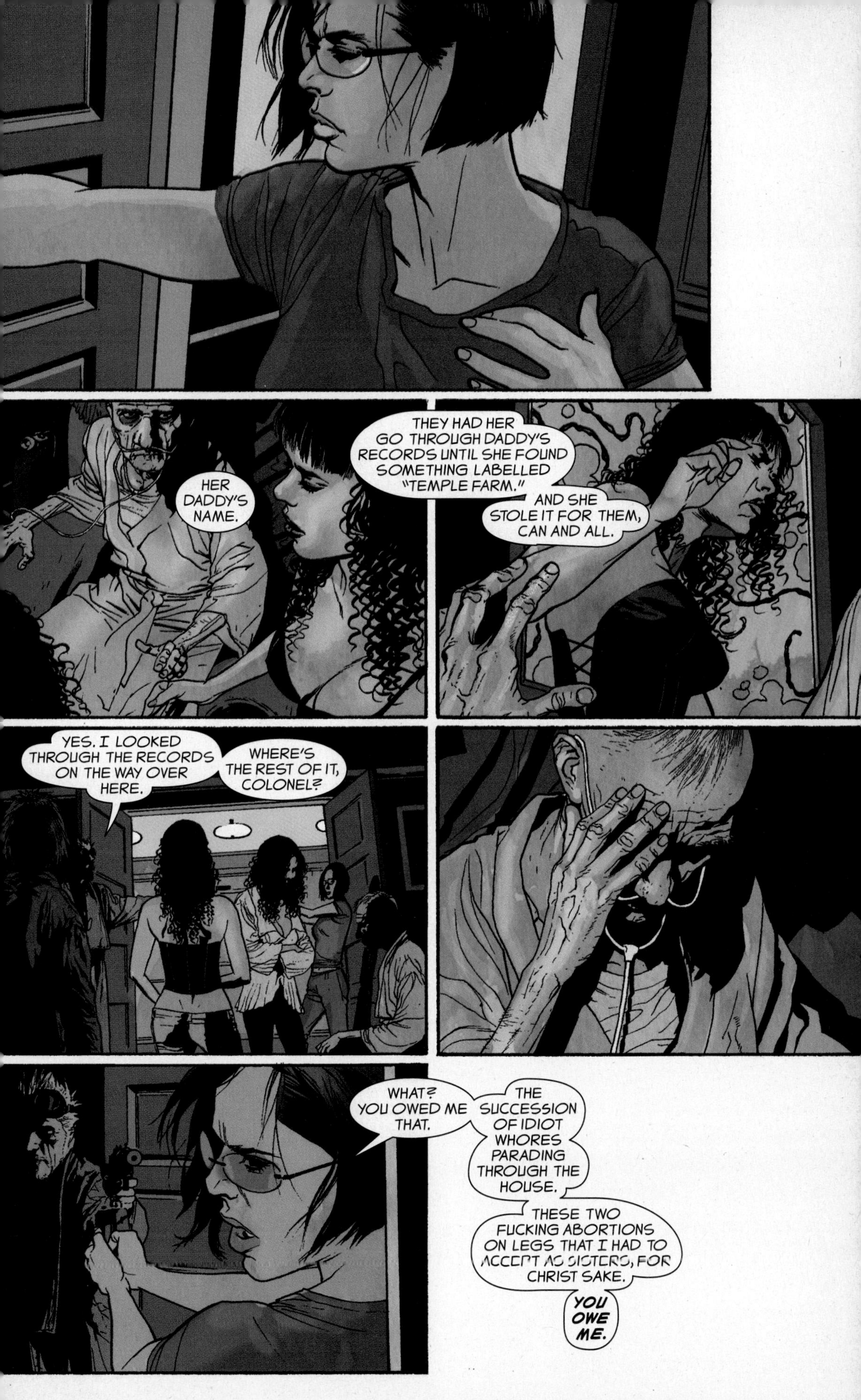
HER DADDY'S NAME.
THEY HAD HER GO THROUGH DADDY'S RECORDS UNTIL SHE FOUND SOMETHING LABELLED "TEMPLE FARM."
AND SHE STOLE IT FOR THEM, CAN AND ALL.
YES. I LOOKED THROUGH THE RECORDS ON THE WAY OVER HERE.
WHERE'S THE REST OF IT, COLONEL?
WHAT? YOU OWED ME THAT.
THE SUCCESSION OF IDIOT WHORES PARADING THROUGH THE HOUSE.
THESE TWO FUCKING ABORTIONS ON LEGS THAT I HAD TO ACCEPT AS SISTERS, FOR CHRIST SAKE.
YOU OWE ME.

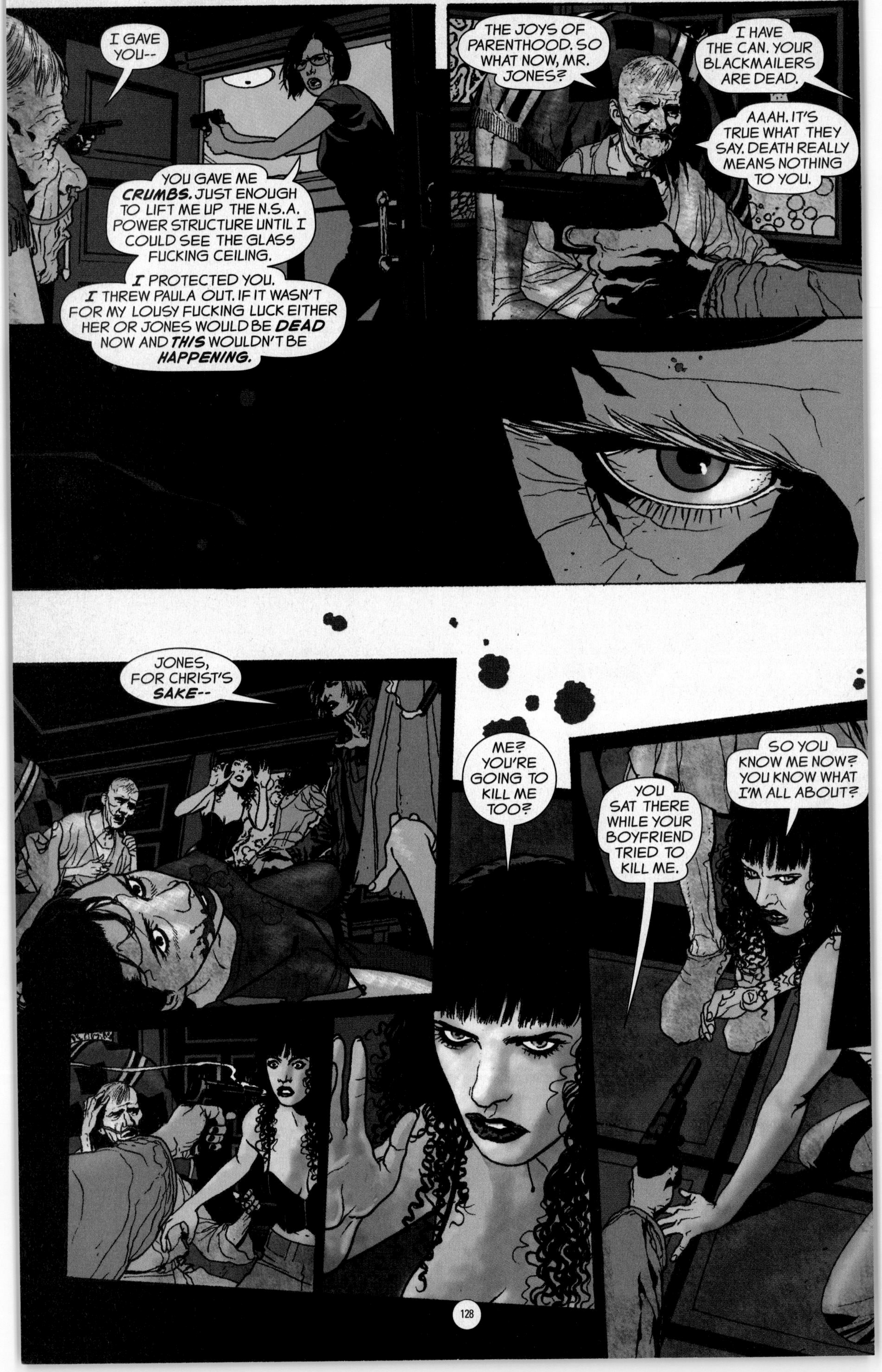
I GAVE YOU--
YOU GAVE ME CRUMBS. JUST ENOUGH TO LIFT ME UP THE N.S.A. POWER STRUCTURE UNTIL I COULD SEE THE GLASS FUCKING CEILING.
I PROTECTED YOU. I THREW PAULA OUT. IF IT WASN'T FOR MY LOUSY FUCKING LUCK EITHER HER OR JONES WOULD BE DEAD NOW AND THIS WOULDN'T BE HAPPENING.
THE JOYS OF PARENTHOOD. SO WHAT NOW, MR. JONES?
I HAVE THE CAN. YOUR BLACKMAILERS ARE DEAD.
AAAH. IT'S TRUE WHAT THEY SAY. DEATH REALLY MEANS NOTHING TO YOU.
JONES, FOR CHRIST'S SAKE--
ME? YOU'RE GOING TO KILL ME TOO?
SO YOU KNOW ME NOW? YOU KNOW WHAT I'M ALL ABOUT?
YOU SAT THERE WHILE YOUR BOYFRIEND TRIED TO KILL ME.

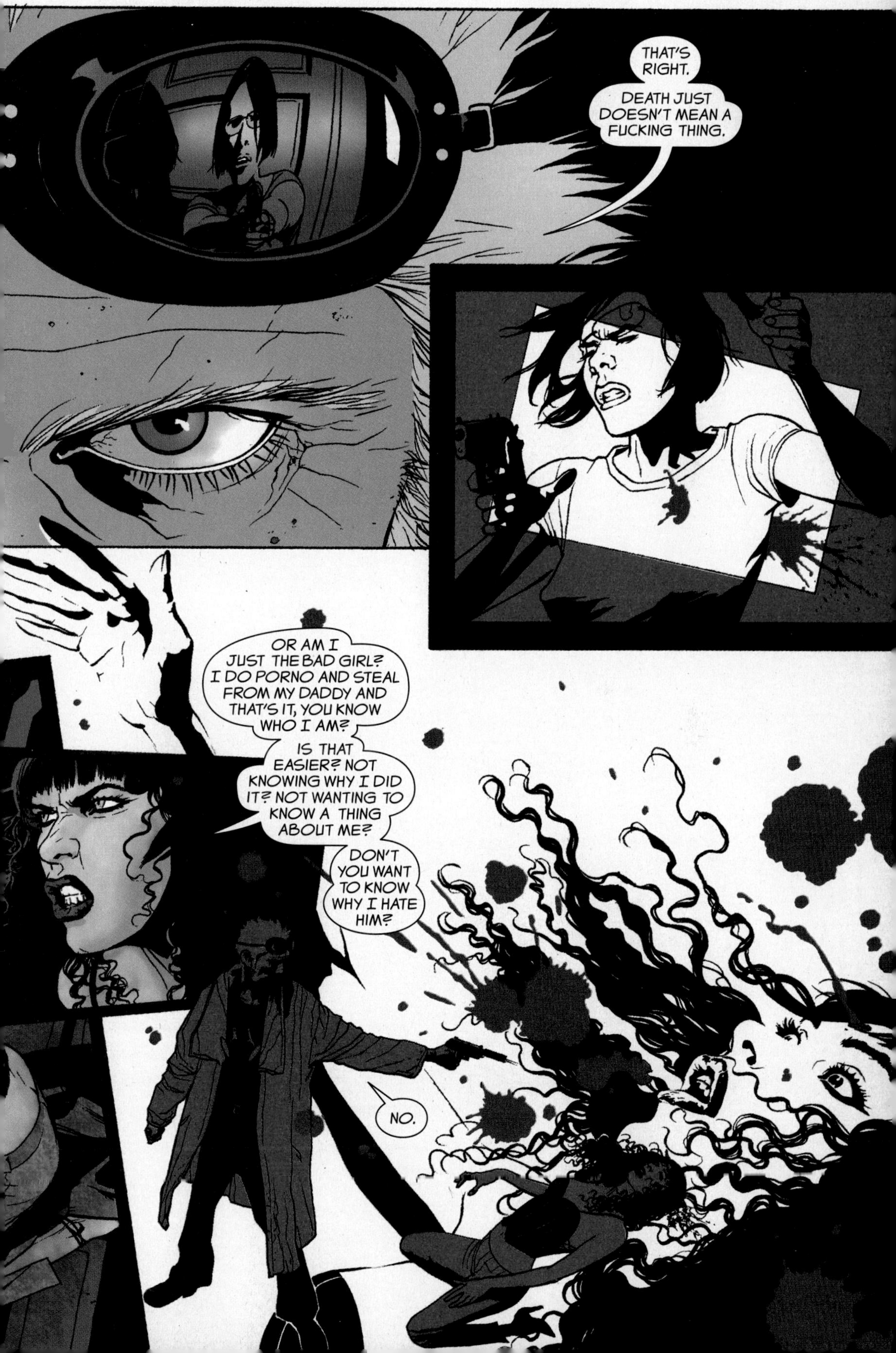
THAT'S RIGHT.
DEATH JUST DOESN'T MEAN A FUCKING THING.
OR AM I JUST THE BAD GIRL? I DO PORNO AND STEAL FROM MY DADDY AND THAT'S IT, YOU KNOW WHO I AM?
IS THAT EASIER? NOT KNOWING WHY I DID IT? NOT WANTING TO KNOW A THING ABOUT ME?
DON'T YOU WANT TO KNOW WHY I HATE HIM?
NO.

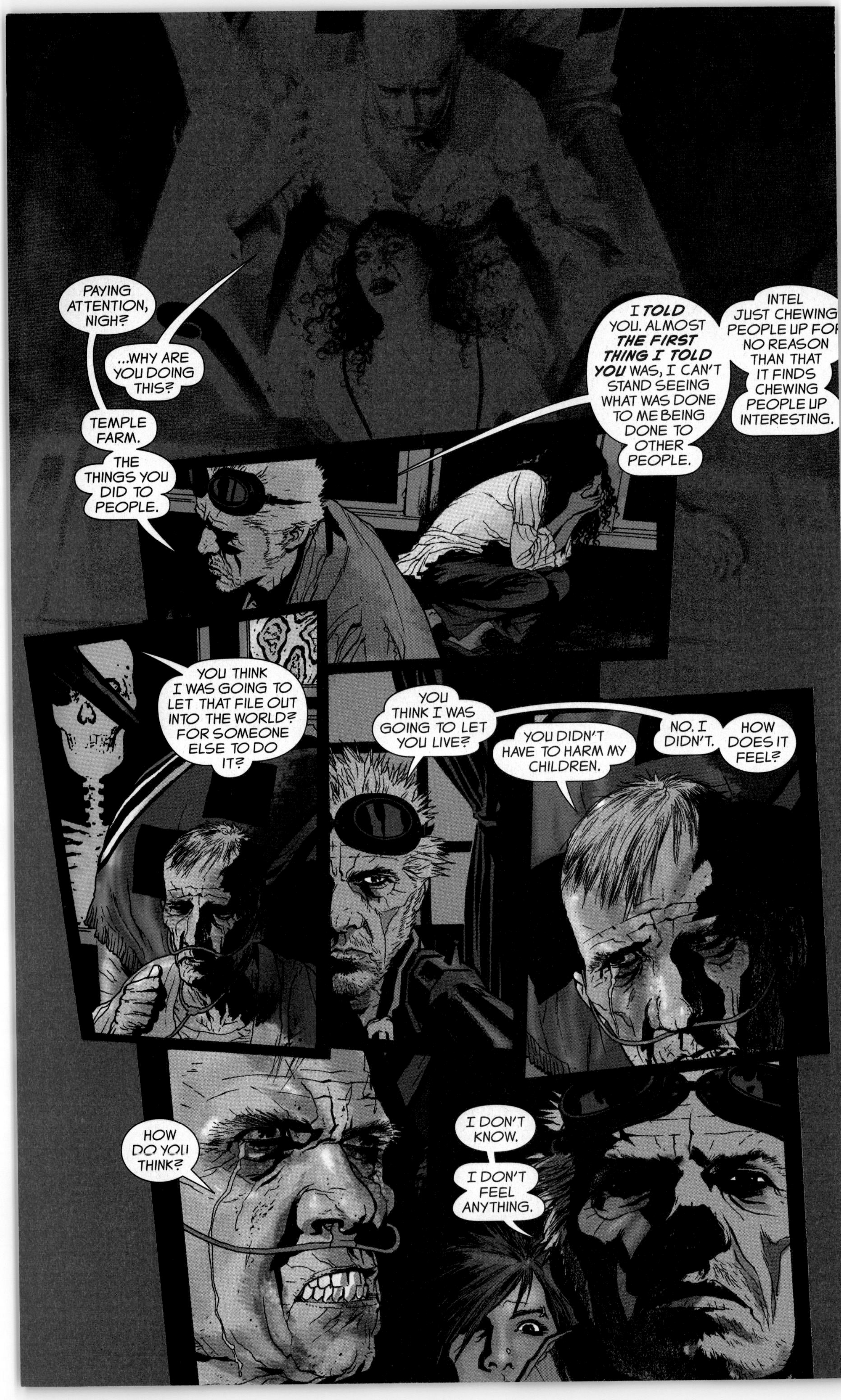
PAYING ATTENTION, NIGH?
...WHY ARE YOU DOING THIS?
TEMPLE FARM.
THE THINGS YOU DID TO PEOPLE.
I *TOLD* YOU. ALMOST ***THE FIRST THING I TOLD YOU*** WAS, I CAN'T STAND SEEING WHAT WAS DONE TO ME BEING DONE TO OTHER PEOPLE.
INTEL JUST CHEWING PEOPLE UP FOR NO REASON THAN THAT IT FINDS CHEWING PEOPLE UP INTERESTING.
YOU THINK I WAS GOING TO LET THAT FILE OUT INTO THE WORLD? FOR SOMEONE ELSE TO DO IT?
YOU THINK I WAS GOING TO LET YOU LIVE?
YOU DIDN'T HAVE TO HARM MY CHILDREN.
NO. I DIDN'T.
HOW DOES IT FEEL?
HOW DO YOU THINK?
I DON'T KNOW.
I DON'T FEEL ANYTHING.

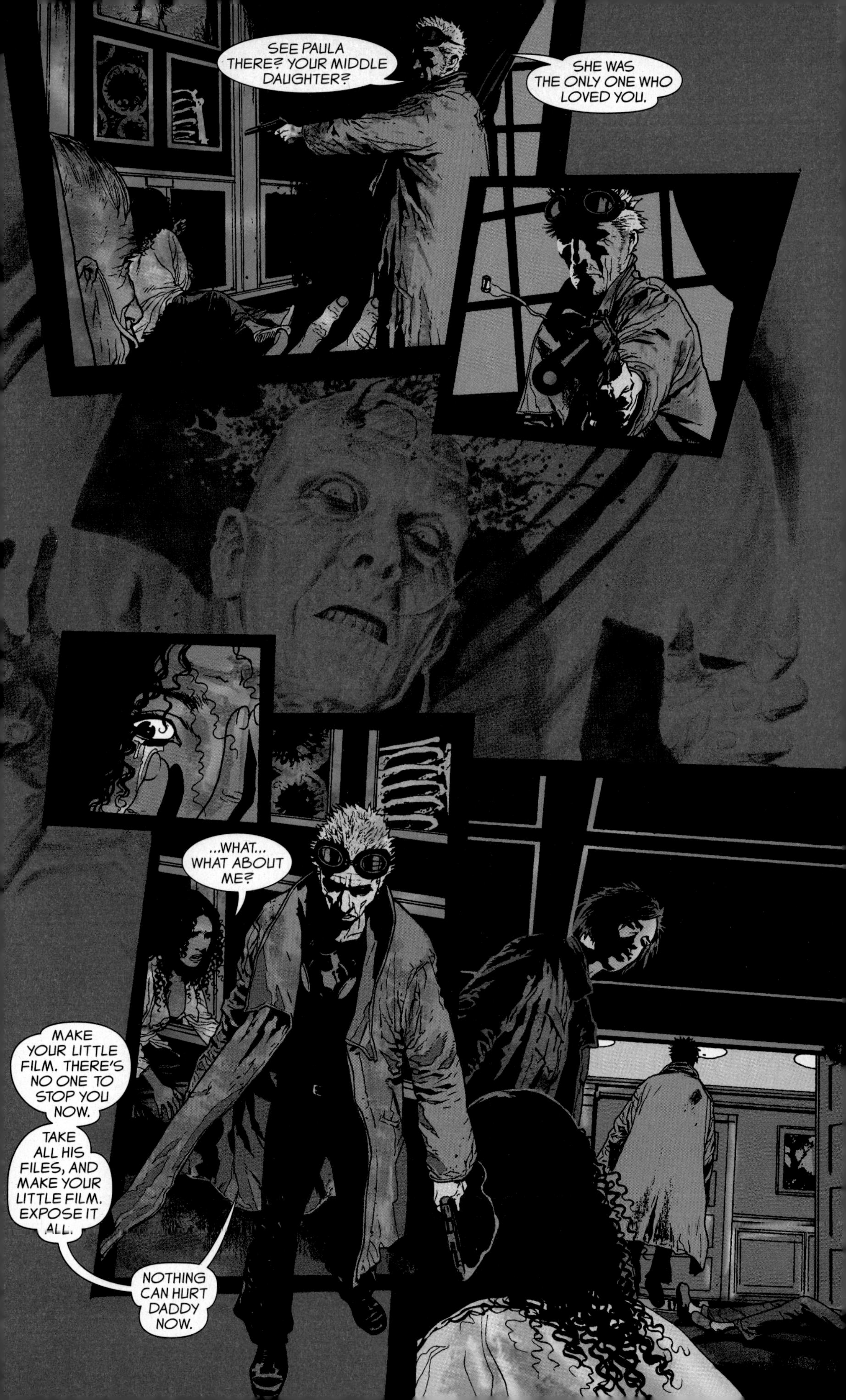
SEE PAULA THERE? YOUR MIDDLE DAUGHTER?
SHE WAS THE ONLY ONE WHO LOVED YOU.
...WHAT... WHAT ABOUT ME?
MAKE YOUR LITTLE FILM. THERE'S NO ONE TO STOP YOU NOW.
TAKE ALL HIS FILES, AND MAKE YOUR LITTLE FILM. EXPOSE IT ALL.
NOTHING CAN HURT DADDY NOW.

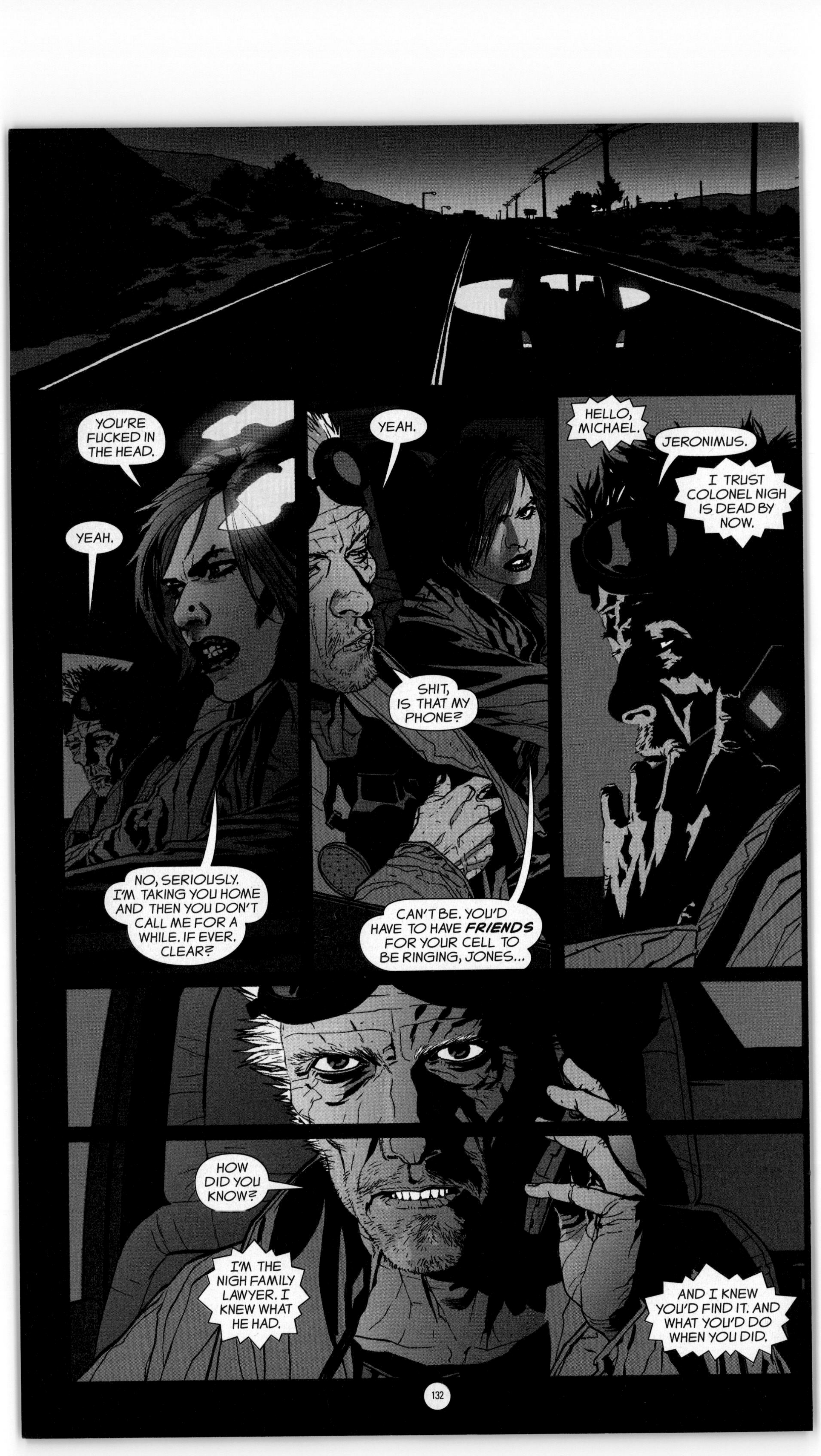

YOU'RE FUCKED IN THE HEAD.
YEAH.
NO, SERIOUSLY. I'M TAKING YOU HOME AND THEN YOU DON'T CALL ME FOR A WHILE. IF EVER. CLEAR?
YEAH.
SHIT, IS THAT MY PHONE?
CAN'T BE. YOU'D HAVE TO HAVE **FRIENDS** FOR YOUR CELL TO BE RINGING, JONES...
HELLO, MICHAEL.
JERONIMUS.
I TRUST COLONEL NIGH IS DEAD BY NOW.
HOW DID YOU KNOW?
I'M THE NIGH FAMILY LAWYER. I KNEW WHAT HE HAD.
AND I KNEW YOU'D FIND IT. AND WHAT YOU'D DO WHEN YOU DID.

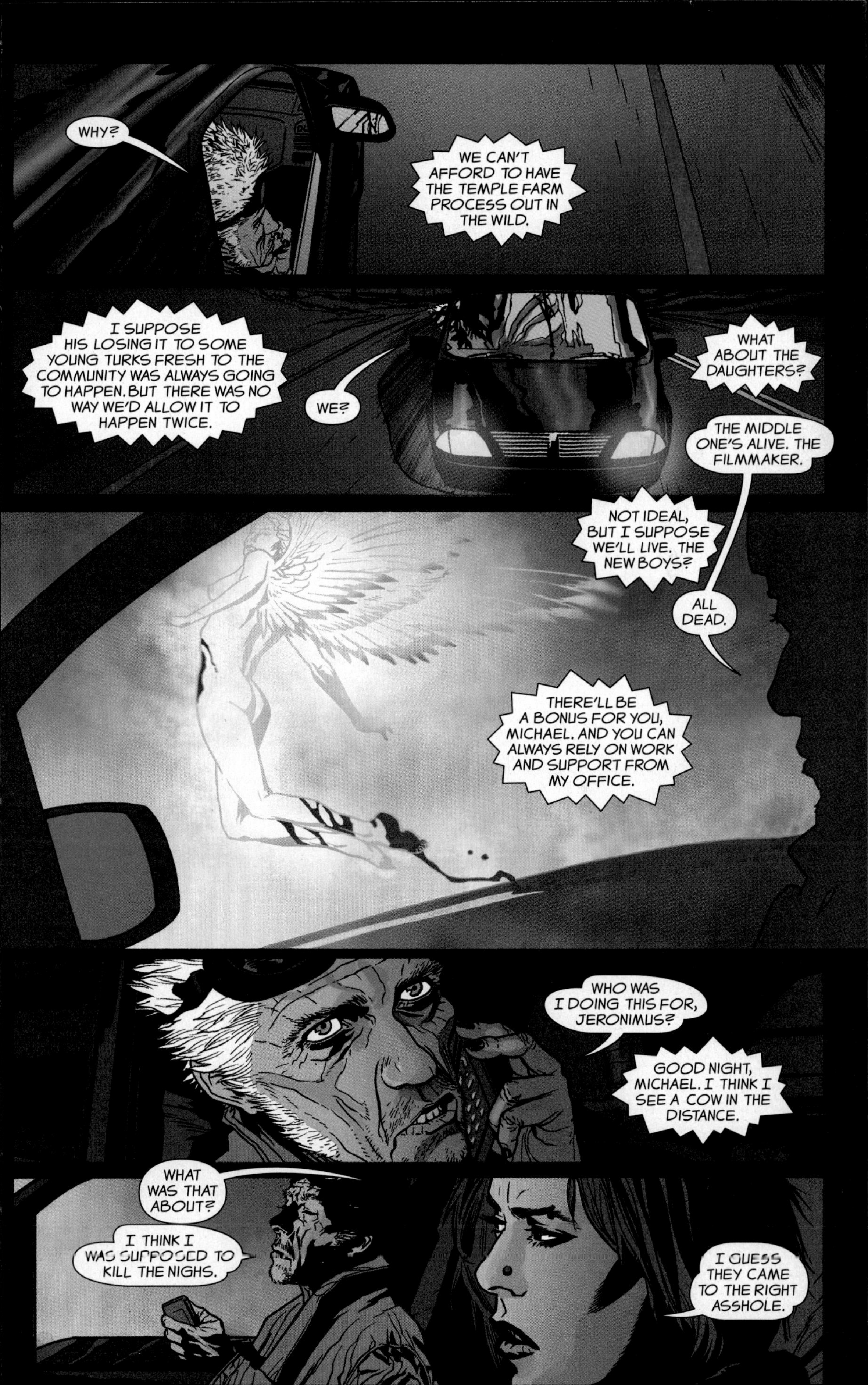
WHY?
WE CAN'T AFFORD TO HAVE THE TEMPLE FARM PROCESS OUT IN THE WILD.
I SUPPOSE HIS LOSING IT TO SOME YOUNG TURKS FRESH TO THE COMMUNITY WAS ALWAYS GOING TO HAPPEN. BUT THERE WAS NO WAY WE'D ALLOW IT TO HAPPEN TWICE.
WE?
WHAT ABOUT THE DAUGHTERS?
THE MIDDLE ONE'S ALIVE. THE FILMMAKER.
NOT IDEAL, BUT I SUPPOSE WE'LL LIVE. THE NEW BOYS?
ALL DEAD.
THERE'LL BE A BONUS FOR YOU, MICHAEL. AND YOU CAN ALWAYS RELY ON WORK AND SUPPORT FROM MY OFFICE.
WHO WAS I DOING THIS FOR, JERONIMUS?
GOOD NIGHT, MICHAEL. I THINK I SEE A COW IN THE DISTANCE.
WHAT WAS THAT ABOUT?
I THINK I WAS SUPPOSED TO KILL THE NIGHS.
I GUESS THEY CAME TO THE RIGHT ASSHOLE.

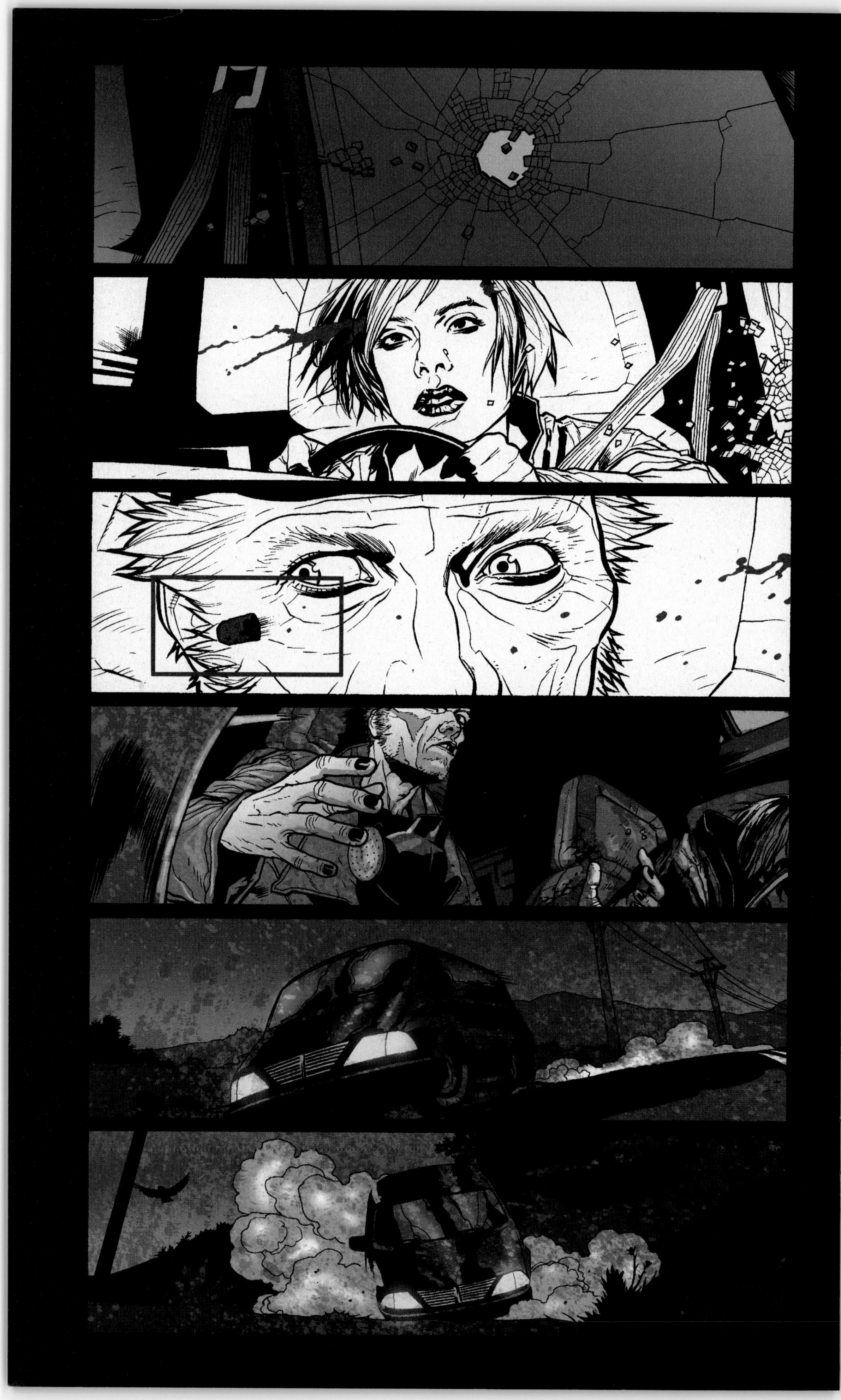

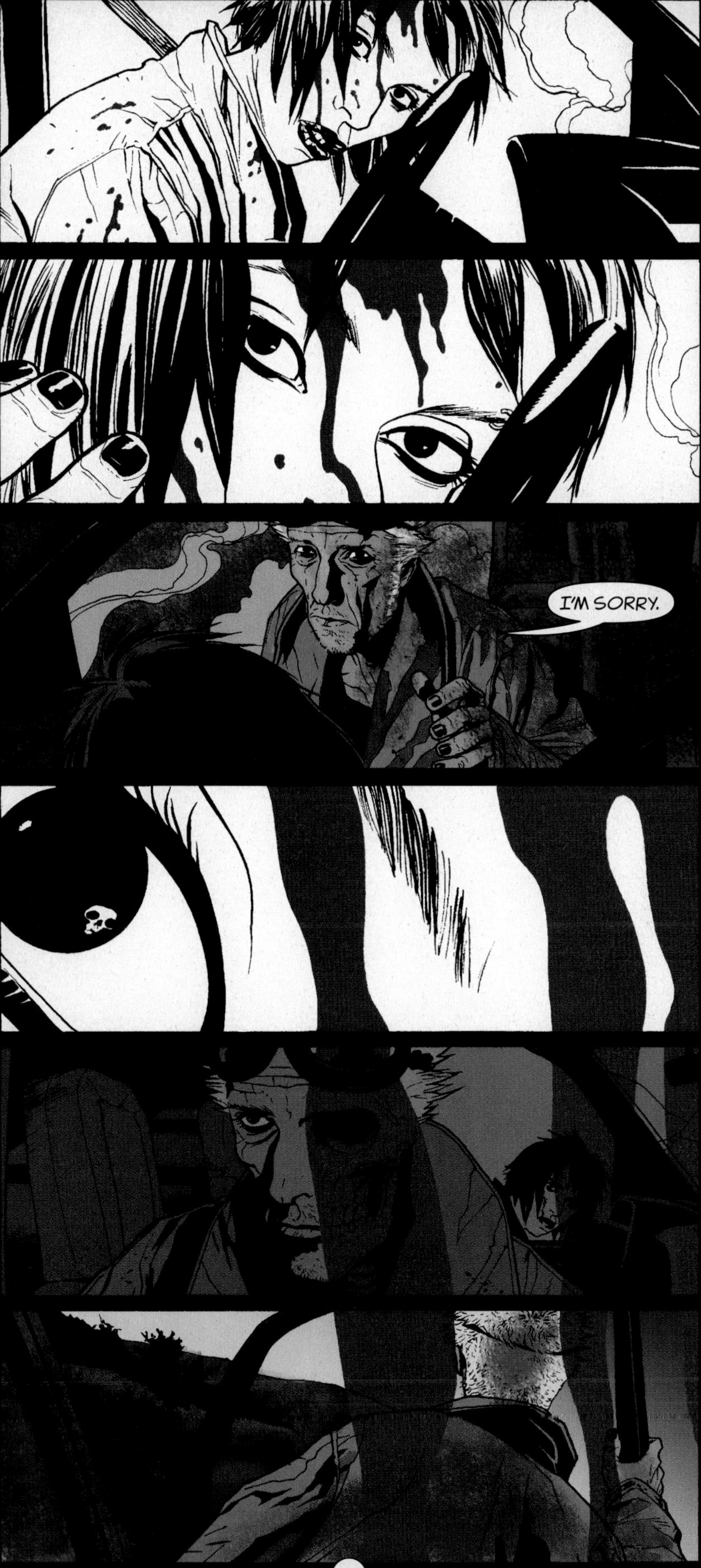
I'M SORRY.

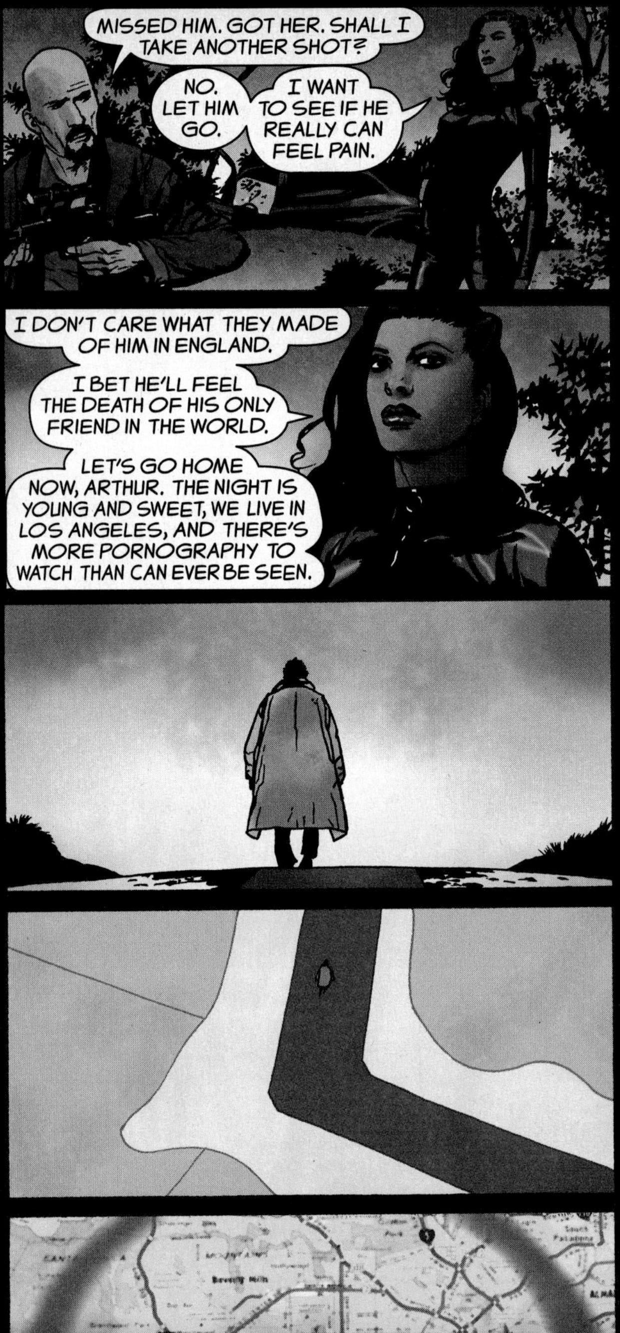
MISSED HIM. GOT HER. SHALL I TAKE ANOTHER SHOT?
NO. LET HIM GO.
I WANT TO SEE IF HE REALLY CAN FEEL PAIN.
I DON'T CARE WHAT THEY MADE OF HIM IN ENGLAND.
I BET HE'LL FEEL THE DEATH OF HIS ONLY FRIEND IN THE WORLD.
LET'S GO HOME NOW, ARTHUR. THE NIGHT IS YOUNG AND SWEET, WE LIVE IN LOS ANGELES, AND THERE'S MORE PORNOGRAPHY TO WATCH THAN CAN EVER BE SEEN.
LOS ANGELES

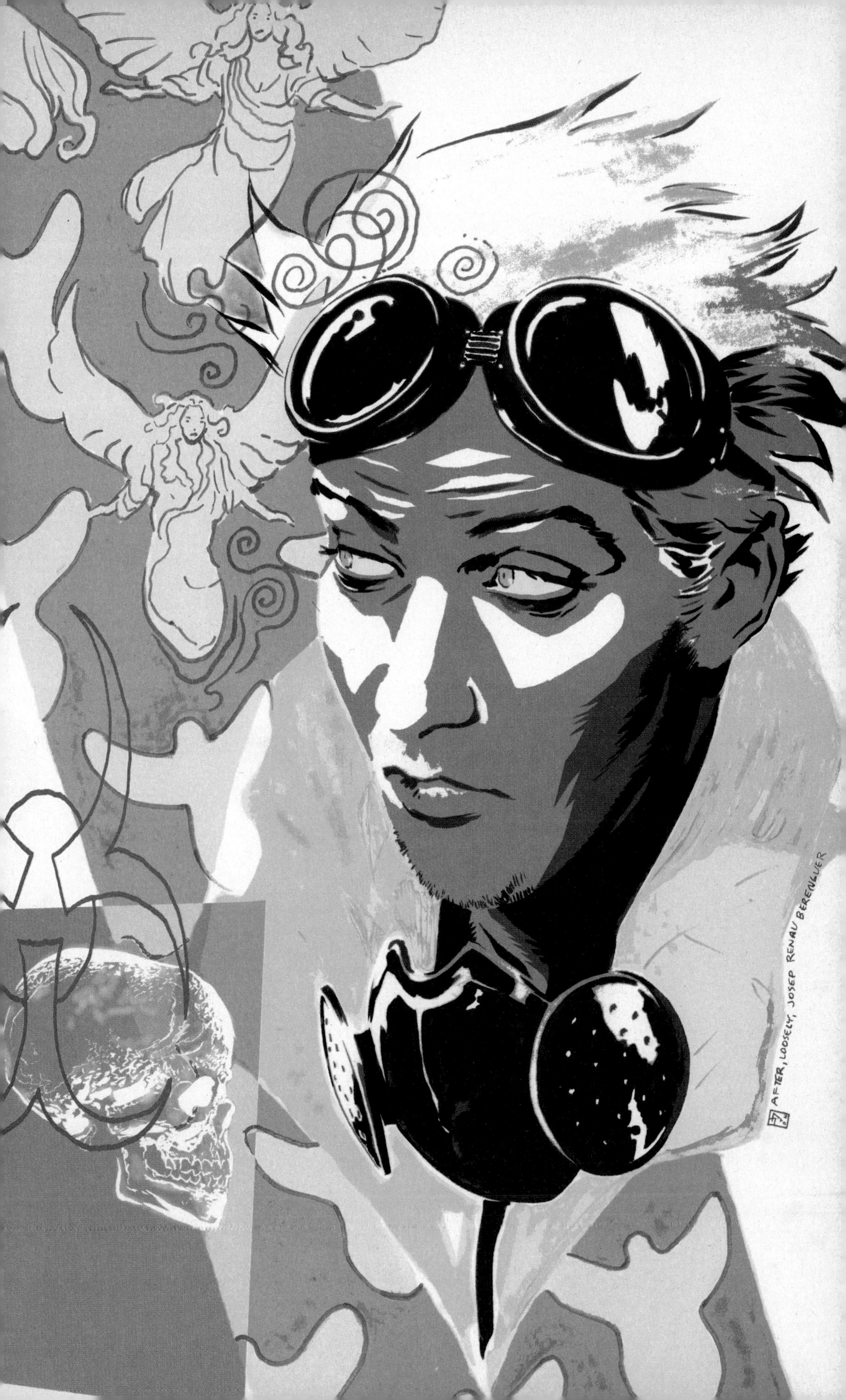
AFTER, LOOSELY, JOSEP RENAU BERENGUER

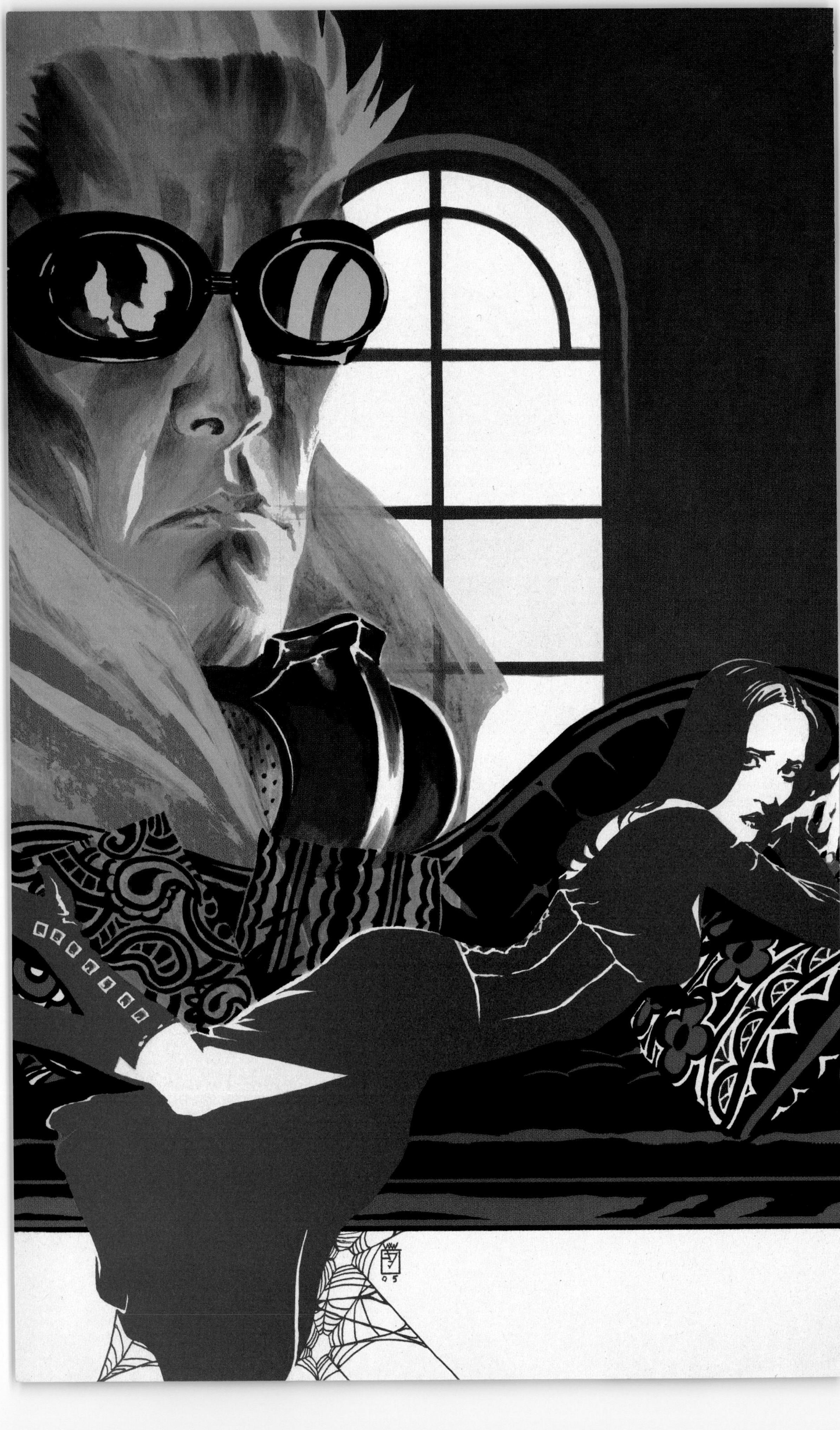

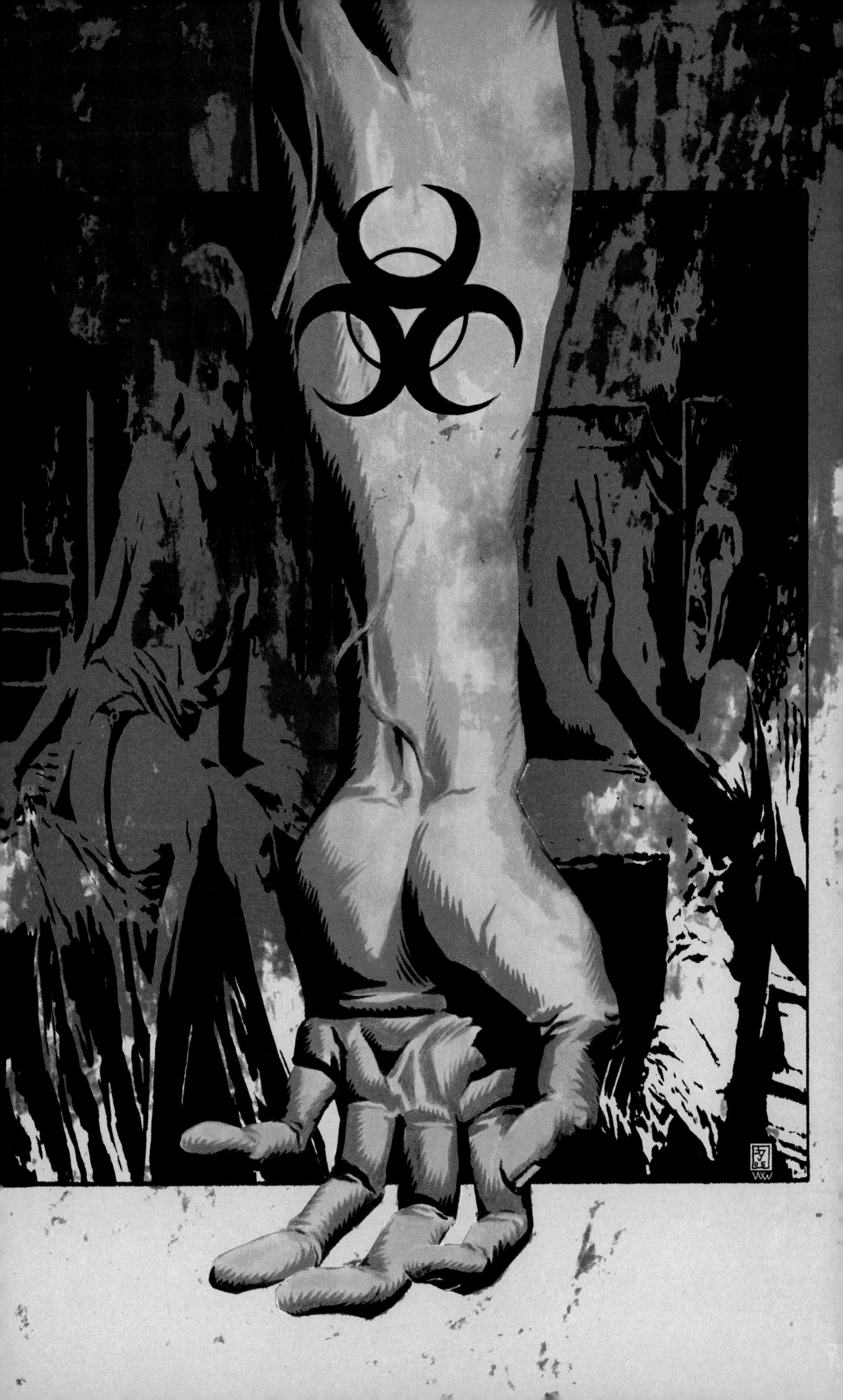

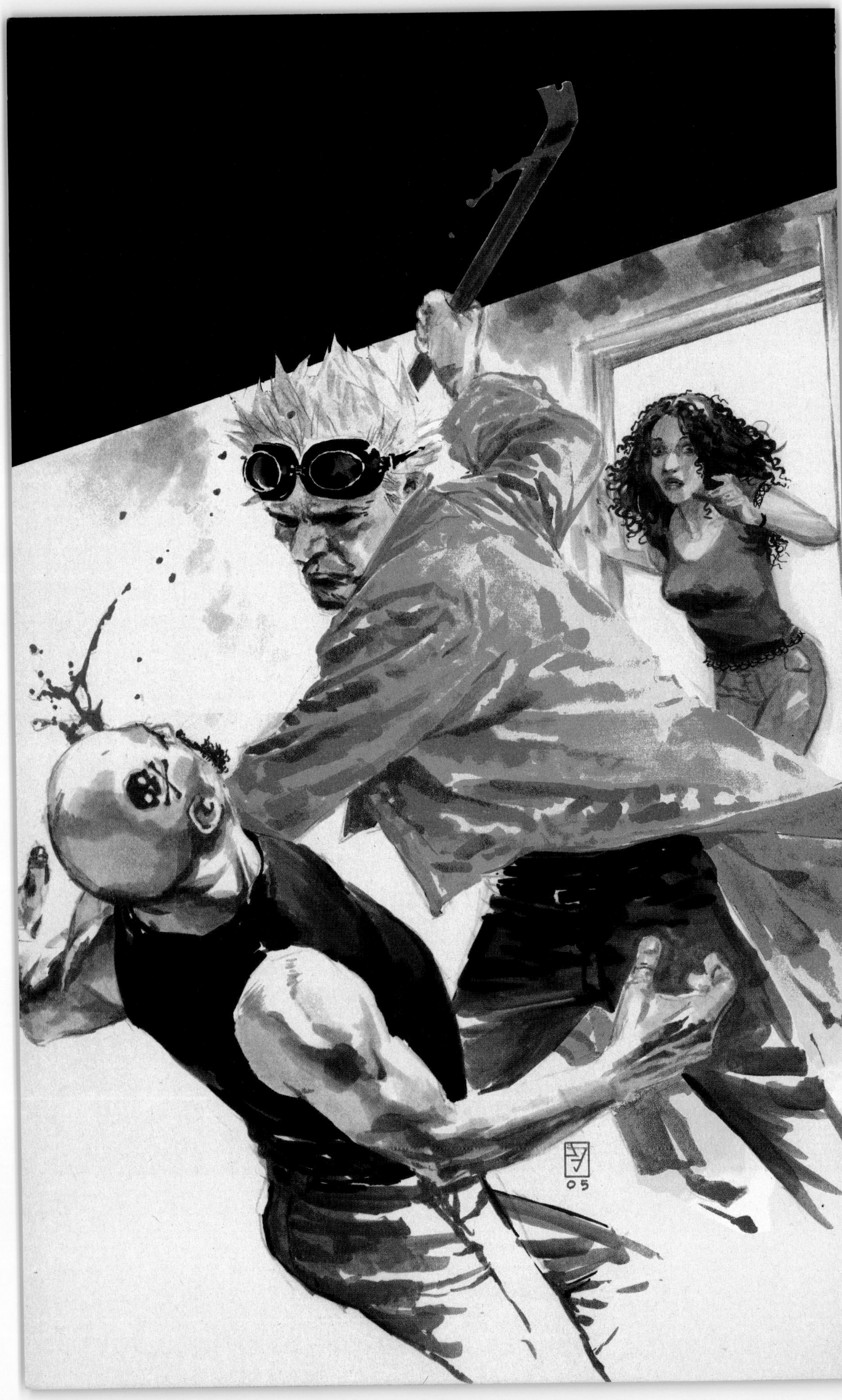

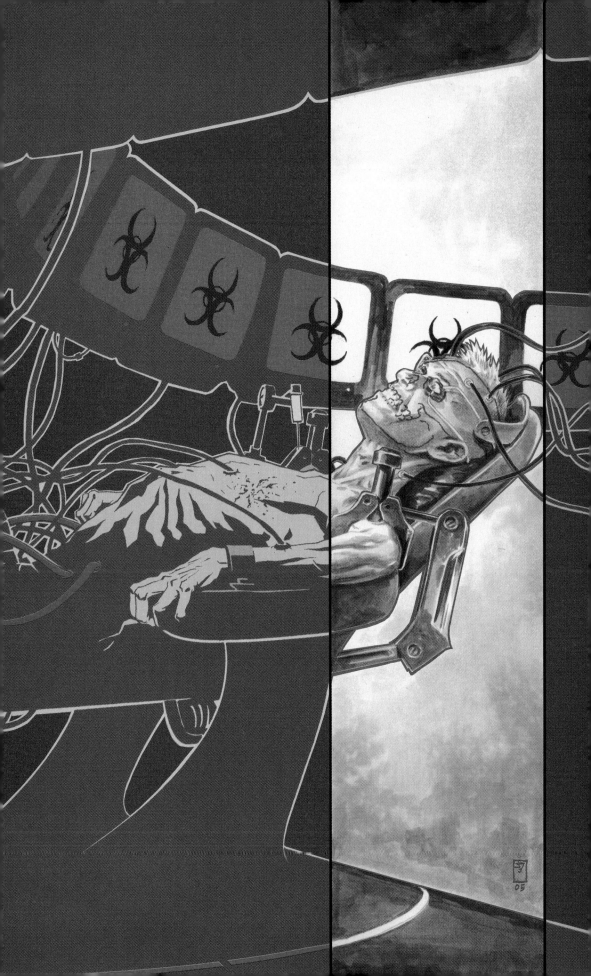

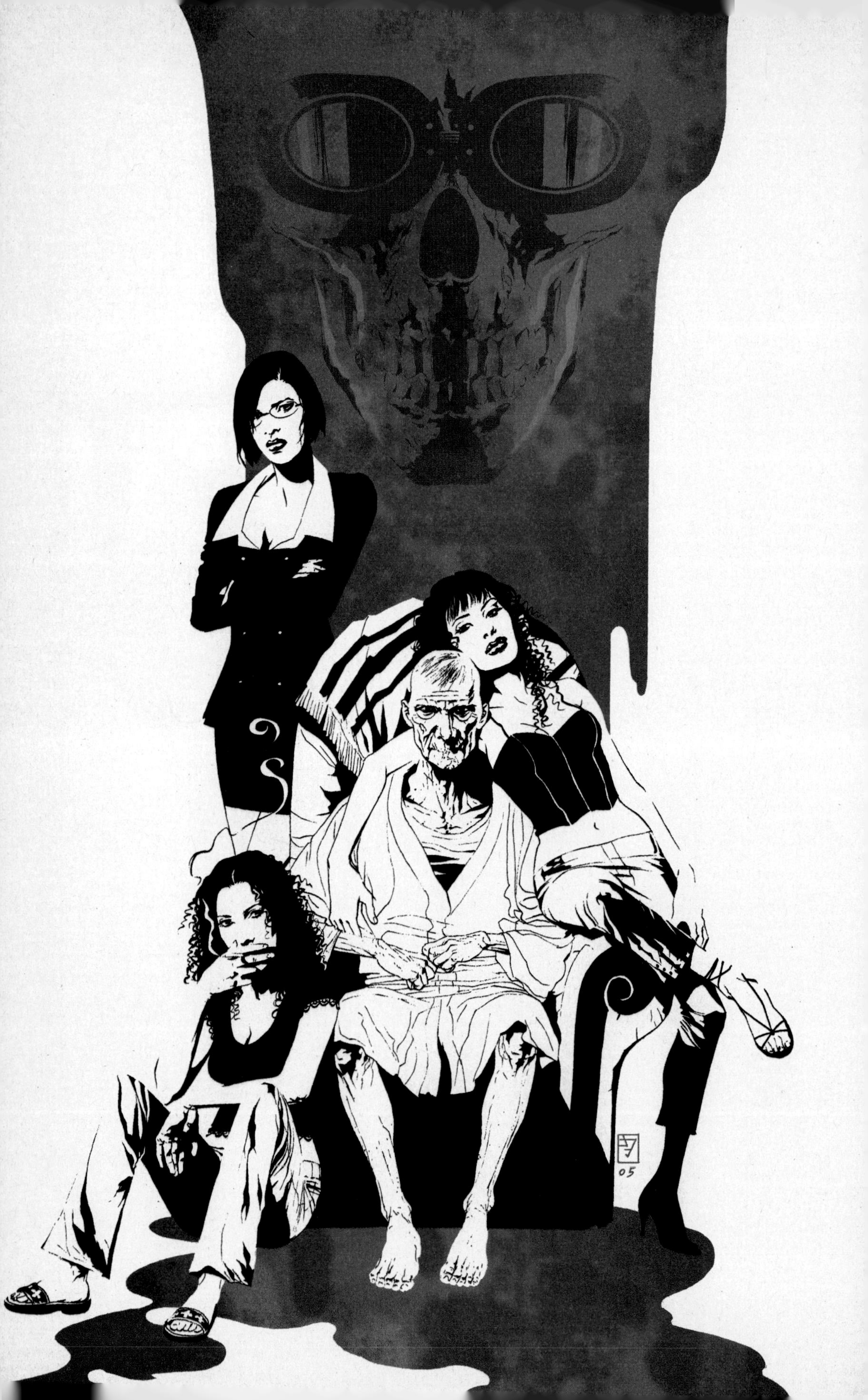

THERE'S A WHOLE WORLD
TO EXPLORE IN

PLANETARY

BY WARREN ELLIS AND JOHN CASSADAY.

This is Planetary: three people who walk the world for strangeness and wonder, uncovering things others wish were left covered. They are the mystery archaeologists, explorers of the planet's secret history, charting the unseen borders of a fantastic world.

VOL. 1: ALL OVER THE WORLD
AND OTHER STORIES
VOL. 2: THE FOURTH MAN
VOL. 3: LEAVING THE 20TH CENTURY

DON'T MISS THESE OTHER WILDSTORM BOOKS BY ELLIS:

GLOBAL FREQUENCY	OCEAN	STORMWATCH
BOOKS 1 & 2		BOOKS 1–5

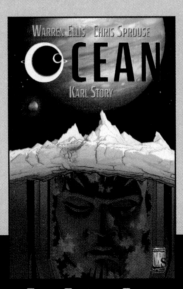

ELLIS•VARIOUS   **ELLIS•SPROUSE•STORY**   **ELLIS•VARIOUS ARTISTS**

TO FIND MORE COLLECTED EDITIONS AND MONTHLY COMIC BOOKS FROM WILDSTORM AND DC COMICS

CALL 1-888-COMIC BOOK

FOR THE NEAREST COMICS SHOP OR GO TO YOUR LOCAL BOOK STORE

THERE'S A WHOLE UNIVERSE OF MAGIC IN

PROMETHEA

BY ALAN MOORE, J.H. WILLIAMS III
AND MICK GRAY.

University student Sophie Bangs
was ordinary—until her studies
introduced her to the power of
Promethea. Now, caught up in a
living myth, she explores the vast
wonders of human imagination and
the worlds of magic that surround
us all.

Catch the whole story in Books 1-5!

DISCOVER THE REST OF THE **ABC** UNIVERSE IN:

THE LEAGUE OF
EXTRAORDINARY GENTLEMEN
VOLUMES 1 & 2

TOM STRONG
BOOKS 1–6

TOP10
BOOKS 1 & 2

MOORE•O'NEILL

MOORE•SPROUSE
GORDON•STORY

MOORE•HA•CANNON

SEARCH THE GRAPHIC NOVELS SECTION OF

WWW.WILDSTORM.COM

FOR ART AND INFORMATION ON ALL OUR BOOKS!